JOURNAL FOR THE STUDY OF THE NEW TESTAMENT SUPPLEMENT SERIES

228

Executive Editor
Stanley E. Porter

Editorial Board
Craig Blomberg, Elizabeth A. Castelli, David Catchpole,
Kathleen E. Corley, R. Alan Culpepper, James D.G. Dunn,
Craig A. Evans, Stephen Fowl, Robert Fowler,
George H. Guthrie, Robert Jewett, Robert W. Wall

COPENHAGEN INTERNATIONAL SEMINAR

10

General Editors
Thomas L. Thompson
Niels Peter Lemche

Associate Editors
Mogens Müller
Hakan Ulfgard

Sheffield Academic Press
A Continuum imprint

'Have Mercy on Me'

The Story of the Canaanite
Woman in Matthew 15.21-28

Glenna S. Jackson

Journal for the Study of the New Testament
Supplement Series 228

Copenhagen International Seminar 10

Copyright © 2002 Sheffield Academic Press
A Continuum imprint

Published by
Sheffield Academic Press Ltd
The Tower Building, 11 York Road, London SE1 7NX
371 Lexington Avenue, New York, NY 10017-6550

www.SheffieldAcademicPress.com
www.continuumbooks.com

British Library Cataloguing-in-Publication Data
A catalogue record for this book is available from the British Library

Typeset by Sheffield Academic Press
Printed on acid-free paper in Great Britain by Bookcraft Ltd, Midsomer Norton, Bath

ISBN   0-8264-6148-4

To Marian Sessler Hoffman
and to the memory of Maggie Giese
(1948–1989)
who served homemade bread after many a long day
in the library

CONTENTS

ABBREVIATIONS

AB	Anchor Bible
ABRL	The Anchor Bible Reference Library
AnBib	Analecta biblica
ANF	The Ante-Nicene Fathers: Translations of *The Writings of the Fathers down to A.D. 325*
ASOR	American Schools of Oriental Research
BA	*Biblical Archaeologist*
BAGD	Walter Bauer, William F. Arndt, F. William Gingrich and Frederick W. Danker, *A Greek–English Lexicon of the New Testament and Other Early Christian Literature* (Chicago: University of Chicago Press, 2nd edn, 1958)
BARev	*Biblical Archaeology Review*
BASOR	*Bulletin of the American Schools of Oriental Research*
BDB	Francis Brown, S.R. Driver and Charles A. Briggs, *A Hebrew and English Lexicon of the Old Testament* (Oxford: Clarendon Press, 1907)
Bib	*Biblica*
BibOr	Biblica et orientalia
BibTod	*The Bible Today*
BJS	Brown Judaic Studies
BLE	*Bulletin de littérature ecclésiastique*
BN	*Biblische Notizen*
BNTC	Black's New Testament Commentaries
BR	*Bible Review*
BTB	*Biblical Theology Bulletin*
BZNW	Beihefte zur *ZNW*
CBQ	*Catholic Biblical Quarterly*
CBQMS	*Catholic Biblical Quarterly*, Monograph Series
CGTC	Cambridge Greek Testament Commentary
CIS	Copenhagen International Seminar
EA	Epigraphica Anatolica
ETL	*Ephemerides theologicae lovanienses*
ExpTim	*Expository Times*
FemTh	*Feminist Theology*
Gul	Geist und Leben
HAR	*Hebrew Annual Review*

HSM	Harvard Semitic Monographs
HTR	*Harvard Theological Review*
ICC	International Critical Commentary
IDB	George Arthur Buttrick (ed.), *The Interpreter's Dictionary of the Bible* (4 vols.; Nashville: Abingdon Press, 1962)
Int	*Interpretation*
IrTQ	Irish Theological Quarterly
JAAR	*Journal of the American Academy of Religion*
JBL	*Journal of Biblical Literature*
JES	*Journal of Ecumenical Studies*
JFSR	*Journal of Feminist Studies in Religion*
JJS	*Journal of Jewish Studies*
JNES	*Journal of Near Eastern Studies*
JNSL	*Journal of Northwest Semitic Languages*
JQR	*Jewish Quarterly Review*
JR	*Journal of Religion*
JSJ	*Journal for the Study of Judaism in the Persian, Hellenistic and Roman Period*
JSNT	*Journal for the Study of the New Testament*
JSOT	*Journal for the Study of the Old Testament*
JSOTSup	*Journal for the Study of the Old Testament*, Supplement Series
JSP	*Journal for the Study of the Pseudepigrapha*
LCL	Loeb Classical Library
LSJ	H.G. Liddell, Robert Scott and H. Stuart Jones, *Greek–English Lexicon* (Oxford: Clarendon Press, 9th edn, 1968)
NCB	New Century Bible
NovT	*Novum Testamentum*
NovTSup	*Novum Testamentum*, Supplements
NRSV	New Revised Standard Version
NTS	*New Testament Studies*
OTL	Old Testament Library
OTP	James Charlesworth (ed.), *Old Testament Pseudepigrapha*
PJ	*Palästina-Jahrbuch*
RB	*Revue biblique*
SBLDS	SBL Dissertation Series
SBLMS	SBL Monograph Series
SBLSP	SBL Seminar Papers
SBLSS	SBL Semeia Studies
SBT	Studies in Biblical Theology
SBTS	Sources for Biblical and Theological Study
SEÅ	*Svensk exegetisk årsbok*
SFSHJ	South Florida Studies in the History of Judaism
SHANE	Studies in the History of the Ancient Near East
SJLA	Studies in Judaism in Late Antiquity
SNT	Studien zum Neuen Testament

SPB	Studia postbiblica
SJOT	*Scandinavian Journal of the Old Testament*
SSSBL	Symposium Series SBL
ST	*Studia theologica*
Str-B	Strack and Billerbeck, *Kommentar zum New Testament aus Talmud und Midrash*
TDNT	Gerhard Kittel and Gerhard Friedrich (eds.), *Theological Dictionary of the New Testament* (trans. Geoffrey W. Bromiley; 10 vols.; Grand Rapids: Eerdmans, 1964–)
ThWAT	G.J. Botterweck and H. Ringgren (eds.), *Theologisches Wörterbuch zum Alten Testament* (Stuttgart: W. Kohlhammer, 1970–)
TQ	*Theologische Quartalschrift*
TT	*Teologisk Tidsskrift*
TZ	*Theologische Zeitschrift*
UF	*Ugarit-Forschungen*
USQR	*Union Seminary Quarterly Review*
VT	*Vetus Testamentum*
VTSup	*Vetus Testamentum*, Supplements
WW	*Word and World*
ZAW	*Zeitschrift für die alttestamentliche Wissenschaft*
ZKT	*Zeitschrift für katholische Theologie*
ZNW	*Zeitschrift für die neutestamentliche Wissenschaft*
ZTK	*Zeitschrift für Theologie und Kirche*

The discovery of new data or the emergence of a new methodology are the prime factors for progress in the scientific study of any area of human concern, according to John R. Donahue.[1] I cannot claim either, the fact being that I am working with centuries-old data and a conglomerate of established methods. What I do claim is a gnawing hunger for a valid, non-patronizing hypothesis concerning the role of the story of the Canaanite Woman in the Gospel of Matthew.

There are four stories in addition to a genealogy in the Gospel of Matthew in which women play a major role. The small number of Gospel narratives that include women has occasioned no surprise among scholars because of what has been traditionally considered to be the sociocultural norm of the times. However, traditional thought on women's status and role in the first century CE does not necessarily reflect the actual situation. Modern social scientists, anthropologists and social historians have delineated descriptive vs. prescriptive categories for studying comparative social organization of ancient Mediterranean culture. This delineation demands a further look at biblical texts that have appeared to portray women in certain traditional and immovable categories. It is now widely recognized that each of these Gospel stories has a life setting, one that does not necessarily fit the widespread scholarly consensus. The purpose of this thesis, which is a slight revision of my dissertation at Marquette University, is to reconstruct the communal setting for Mt. 15.21-28, the story of Jesus' encounter with a Canaanite woman.

Biblical texts are most frequently quoted from the RSV or NRSV; my translations are indicated. Quotations from Diogenes Laertius, Jerome, Josephus and Philo are from the translations in the Loeb Classical Library; quotations from Origen are taken from the Ante-Nicene Christian Library. Other sources are acknowledged at the appropriate places within the text.

There are many persons to whom I owe a debt of gratitude. First, my

1. John R. Donahue, *Are You the Christ? The Trial Narrative in the Gospel of Mark* (SBLDS, 10; Atlanta: Scholars Press, 1973), p. 1.

heartfelt thanks go to Julian V. Hills, who, over a period of eight years was teacher, mentor, advisor and dissertation director at Marquette University; for the past eight years, he has continued as friend and colleague, and deserves special credit for his guidance in this final manuscript on the story of the Canaanite Woman. I also thank Thomas L. Thompson for reading an early draft of the dissertation several years ago and for maintaining interest and encouragement. Deep appreciation is extended to many colleagues at Otterbein College, including Dean Patricia A. Frick, the Courtright Memorial Library staff, to departmental colleagues, Paul A. Laughlin, Andrew P. Mills and Charles E. Zimmerman for, above all else, their friendship and sense of humor, and to Patti Welch and Terri Tracy for their computer programming expertise. Special thanks go to Elizabeth Struthers Malbon and Daryl Schmidt for reading the manuscript and offering helpful advice and to Wendy L. Jackson for her editorial assistance. A final word of thanks and appreciation goes to my family: Gary, my husband of 35 years and our children, Wendy, Thad, Mandy and Adam, have supported me unconditionally on every venture and are the sources of all happiness. 'Every evening I sit down to dine with you—if not in body, always with your presence—because in this beautiful world of ours, all things are possible' (paraphrase from the film, *Babette's Feast*).

Introduction

1. *The Project*

The focus of research on the story of the Canaanite Woman in Mt. 15.21-28 has traditionally been on content rather than context. That is, the story in both Matthew's and Mark's Gospels has received attention because it illustrates Jesus' growing popularity, inaugurates the mission to the Gentiles, exemplifies the stamina that faith requires, and demonstrates the reward—that is, a miraculous healing—for such perseverance. This study shows that the preoccupation with these elements of the story in the history of interpretation provides an incomplete and perhaps distorted picture. There are issues in this story that have perplexed scholars, for example, why does Matthew portray Jesus in v. 23 as first seemingly ignoring the woman and why is he then conspicuously rude to her? The troublesome words in v. 26 about the children's bread have been softened or explained away by scholars, but not convincingly. For example, Jesus' apparent rebuke of the woman has been trivialized by claims that irony and humor are used by the author of Matthew in this text merely for rhetorical effect.

I argue that this story must be seen in its proper setting and that it was not included in Matthew's Gospel only to document the evangelizing of Gentiles. Quite the contrary: it is a story that reflects tension between Jews and proselytes in Matthew's community and responds to the question, 'What must one do to become a member of the community?' I also argue that while the text portrays the woman in a penitential role, it more importantly demonstrates a desire on the woman's part to become a member of the community.

Matthew has a preoccupation with qualifications for inclusion in the community. If Jews were 'in' and Gentiles were 'out', if men were 'in' and women were 'out' in Matthew's church, then Gentile women were probably the most marginalized. Already, feminist scholars such as Elisabeth Schüssler Fiorenza and Alice Dermience have alluded to the possibility of a setting for this text that goes beyond the traditional interpretation of submissive faith. Some of the elements of this thesis have previously been seen, therefore, but the pieces have thus far not been put together.

It is possible to retrace the evangelist's steps and see that the story of the Canaanite Woman was developed, not just as a paradigm of faith, but as a paradigm for female proselytism in the Matthean community.

2. *The History of Research*

The conventional understanding of the pericope is that as a result of the encounter with the woman from Tyre and Sidon, Jesus will no longer restrict his attention to the Jews, with whom he is seemingly having very little success anyway. He is now open to a broader, more universal concept of humanity's need for God.[1] W.D. Davies and Dale C. Allison, Jr, review contemporary scholarship on this pericope and compare it with that of the centurion in Mt. 8.5-13, concluding that:

> Matthew's contributions to the list of parallels [of the stories of the Centurion and the Canaanite Woman] by and large focus on two themes: faith, and the place of Israel. The reason is not hard to figure. There are only two episodes in our gospel in which Jesus clearly helps a Gentile: 8.5-13 and 15.21-28. Given Matthew's understanding of salvation-history, he cannot let these exceptional episodes go by without making it perfectly clear that when Gentiles are granted salvation it is solely on the basis of their faith: they are not expected to become Jews.[2]

Gerd Theissen also fuses faith and salvation history in Matthew's revised account of the story of the Syrophoenician Woman:

> Faith in miracles has an important function in salvation history; it does have the power to break through barriers and open a path for salvation into the whole world. This idea certainly contains a historically accurate observation: all nations are susceptible to belief in miracles.[3]

---

1. As an example of this view, J. Martin C. Scott ('Matthew 15.21-28: A Test-Case for Jesus' Manners', *JSNT* 63 [1996], pp. 21-44 [44]) argues that 'the conversion of Jesus by an "outsider" in turn encourages the reader to move from an exclusive to an inclusive understanding of Christian discipleship'.

2. W.D. Davies and Dale C. Allison, Jr, *A Critical and Exegetical Commentary on the Gospel According to Saint Matthew* (ICC; 3 vols.; Edinburgh: T. & T. Clark, 1991–97), II, pp. 558-59. While others also focus on the similarities between the stories of the Centurion's Servant and the Syrophoenician//Canaanite Woman, John P. Meier (*A Marginal Jew: Rethinking the Historical Jesus* [ABRL; 2 vols.; New York: Doubleday, 1991–94], II, p. 719), for example, points out the differences as well.

3. Gerd Theissen, *The Miracle Stories of the Early Christian Tradition* (Philadelphia: Fortress Press, 1983), p. 138.

Faith and salvation history are undoubtedly major concerns for Matthew, but that is not the sum of the story of the Canaanite Woman.[4] An earlier scholar, Benjamin W. Bacon, also connects the stories of the Canaanite Woman and the Centurion, and states that 'the believing suppliant [the Canaanite Woman] stands in exactly the same relation to unbelieving Israel as the Believing Centurion of 8.5-13'.[5] He then adds: 'Of course

4.   Karl Matthäus Woschitz ('Erzählter Glaube: Die Geschichte vom starken Glauben als Geschichte Göttes mit Juden und Heiden [Mt 5, 21-28 par]', *ZKT* 107 [1985], pp. 319-32 [320]) suggests that the story of the Canaanite Woman links faith and salvation history by providing a 'seam' between the 2000 year-old Jewish belief in being chosen by God and the old cults of the Canaanite religion. I oppose that view because the 'seam', if there is one, is not between Judaism and the old cults, but between Judaism and the enemies of Israel made possible by their conversion to Judaism. A number of articles, many of them hermeneutical, have been written with the story of the Canaanite Woman as their springboard for both faith and empowerment; for example: Ofelia Alvarez, 'Bible Study III—Matthew 15.21-28', *Ministerial Formation* (Geneva: World Council of Churches, 1998), pp. 12-15; Diane Blanchard, 'The Gentile Woman: Engagement with Suffering', *Consensus* 20.2 (1994), pp. 11-23; Robert W. Dahlen, 'The Savior and the Dog: An Exercise in Hearing', *WW* 17 (1997), pp. 269-77; Musa W. Dube, 'Consuming a Colonial Cultural Bomb: Translating *Badimo* into "Demons" in the Setswana Bible (Matthew 8.28-34; 15.22; 10.8)', *JSNT* 73 (1999), pp. 33-59; *idem*, 'Readings of Semoya: Batswana Women's Interpretations of Mt. 15.21-28', *Semeia* 73 (1996), pp. 111-29; Joyce M. Graue, 'A Problem…or a Moonbeam? Sermon Study on Matthew 15.21-28', *Lutheran Theological Journal* 30 (1996), pp. 75-80; Leticia A. Guardiola-Saenz, 'Borderless Women and Borderless Texts: A Cultural Reading of Matthew 15.21-28', *Semeia* 78 (1997), pp. 69-81; Judith Gundry-Volf, 'Spirit, Mercy, and the Other', *TT* 51 (1995), pp. 508-23; Bengt Holmberg, 'Debatten Jesus inte vann', *SEÅ* 63 (1998), pp. 167-76; Anita Monro, 'Alterity and the Canaanite Woman: A Postmodern Feminist Theological Reflection on Political Action', *Colloquium: The Australian and New Zealand Theological Review* 26 (1994), pp. 32-43; Margaret James Neill, 'The Canaanite Woman's Challenge', *The Other Side* 34 (1998), pp. 42-44; Gail O. O'Day, 'Surprised by Faith: Jesus and the Canaanite Woman', *Listening: Journal of Religion and Culture* 24 (1989), pp. 290-301 (299); Jim Perkinson, 'A Canaanitic Word in the Logos of Christ; or the Difference the Syro-Phoenician Woman Makes to Jesus', *Semeia* 75 (1996), pp. 61-85; James Treat, 'The Canaanite Problem', *Daughters of Sarah* 20 (1994), pp. 20-24.

5.   Benjamin W. Bacon, *Studies in Matthew* (2 vols.; New York: Holt, Rinehart & Winston, 1930), II, p. 219. R.T. France (*Matthew: Evangelist and Teacher* [Exeter: Paternoster Press, 1989], p. 228) and Heinz Joachim Held ('Matthew as Interpreter of the Miracle Stories', in Gunther Bornkamm, Gerhard Barth and Heinz Joachim Held [eds.], *Tradition and Interpretation in Matthew* [Philadelphia: Westminster Press, 1963], pp. 165-299 [193, 195]) also pair the stories of the Centurion and the Canaanite Woman as examples of non-Jews who receive the blessings of Israel through Jesus.

there could be no objection even from the Synagogue's point of view to the welcoming of a humble, believing proselyte'.[6] He has stated the case perfectly. In fact, the author of Pseudo-Clementine assigns the Syrophoenician/Canaanite woman the name of Justa and describes her as a proselyte.[7] Another early interpretation of the story of the Canaanite Woman is an allegorical one in which, according to Hilary (fourth century CE), the woman is a proselyte who intercedes for her child (that is, the dogs), the pagans.[8] But for whatever reason, that association has been lost,

6.   Bacon, *Matthew*, II, p. 219. J. Duncan M. Derrett ('Law in the New Testament: The Syro-Phoenician Woman and the Centurion of Capernaum', *NovT* 15 [1973], pp. 161-86) sees the connection between the two stories, entertains the notion that 'the Centurion reminded St. Luke of Jethro, proselyte and maker of proselytes', but apparently does not detect proselytism in Mark's story of the Syrophoenician Woman. In another context, Nicholas H. Taylor ('The Social Nature of Conversion in the Early Christian World', in Philip F. Esler [ed.], *Modelling Early Christianity: Social-Scientific Studies of the New Testament in Its Context* [London: Routledge, 1995], pp. 128-36 [131]) does not see the Syrophoenician woman as an example of conversion to Jesus' preaching.

7.   Pseudo-Clementine Homilies II, p. 19 in Alexander Roberts and James Donaldson (eds.), ANF: Translations of *The Writings of the Fathers down to A.D. 325* (Grand Rapids, MI: Eerdmans, repr. 1987), VIII, pp. 232, 301. The homilies are usually given third or fourth-century dating, but the materials obviously originated earlier. Elisabeth Schüssler Fiorenza (*But She Said: Feminist Practices of Biblical Interpretation* [Boston: Beacon Press, 1992], p. 100) includes Justa in her exploration of the story of the Syro-Phoenician woman in the context of boundary constructions and transgressions within early Christian communities.

8.   Ulrich Luz, *Matthew in History: Interpretation, Influence, and Effects* (Minneapolis: Fortress Press, 1994), p. 27. Similarly, P. Smulders, *Hilary of Poitiers' Preface to His Opus Historicum: Translation and Commentary* (Leiden: E.J. Brill, 1995), p. 33. This interpretation was dominant from the fourth until the eighteenth century. As Luz rehearses the tradition, 'the dogs in the metaphor are the pagans; the children, the Israelites; the bread is the doctrine of the gospel; the table is the Holy Scriptures... The church, in Matthew's time a Jewish-Christian minority group breaking down old borders, became a successful rival of the synagogue and finally triumphed over it and suppressed it. The text, originally a promise to a "little flock", gradually became an expression of self-confirmation of a powerful church with a negative impact on those who now were the small minority group, namely, the Jews. The interpretation remained verbally the same, but the situation changed. In this case it was the changed situation that transformed the interpretation into the opposite of what it was originally meant to be.' Also in the fourth century, according to P. Frisch ('Über die lydisch-phrygischen Sühneinschriften and die "Confessiones" des Augustinus', *EA* 2 [1983], pp. 41-45, as cited in G.H.R. Horsley and S.R. Llewelyn [eds.], *New Documents*

for the most part, in the history of interpretation.

Anthony J. Saldarini does acknowledge the proselytic overtones of the text, but still insists that the Canaanite Woman's great faith effects the reward, that is, in her case a healing for her daughter, and in Matthew's time, causes membership in his assembly, but as a Gentile, not a Jew.[9] I agree with Saldarini's statement that 'Israel remains the context and concern of Matthew', but would say not that Matthew is 'cautiously seek[ing] to include Gentiles in the reformed Christian-Jewish community of believers-in-Jesus',[10] but that, at least in the case of the Canaanite Woman, she must become a Jew in a Jewish community.

Fiorenza focuses on the issue of women's status and role in the Jesus movement:

> [Mark's Syro-Phoenician woman] does not argue for equal access; she begs for crumbs... She acts like a dog who is grateful even when kicked. Hence it is not surprising that commentators praise her for her humble submission. This is indeed a sacred text that advocates and reinscribes patriarchal power-relations, anti-Jewish prejudices, and women's feminine identity and submissive behavior.[11]

I hope to show that Matthew takes Mark's Syro-Phoenician Woman and transforms the story into one that reinforces Jewish Law[12] and grants equality to the woman who aggressively seeks membership, rather than a story that promotes anti-Jewish prejudice and reinforces female submissive behavior.

Illustrating Early Christianity (8 vols.; The Ancient History Documentary Research Centre; New South Wales, Australia: Macquarie University, 1981–98), VIII, p. 173, are points of contact between early confessional inscriptions and Augustine's Confessions; he notes that Augustine understood conversion as a miraculous healing.

9.   Anthony J. Saldarini, *Matthew's Christian-Jewish Community* (Chicago: University of Chicago Press, 1994), pp. 73-74. And so I would argue against his note (p. 249 n. 13) that 'Matthew is justifying the integration of non-Jews into his Christian-Jewish group on the basis of their faith in Jesus'. J. Andrew Overman (*Church and Community in Crisis: The Gospel According to Matthew* [The New Testament in Context; Valley Forge, PA: Trinity Press International, 1996], p. 229) wants it both ways: 'Although a Gentile, she is a Matthean Jew in good standing. She behaves and believes in accordance with the community rules'; later (p. 231), 'This Gentile has become a follower and believer, if not a member, within the Matthean community'.

10.   Saldarini, *Matthew's Christian-Jewish Community*, p. 75.

11.   Fiorenza, *But She Said*, p. 161.

12.   Seldom, if ever, is the story of the Canaanite Woman examined in terms of its relationship to Matthew's concept of Law.

This is not to say that first-century biblical texts are not used for these purposes because, of course, they are and we must be attentive to the damage and destruction that occur as a result. All too often, placing Jesus on a pedestal because he relates to women positively (at least from a Christian perspective) is at a cost to first-century Judaism and twenty-first century Jewish women. As Robert W. Funk suggests, 'The [basic] question for both Christians and Jews is what role to assign Jesus the Jew in the Jewish sect known as Christianity'.[13] Judith Plaskow was one of the first to challenge Christian feminists to deepen their understanding of Judaism before evaluating 'the uniqueness or non-uniqueness of Jesus' attitudes toward women'.[14]

Two previous studies have provided valuable insights into Matthew's story of the Canaanite Woman: *The Social and Ethnic Dimensions of Matthean Social History* by Amy-Jill Levine, and *Towards a Feminist Critical Reading of the Gospel According to Matthew*, an extensive narrative-critical work on the role of women in Matthew's Gospel by Elaine Mary Wainwright. These two authors have gone beyond the traditional views of interpretation by raising questions about the difficult issues of Jesus' apparent rudeness, the woman's ethnicity and her gender.[15] A.-J.

13. Robert W. Funk, *Honest To Jesus: Jesus for a New Millennium* (San Francisco: Harper & Row, 1996), p. 32.

14. Judith Plaskow, 'Blaming Jews for Inventing Patriarchy', *Lilith* 7 (1980), pp. 11-12. There are a number of other studies that address this issue; for example, Elisabeth Schüssler Fiorenza, *In Memory of Her: A Feminist Theological Reconstruction of Christian Origins* (New York: Crossroads, 1983); Susannah Heschel, 'Anti-Judaism in Christian Feminist Theology', *Tikkun* 5.3 (1990), pp. 25-28, 95-97; 'Jesus as Theological Transvestite', in Miriam Peskowitz and Laura Levitt (eds.), *Judaism Since Gender* (New York: Routledge & Kegan Paul, 1997), pp. 188-99; Glenna S. Jackson, 'Jesus as First-Century Feminist: Christian Anti-Judaism?', *FemTh* 19 (1998), pp. 85-98; Judith Plaskow, 'Feminist Anti-Judaism and the Christian God', *JFSR* 7.2 (1991), pp. 99-108; *idem*, 'Anti-Judaism in Feminist Christian Interpretation', in Elisabeth Schüssler Fiorenza (ed.), *Searching the Scriptures: A Feminist Introduction* (2 vols.; New York: Crossroad, 1993), I, pp. 117-29; Elisabeth Schüssler Fiorenza, *Jesus: Miriam's Child, Sophia's Prophet: Critical Issues in Feminist Christology* (New York: Continuum, 1994), especially chapter 3 'The Power of Naming: Jesus, Women, and Christian Anti-Judaism', pp. 67-96; *idem*, *Sharing Her Word: Feminist Biblical Interpretation in Context* (Boston: Beacon Press, 1998).

15. Marla J. Selvidge ('Violence, Woman, and the Future of the Matthean Community: A Redactional Critical Essay', *USQR* 39 [1984], pp. 213-23 [215]) also raises the issue of ethnicity by suggesting that 'Matthew stirs the strings of racism...by characterizing her as a Canaanite, an arch-enemy of the Jews'. Gerd Theissen

Levine opposes the idea of an anti-Jewish polemic[16] through a study of two seemingly opposing texts, the exclusivity logion found both in 10.5b-6 and the story of the Canaanite Woman in 15.24 against the Great Commission in 28.16-20.[17] One of her conclusions is relevant to mine: 'The exclusivity logion is strategically located in the account of the Canaanite woman, and it is programmatic for the first evangelist's redactional concerns... The privileged position of the Jews is retained during Jesus' ministry.'[18]

(*Sociology of Early Palestinian Christianity* [Philadelphia: Fortress Press, 1988], p. 51) suggests the same.

16. A.-J. Levine, *The Social and Ethnic Dimensions of Matthean Social History* (Studies in the Bible and Early Christianity, 14; Lewiston, NY: Edwin Mellen Press, 1988). Howard Clark Kee (*Christian Origins in Sociological Perspective: Methods and Resources* [Philadelphia: Westminster Press, 1980], p. 141), for example, mistakenly generalizes 'Jews' for 'scribes and Pharisees' in Mt. 23: '[Mt. 23] is without parallel in the New Testament for its vindictive, vengeful denunciation of the Jews'. Kee at times, however, is more specific about the target of castigation: 'Clearly, the community behind Matthew stands in bitterest conflict and competition with Pharisaic Judaism' (p. 142).

17. See also Donald A. Hagner, 'The *Sitz im Leben* of the Gospel of Matthew', in David R. Bauer and Mark Allan Powell (eds.), *Treasures New and Old: Recent Contributions to Matthean Studies* (SSSBL; Atlanta: Scholars Press, 1996), pp. 27-68 [29-32]) for the tensions in Matthew between particularism and universalism. Others, for example, Helmut Koester (*Ancient Christian Gospels: Their History and Development* [London: SCM Press; Philadelphia: Trinity Press International, 1990], p. 152), have investigated the two seemingly opposing texts in 10.5-6b and 28.16-20, but most do not include the story of the Canaanite Woman as Levine does. Bruce J. Malina and Jerome H. Neyrey (*Calling Jesus Names: The Social Value of Labels in Matthew* [Sonoma: Polebridge Press, 1988], p. 5) attribute the presumed difference to 'information about Jesus [being] "traditioned"...[i.e.,] different sources or layers of tradition in the gospel that in turn reflect different experiences and interpretations of those experiences'. Wolfgang Schrage (*The Ethics of the New Testament* [Philadelphia: Fortress Press, 1988], p. 144) calls it a difference of pre-Easter and post-Easter mission, that is, 'the mission to Israel in 10.5-6, 23 becomes a mission to the nations'. I hope to show that these texts need to be re-examined through the lens of Matthew's Jewish bias rather than with the assumption that there are 'layers of tradition' or 'a pre-Easter and post-Easter mission'. I argue that Matthew is more consistent than scholars suggest; this consistency is reflected in the story of the Canaanite Woman.

18. A.-J. Levine, *Social and Ethnic Dimensions*, pp. 163-64. Meier (*Marginal Jew*, II, p. 374) goes a step further and argues that from a reading of all the sources of all four Gospels, 'nowhere does Jesus undertake a programmatic mission to the Gentiles'. Edwin D. Freed ('The Women in Matthew's Genealogy', *JSNT* 29 [1987], pp. 3-19 [5])

Wainwright, after Fiorenza, concludes that the story of the Canaanite Woman suggests a 'legitimation of women's active role in liturgy, their participation in the community's theological reflection on the life and ministry of Jesus in the light of their scriptures, and their leadership role'.[19] Our purposes, however, are obviously divergent: Wainwright's narrative study is done with a wide-angle lens on all of the women in Matthew's Gospel in an attempt to develop a comprehensive picture of the role of women in that particular community; conversely, my lens magnifies one story in an attempt to more clearly develop one scene in the Gospel narrative that provides detail on a previously overlooked controversy in the social world of Matthew's community.

Janice Capel Anderson also addresses gender, but relegates women's roles in the narrative to that of 'foils for various character groups':

> Their very 'otherness' makes them suitable foils. The Canaanite woman…is doubly marginal as a Gentile and a woman. As a mother she seeks healing for her daughter. Her faith and initiative are contrasted favorably with those of [the Jewish leaders, the disciples and the crowds]. Nevertheless, she does not become a disciple, a privileged male group in Matthew. Nor does she have a continuing role in the narrative.[20]

holds the opposite thesis: 'Throughout the Gospel Matthew reflects a Christian polemic against the Jews or a polemic of the church against the synagogue'. Of the same texts, Jerome H. Neyrey ('Decision Making in the Early Church: The Case of the Canaanite Woman [Mt 15.21-28]', *Science et Esprit* 33 [1981], pp. 373-78 [373-74]) posits the story of the Canaanite Woman as a transitional text between the 'exclusive Jewish mission and the catholic mission', thereby demonstrating the decision-making process of an early church.

19. Elaine Mary Wainwright, *Towards a Feminist Critical Reading of the Gospel According to Matthew* (BZNW, 60; New York: W. de Gruyter, 1991), p. 245; Fiorenza, *In Memory of Her*, p. 138. George T. Montague (*Companion God: A Cross-Cultural Commentary on the Gospel of Matthew* [New York: Paulist Press, 1989], p. 174) also maintains that the Canaanite woman's cry 'both echoes the Psalms and foreshadows the liturgical prayer of the church'.

20. J. Anderson, 'Mary's Difference: Gender and Patriarchy in the Birth Narratives', *JR* 67 (1987), pp. 183-202 (200). Russell Pregeant ('The Wisdom Passages in Matthew's Story', in Bauer and Powell [eds.], *Treasures*, pp. 197-232 [217]) likewise contends that one of the reasons for the story of the Canaanite Woman is to 'reinforce the reader's negative impression of the attitude of the religious leaders'. Rosemary Radford Ruether (*Sexism and God-Talk: Toward a Feminist Theology* [Boston: Beacon Press, 1983], pp. 136-37) also concludes that women represent the doubly despised in the gospels and 'have no honor within the religious groups. The protest of the Gospels is directed at the concrete sociological realities in which

Women undoubtedly served as more than foils for various character groups, and while the Canaanite woman is not credited with a further role in the narrative, the story is one of the girders on which the Gospel is built.

As Levine and Wainwright have aptly pointed out, the history of interpretation has missed some key points because the woman has been viewed strictly through the eyes of the early church's mission to the Gentiles. The story needs instead to be seen with binocular vision: first, through the wide-angle lens focused on the narrative world of the gospel writer and the sources and traditions that the evangelist knew and used; and second, through the narrow-spectrum lens with a fix on the story of the woman from Tyre and Sidon and its narrative purpose in the Matthean community.

Dennis Ronald MacDonald points out the importance of looking at independent tales that have been written down in larger narratives intertextually and not atomistically; he cites for example, the story of the Syrophoenician Woman.[21] In other words, each tale can function differently in each context in which it is used. Fiorenza states:

> form and redaction criticism have demonstrated that the biblical tradition is not a doctrinal or exegetical tradition, but a living tradition of the community of faith... Thus the Gospel writers were not content to repeat formulas and stories just because they belonged to the tradition; instead they reformulated them in order to respond to the needs of the Christians of their own day.[22]

maleness and femaleness are elements, along with class, ethnicity, religious office, and law, that define the network of social status.' So Celia M. Deutsch, *Lady Wisdom, Jesus, and the Sages: Metaphor and Social Context in Matthew's Gospel* (Valley Forge, PA: Trinity Press International, 1996), p. 138. Fiorenza (*But She Said*, p. 12) goes a step further and calls the Canaanite//Syrophoenician Woman a 'triple outsider', that is, gender, ethnic//cultural//religious affiliation, and she 'enters the site of canonical male discourse'. Mary Rose D'Angelo ('[Re]Presentations of Women in the Gospels: John and Mark', in Ross Shepard Kraemer and Mary Rose D'Angelo [eds.], *Women and Christian Origins* [New York: Oxford University Press, 1999], pp. 129-49 [139]) disagrees and argues that the woman is very much an insider, indeed a 'triple insider', because Mark's audience could identify with her. E.A. Russell ('The Canaanite Woman and the Gospels [Mt 15.21-28]', in E.A. Livingstone [ed.], *Studia Biblica 1978*. II. *Papers on the Gospels* [JSNTSup, 2; Sheffield: JSOT, 1980], pp. 263-300 [270]) inappropriately suggests that the woman may be a prostitute since no father is mentioned.

21. Dennis Rowland MacDonald, 'From Audita to Legenda: Oral and Written Miracle Stories', *Forum* 2.4 (1986), pp. 15-26 (24).

22. Elizabeth Schüssler Fiorenza, *Bread Not Stone: The Challenge of Feminist Biblical Interpretation* (Boston: Beacon Press, 1984), pp. 33-34.

This 'reformulation' can be demonstrated by looking at the differences in the story of the Syrophoenician Woman in Mark's Gospel and the story of the Canaanite Woman in Matthew's Gospel.

3. *The Syrophoenician Woman and the Canaanite Woman*

Mark's account of the Syrophoenician Woman in 7.24-30 is generally accepted as Matthew's primary source for the story of the Canaanite Woman in 15.21-28.[23] Scholars differ, of course, on the priority of Mark or Matthew,[24] and even of those who subscribe to the two-document theory, some sense that Matthew's version of the Canaanite Woman may be independent of Mark's story of the Syrophoenician Woman. For instance, B.H. Streeter discusses the Syrophoenician Woman as one of three specific cases in the 'overlapping of Mark and M'. He claims that in the pericopes on Divorce (Mt. 19.3-12//Mk 10.2-12), the Healing of the Withered Hand (Mt. 12.9-12//Mk 3.1-6), and the Syrophoenician Woman (Mt. 15.21-28//Mk 7.24-30), the writer of Matthew's Gospel had a parallel version in M, but chose to tell the stories in the Markan context.[25] Rudolf Bultmann disagrees with Streeter, and argues:

23. For Mark's sources, see W.D. Davies, *Invitation to the New Testament: A Guide to Its Main Witnesses* (Garden City, NY: Doubleday, 1966), pp. 98-100; Barnabas Flammer, 'Die Syrophoenizerin: Mk 7, 24-30', *TQ* 148 (1968), pp. 463-78; France (*Matthew*, especially chapter 3, 'The Gospel [Matthew] as a Drama', pp. 149-53; Joachim Gnilka, *Das Evangelium nach Markus* (EKKNT; 2 vols.; Zürich: Benzinger Verlag, 1978), I, pp. 289-95; Koester, *Ancient Christian Gospels*, pp. 203, 285, 287; Burton L. Mack, *A Myth of Innocence: Mark and Christian Origins* (Philadelphia: Fortress Press, 1988); William Telford (ed.), *The Interpretation of Mark* (Issues in Religion and Theology, 7; Philadelphia: Fortress Press, 1985). For narrative-critical studies of Mark's story, see, for example, Pierre-Yves Brandt, 'De l'usage de la frontière dans la rencontre entre Jésus et al Syrophénicienne (Mc 7/24-30)', *ETR* 74 (1999), pp. 173-88; David Rhoads, 'Jesus and the Syrophoenician Woman in Mark: A Narrative-Critical Study', *JAAR* 62 (1994), pp. 343-75.

24. See, for example, Helmut Koester, (*Introduction to the New Testament* [2 vols.; Berlin: W. de Gruyter, 1980], II, pp. 44-49, 164-77) for a discussion of 'The Synoptic Problem and the Sources of the Gospels' and 'The Oldest Gospel of the Church: The Gospel of Mark'. See further Robert W. Funk, Roy W. Hoover and The Jesus Seminar, *The Five Gospels: The Search for the Authentic Words of Jesus* (New York: Macmillan, 1993), pp. 9-12.

25. B.H. Streeter, *The Four Gospels* (New York: Macmillan, 1956), p. 260. Those who also note the overlapping of Matthew and Mark in the story of the Canaanite woman, but with no conclusions, include Roy A. Harrisville, 'The Woman of Canaan:

It is possible to ask whether Matthew used an older version of the story than lay before our Mark. But the discussion with the disciples does not support that, for the heightening of the element of dialogue is normally a sign of a secondary form...the saying of Jesus in Matt. 15.24 certainly gives the impression of being old, and Matt. probably knew it as a logion in independent circulation which he wove into the middle of Mark's dialogue at v. 23.[26]

The story of the Canaanite Woman is classified by Bultmann as an apophthegm, or controversy dialogue, rather than a miracle story.[27] He

A Chapter in the History of Exegesis', *Int* 20 (1966), pp. 274-87 (276); Held, 'Matthew as Interpreter', pp. 198-99; G.D. Kilpatrick, *The Origins of the Gospel According to St. Matthew* (Oxford: Clarendon Press, 1946), p. 50; E.A. Russell, 'Canaanite Woman', pp. 263-64, 280.

26. Rudolf Bultmann, *History of the Synoptic Tradition* (New York: Harper & Row, rev. edn, 1963), p. 38. Bultmann also observes that Dobschütz and Bussmann are in agreement with Streeter. See further T.A. Burkill, 'The Syrophoenician Woman: The Congruence of Mark 7.24-31', *ZNW* 57 (1966), pp. 23-37 (25-28). Burkill ('The Historical Development of the Story of the Syrophoenician Woman [Mark vii.24-30]', *NovT* 9 [1967], pp. 161-77) posits four phases in the life-history of the story of the Syrophoenician Woman; the Matthean account is included as the fourth phase. Part of Fiorenza's history of interpretation (*But She Said*, p. 97) includes a 'simple Galilean miracle story about a woman asking Jesus to exorcise her daughter, with Jesus granting her request' (Mk 7.25, 26b, 29b, 30), followed by the addition of a connection with feeding miracle stories (vv. 26a, 27-29a) and the introduction of the opposition between a Syro-Phoenician—Greek—woman and Jesus—Galilean—male. This scenario, according to Fiorenza, is then taken over by Mark and tied into the gospel narrative with v. 24 and *proton* in v. 27. Since Mark and Matthew each write a story about a Gentile woman from Tyre, a legitimate question arises as to why the author of Luke did not include a similar story. There are a variety of explanations. T.A. Burkill (*New Light on the Earliest Gospel* [Ithaca, NY: Cornell University Press, 1972], p. 75), for instance, contends that 'St. Luke may have been offended by the reference to Gentiles as dogs in Mark 7.27, and for this reason decided to omit the story'. Derrett ('Law', p. 184) perceives that Luke's omission is not so much because the content of Mark's Syrophoenician Woman is offensive, as because it is unnecessary: 'parts of her tale are scattered elsewhere in his gospel, verbally or by implication'. For a discussion of the omission in both Luke's and John's Gospels, see E.A. Russell, 'Canaanite Woman', pp. 282-90. See further Jeffrey S. Siker, ' "First to the Gentiles": A Literary Analysis of Luke 4.16-30', *JBL* 111 (1992), pp. 73-90. Arland D. Jacobson (*The First Gospel: An Introduction to Q* [Sonoma, CA: Polebridge Press, 1992], p. 154) includes this story in 'Luke's "greater omission" '.

27. Bultmann, *History*, pp. 38, 41, 63, 209. See also Davies and Allison (*Matthew*, p. 544) and Held ('Matthew as Interpreter', p. 199). Robert C. Tannehill ('Varieties of Synoptic Pronouncement Stories', *Semeia* 20 [1981], pp. 101-19 [107, 113]) classifies

claims that even though the story of the Syrophoenician Woman contains a miracle of healing, '[it is] not told in the style of miracle stories, for the miracle has been completely subordinated to the point of the apophthegm'.[28] According to Bultmann's definition, 'controversy dialogues are imaginary scenes illustrating in some concrete occasion a principle which the Church ascribed to Jesus'.[29] However, in this case the form does not fit because the principle is spoken by the Canaanite woman, not Jesus.

In his discussion of the 'Form and History of Apophthegms', Bultmann includes rabbinic history:

> To carry on disputes in this way is typically Rabbinic. So we have to look for the *Sitz im Leben* of the controversy dialogues in the discussions the Church had with its opponents, and as certainly within itself, on questions of law.[30]

As will be shown, rabbinic traditions and forms may have played a significant role in the genesis of the story of the Canaanite Woman.[31]

Mk 7.24-30//Mt. 15.21-28 as a 'Pronouncement Story', with sub-classifications such as 'Objection Story' and 'Quest Story', in fact a hybrid story that combines both objection and commendation or objection-quest. Clear summaries of the importance of the form can be found in, for example, Martin Dibelius, *From Tradition to Gospel* (New York: Charles Scribner's Sons, 1935); Mack, *Myth*, esp. ch. 7, 'The Pronouncement Stories', pp. 172-207, and 'The Miracle Stories', pp. 208-45; Burton Mack and Vernon K. Robbins, *Patterns of Persuasion in the Gospels* (Sonoma, CA: Polebridge Press, 1989), esp. chs. 1 and 2, 'Chreia and Pronouncement Story in Synoptic Studies', pp. 1-29 and 'Elaboration of the Chreia in the Hellenistic School', pp. 31-67; Vernon K. Robbins, 'Pronouncement Stories from a Rhetorical Perspective', *Forum* 4.2 (1988), pp. 3-32; Gerd Theissen, *The Gospels in Context: Social and Political History in the Synoptic Tradition* (Minneapolis: Fortress Press, 1991), pp. 112-22.

28. Bultmann, *History*, p. 209.

29. Bultmann, *History*, p. 41.

30. Bultmann, *History*, pp. 41-54 (41). He maintains that while inquiry into rabbinic forms and their relationship to the Synoptics is complicated, they must be considered in parallel fashion.

31. S. Solomon Schechter (*Studies in Judaism* [New York: Meridian, 1958], p. 102), in spite of saying that 'the Rabbis have nothing to tell us about the personality of Jesus', invites study of rabbinic literature in order to 'help us to a better understanding of the writings attributed to Jesus and his disciples'. Samuel Tobias Lachs ('Rabbinic Sources for New Testament Studies—Use and Misuse', *JQR* 74 [1983], pp. 159-73 [160]) echoes that invitation: 'preference for the Bible and the intertestamental literature [while ignoring Rabbinic material even of the second century CE]…is widespread. It stems either from ignorance of that literature or from a misguided notion that it is not applicable, since it comes from too late a period. This ignores the fact that

For now, it must be recognized that a miracle of healing[32] is contained in the chreia, and the account is longer in Matthew than in Mark, unlike the other ten miracle stories that the two gospels have in common.[33] While a cursory look at the Markan source shows that the story is used by the author of Matthew, it can also be seen that the Matthean narrative is filled out with a personal repertoire of traditions and motivations.[34]

An element of Matthew's social world can be detected through that expansion which includes the presence of the male group of Jewish disciples. A most conspicuous development centers on the description of the woman, the disciples' reaction to her, and her argument with Jesus. This study will consider Matthew's sources for the expansion and development, along

much of the literature stemming from the 2nd through the 4th centuries represents a continuum from the 1st century and perhaps even earlier.' So Overman, *Church and Community*, p. 15: 'Rabbinic Judaism, too, was concentrated in the north in Israel—it was largely a Galilean movement at the outset—and rabbinic Judaism retained many of the features of post-70 Judaism we hear debated in the pages of Matthew's Gospel'.

32. Studies on the history and significance of miracle stories in the first century are numerous. See, for example: Colin Brown, 'Synoptic Miracle Stories: A Jewish Religious and Social Setting', *Forum* 2.4 (1986), pp. 55-76; G. Adolf Deissmann, *Light From the Ancient East: The New Testament Illustrated by Recently Discovered Texts of the Graeco-Roman World* (London: Hodder & Stoughton, 1908), pp. 393-94; Schüssler-Fiorenza (ed.), *Aspects of Religious Propaganda in Judaism and Early Christianity* (University of Notre Dame Center for the Study of Judaism and Christianity in Antiquity, 2; Notre Dame: University of Notre Dame Press, 1976), especially ch. 1, 'Miracles, Mission, and Apologetics', pp. 1-25; John Paul Heil, 'Significant Aspects of the Healing Miracles in Matthew', *CBQ* 41, 1979, pp. 274-87; David Lenz Tiede, *The Charismatic Figure As Miracle Worker* (SBLDS, 1; Missoula, MT: Society of Biblical Literature, 1972).

33. The list includes the Healing of Peter's Mother-in-Law (Mk 1.29-31//Mt. 8.14-15); the Cleansing of the Leper (Mk 1.40-45//Mt. 8.1-4); the Healing of the Paralytic (Mk 2.1-12//Mt. 9.1-8); the Man with a Withered Hand (Mk 3.1-6//Mt. 12.9-14); the Gerasene Demoniac (Mk 5.1-20//Mt. 8.28-34); Jairus' Daughter (Mk 5.21-24, 35-43//Mt. 9.18-19, 23-26); the Woman with a Hemorrhage (Mk 5.25-34//Mt. 9.20-22); the Deaf Mute and Many Others (Mk 7.31-37//Mt. 15.29-31); the Epileptic Boy (Mk 9.14-29//Mt. 17.14-21); and the Healing of the Blind Men (Mk 10.46-52//Mt. 29.29-34). Howard Clark Kee (*Miracle in the Early Christian World* [New Haven: Yale University Press, 1983], p. 187) discusses Matthew's 'spatial miraculous preparations for events leading up to and within the career of Jesus, but then the condensation of actual miracle stories'; the story of the Canaanite Woman is the exception.

34. An essay on the development of stories and texts is Paul J. Achtemeier's '*Omne verbum sonat*: The New Testament and the Oral Environment of Late Western Antiquity', *JBL* 109 (1990), pp. 3-27.

with the possibility that Matthew's writing is based on the desire to write a gospel that influences and sets rules for proselytism in the community.[35]

4. *Proselytism*

While A.-J. Levine echoes many scholars in saying that 'first-century Jews were not for the most part engaged in an active proselytizing program... proselytes to Judaism were in many cases heartily welcomed, but their affiliation was not actively sought',[36] it remains that converts to Judaism

35. I agree with Benedict T. Viviano ('The Genres of Matthew 1–2: Light from 1 Timothy 1.4', *RB* [1990], pp. 31-53) that 'the literary genre of Mt. 1–2 is myth, to which are added a genealogy and midrashic expositions of Scripture' (p. 42), although I question his ultimate conclusion (pp. 52-53). See also Robert W. Funk and The Jesus Seminar, *The Acts of Jesus: What Did Jesus Really Do?* (San Francisco: HarperSanFrancisco, 1998), pp. 497-526. On another issue, the evidence will suggest that this is proselytism into Judaism, not Christianity; this is contrary to traditional scholarship on the theme of Matthew's universalism. For example, Guido Tisera reviews literature in his work, *Universalism According to the Gospel of Matthew* (Frankfurt am Main: Peter Lang, 1993) and agrees with the traditional theme.

36. A.-J. Levine, *Social and Ethnic Dimensions*, pp. 20-21. See also, *idem*, 'Anti-Judaism and the Gospel of Matthew', in William R. Farmer (ed.), *Anti-Judaism and the Gospels* (Harrisburg, PA: Trinity Press International, 1999), pp. 9-36 (26). P.M. Casey (*From Jewish Prophet to Gentile God* [Louisville, KY: Westminster/John Knox Press, 1991], p. 70) agrees that 'ethnicity was taken for granted: there was no mission to the Gentiles during the historic ministry, and Gentile faith was regarded as remarkable'. Robert Goldenberg ('The Place of Other Religions in Ancient Jewish Thought, with Particular Reference to Early Rabbinic Judaism', in Martin E. Marty and Frederick E. Greenspahn [eds.], *Pushing the Faith: Proselytism and Civility in a Pluralistic World* [New York: Crossroad, 1988], pp. 27-40 [30-31]) maintains two conflicting positions: 'There is abundant evidence of an active Jewish drive for converts, a quest lasting for centuries that did not come to an end until Roman pressure, especially Christian Roman pressure, made it impossible to continue'. He later speaks of rabbinic activity and writes that 'in contrast to earlier Jewish and contemporary Christian thinkers, ancient rabbis were no longer engaged in a struggle to win over the world... They were content to preserve a Jewish community relatively safe from the depredations and temptations of the outside world, and were willing to give up prospects for continued large-scale recruitment if such self-restraint was the only way to achieve that safety' (p. 34). See also Dieter Georgi, *The Opponents of Paul in Second Corinthians* (Philadelphia: Fortress Press, 1986), especially ch. 2, 'Missionary Activity in New Testament Times', pp. 83-228; Hans Conzelmann, *Gentiles, Jews, Christians: Polemics and Apologetics in the Greco-Roman Era* (Minneapolis: Fortress Press, 1992), pp. 17-19; Martin Hengel, *Judaism and Hellenism: Studies in their Encounter in*

came from a variety of circumstances and became members of the faith in a variety of capacities and in a variety of categories.[37] Miriam S. Taylor points out that:

> Scholars have portrayed isolationism and proselytizing as two exclusive alternatives, and have failed to consider that they might rather be seen as extremes on a continuum, opening the door to the possibility that ancient Judaism defined the relationship between insiders and outsiders in a more complex and more nuanced fashion.[38]

Palestine during the Early Hellenistic Period (2 vols.; Philadelphia: Fortress Press, 1974), especially I, pp. 247-54, 303-309. Carleton Paget ('Jewish Proselytism at the Time of Christian Origins: Chimera or Reality?', *JSNT* 62 [1996], pp. 65-103) assesses the evidence and concludes that Jewish proselytism existed in sufficient measure to argue for the existence of a missionary consciousness among some Jews of the first century. David C. Sim (*The Gospel of Matthew and Christian Judaism: The History and Social Setting of the Matthean Community* [Studies of the New Testament and Its World; Edinburgh: T. & T. Clark, 1998]) points out one of the spectrums that existed: on the one hand, 'the Jews were prepared to relax these boundaries [that is, the social and ethnic distinctions between Jew and Gentile] for those Gentiles who showed interest in the religion of Judaism and the Jewish lifestyle' (p. 15); on the other hand, in the Antiochene church, 'anything less than total conversion to (Christian) Judaism would see them exempt themselves from full participation in the Antiochene church' (p. 103). Evidence from the story of the Canaanite Woman parallels Sim's right end of the spectrum. For a complete review of the literature and the issues, see Louis H. Feldman, *Jew and Gentile in the Ancient World: Attitudes and Interactions from Alexander to Justinian* (Princeton, NJ: Princeton University Press, 1993), especially Chapters 9-11; James LaGrand, *The Earliest Christian Mission to 'All Nations' in the Light of Matthew's Gospel* (Atlanta: Scholars Press, 1995), pp. 9-11. See also Martin Goodman, *Mission and Conversion: Proselytizing in the Religious History of the Roman Empire* (Oxford: Clarendon, 1994), especially ch. 4, 'Judaism before 100 CE: Proselytes and Proselytizing', pp. 60-90.

37. The role of proselytes in Israelite history varies in importance, for example, the story of Rahab (Josh. 2–6), which will be discussed in Chapter 2. It also must be noted that inclusion of the Gentiles did not start with Paul or the gospel communities; see, for example, 1 Chron. 16.8, 24; Pss. 96.3, 10; 105.1; Isa. 12.4; 66.19; Jer. 31.10; Mal. 1.11. In that regard, Terence Donaldson ('"Riches for the Gentiles" [Rom 11.12]: Israel's Rejection and Paul's Gentile Mission', *JBL* 112 [1993], pp. 81-98 [98]) suggests that while Paul's convictions on Jewish proselytism 'differ from the corresponding Jewish ones in *substance*...they are congruent in *form*: God has chosen Israel to be a channel of salvation for all nations; Gentiles are to be welcomed into the community of salvation on equal terms with Jews.' See also Christiana van Houten, *The Alien in Israelite Law* (JSOTSup, 107; Sheffield: JSOT Press, 1991).

38. Miriam S. Taylor, *Anti-Judaism and Early Christian Identity: A Critique of the Scholarly Consensus* (Leiden: E.J. Brill, 1995), p. 13.

By the same token, Samuel Sandmel suggests that 'it is perhaps a viable distinction to differentiate between welcoming into a community an outsider who volunteers to enter, as was the case with Ruth, and pursuing an active, aggressive movement designed to persuade outsiders to enter'.[39] As will be shown, the story of the Canaanite Woman parallels the story of Ruth in its theme of proselytism.

Some scholars theorize that there was widespread success of Jewish proselytism among the Phoenicians during the Diaspora. According to Louis H. Feldman:

> Once the mother-cities of Tyre and Sidon and the chief daughter-city, Carthage, had lost their independence, the Phoenician colonies throughout the world were in effect an orphaned Diaspora and may have been attracted to Judaism because of the parallel with the kindred Jewish Diaspora.[40]

With another bit of evidence, Feldman adds, 'We may also cite the statement of Rav in the third century (*Menaboth* 110a) that "from Tyre to Carthage they know Israel and their Father in Heaven".' But he appends Salo W. Baron's suggestion that 'The success of Jewish missionary activities may help to explain the bitter feelings of Tyre, and to a lesser degree of Sidon, toward the Jews (cf. 1 Macc. 5.15; Josephus' *War* 2. 478-79 and *Against Apion* 1.70)'.[41] These conflicting attitudes between Israel and Phoenician cities like Tyre and Sidon will be discussed in Chapter 1.

'God-fearers'[42] or 'fearers of heaven'[43] were the dominant group; already George F. Moore detects five different categories of converts: religious persons ('those who worship, or revere, God'); *gerim gerurim* (the 'dragged in'); *ger sedek* or *gere emet* ('righteous or true proselytes'); *ger toshab* ('semi-proselyte'); proselytes of the gate, proselytes of righ-

---

39. Samuel Sandmel, *The First Christian Century in Judaism and Christianity: Certainties and Uncertainties* (New York: Oxford University Press, 1969), p. 21.

40. Feldman, *Jew and Gentile*, p. 329.

41. Salo W. Baron, *A Social and Religious History of the Jews* (2 vols.; New York: Columbia University Press; Philadelphia: Jewish Publication Society, 2nd edn, 1952), I, pp. 374-75, as cited in Feldman, *Jew and Gentile*, p. 328.

42. Overman, 'The God-Fearers: Some Neglected Features', *JSNT* 32 (1988), pp. 17-26; D. Flusser, 'Paganism in Palestine', in S. Safrai and M. Stern (eds.), *The Jewish People in the First Century* (2 vols.; Philadelphia: Fortress Press, 1987), II, pp. 1065-100 (1095).

43. M. Stern, 'The Jews in Greek and Latin Literature', in Safrai and Stern (eds.), *Jewish People*, II, pp. 1101-59 (1158).

teousness or full proselytes or God-fearing Gentiles.[44] Samuel Tobias Lachs differentiates between God-fearers and proselytes, the latter being 'those who were formally converted and took up membership in the Jewish people. This required instruction in the principles of Judaism.'[45] Robert S. MacLennan also points out that the terms 'proselyte' and 'God-fearer' are not identical: 'The proselyte is one who does have religious interests, while a God-fearer might have any number of reasons for associating with the synagogue or a community center where Jews would be present'.[46] It is not the purpose of this study to determine what kind of proselyte the Canaanite Woman is in the Gospel of Matthew, nor is it necessary to argue what rites were to follow acceptance into the community. One of the purposes of this study, however, is to show the need for a complete examination of the element of proselytism in Matthew's community as unfolded in the narrative; the story of the Canaanite Woman is only a small part of that examination.

One of the reasons for the neglect is that the term προσήλυτος is used only once in Matthew[47] and the emphasis is not on proselytes, but on Jesus' anger directed toward some of the scribes and Pharisees.[48]

---

44. G.F. Moore, *Judaism in the First Centuries of the Christian Era: The Age of the Tanaaim* (3 vols.; Peabody, MA: Hendrickson, 1997), I, pp. 325-40. Marcus Jastrow (*A Dictionary of the Targumim, the Talmud Babli and Yerushalmi, and the Midrashic Literature* [2 vols.; Brooklyn, NY: P. Shalom, 1967], I, p. 263) also lists the variety of proselytes that the term *ger* can include. Shaye J.D. Cohen ('Crossing the Boundary and Becoming a Jew', *HTR* 82 [1989], pp. 13-34) identifies seven different categories of associations between Gentiles and Jews, including the final step of converting to Judaism.

45. Samuel Tobias Lachs, *A Rabbinic Commentary on the New Testament: The Gospels of Matthew, Mark, and Luke* (Hoboken, NJ: Ktav, 1987), p. 369. See also Terrance Callan ('The Background of the Apostolic Decree [Acts 15.20, 29; 21.25]', *CBQ* 55 [1993], pp. 284-97 [290-95]) for a discussion of the *ger* equal to 'convert' and also equal to 'resident alien as Gentile adherent of the synagogue'.

46. Robert S. MacLennan, *Early Christian Texts on Jews and Judaism* (BJS, 194; Atlanta: Scholars Press, 1990), p. 134.

47. The only additional New Testament citations are in Acts 2.10, 6.5 and 13.43, where in each case the term is in relation to Judaism. In all of the 71 citations in the LXX, the meaning for the term which is translated from the Hebrew *ger*, is 'alien, stranger or sojourner'. It is noteworthy that in all but one of those citations, aliens and the House of Israel not only reside alongside each other, but are also to be treated equally: 'As for the assembly, there shall be for both you and the resident alien a single statute, a perpetual statute throughout your generations; you and the alien shall be alike before the Lord. You and the alien who resides with you shall have the same law and

> Woe to you, scribes and Pharisees, hypocrites! for you traverse sea and land
> to make a single proselyte (προσήλυτον), and at the time when he
> becomes one, you make him twice as much a child of hell as yourselves.
> (Mt. 23.15)

This text is interpreted in a variety of ways, for example, as an indication of active Jewish proselytism existed during the first century CE or that 'the synagogue was in competition with the church for Gentile approval if not for membership'.[49] The text can be seen more accurately as Matthew's narrative use of tension between Jesus and some of the Jewish leaders and cannot be used to develop Matthew's attitude toward proselytes; the negativity is directed towards certain scribes and Pharisees who are recruiting converts.[50] I agree with Saldarini, who argues that 'the author of Matthew seeks specifically to delegitimate rival Jewish leaders and legitimate himself [namely, Matthew] and his group as the true leaders of Israel,

the same ordinance' (Num. 15.15-16); 'Cursed be anyone who deprives the alien, the orphan, and the widow of justice' (Deut. 27.19a); 'Assemble the people—men, women, and children, as well as the aliens residing in your towns—so that they may hear and learn to fear the Lord your God and to observe diligently all the words of this law' (Deut. 31.12); 'So you shall divide this land among you according to the tribes of Israel...the aliens...shall be to you as citizens of Israel' (Ezek. 47.21-23). The exception is found in 2 Chron. 2.16-17 (LXX) where Solomon makes laborers, stonecutters and overseers out of the aliens.

48. So David E. Garland, *The Intention of Matthew 23* (SNT, 52; Leiden: E.J. Brill, 1979), p. 129.

49. A.-J. Levine (*Social and Ethnic Dimensions*, p. 195), citing proof texts of Douglas R.A. Hare and Daniel J. Harrington's theory (' "Make Disciples of All the Gentiles" [Mt 28.19]', *CBQ* 37 [1975], pp. 359-69).

50. Martin Goodman ('Jewish Proselytizing in the First Century', in Judith Lieu, John North and Tessa Rajak [eds.], *The Jews Among Pagans and Christians in the Roman Empire* [New York: Routledge, 1992], pp. 53-78 [60-62]) suggests that the term 'proselyte' in this case may refer to the conversion of *Jews* to Pharisaism. For an abbreviated review of the interpretations of this text, see Paget, 'Jewish Proselytism', pp. 94-96. See also John Kampen ('Communal Discipline in the Social World of the Matthean Community', in Julian V. Hills [ed.], *Common Life in the Early Church: Essays Honoring Graydon F. Snyder* [Harrisburg, PA: Trinity Press International, 1998], pp. 158-74) for the argument that the scribes and Pharisees were not the only Jewish groups which were in conflict with Matthew's community; in fact, they were all in conflict with one another. For our purposes, Kampen's contention that 'debates about the nature and fulfillment of the law in Matthew were probably not representative of various groups within the first-century Christian movement...these followers of Jesus were in competition with a variety of perspectives found within the Jewish community of which they were a part' (174) is also one of my arguments.

accurate interpreters of the Bible and the authentic messengers of God's will'.[51]

A key Hebrew Bible passage for rabbinic teachings regarding the treatment of proselytes is found in Deuteronomy:

> He [God] executes justice for the fatherless and the widow, and loves the sojourner (προσήλυτον), giving him food (ἄρτον) and clothing (ἱμάτιον). Love the sojourner therefore; for you were sojourners in the land of Egypt. (Deut. 10.18-19 LXX)

According to David Daube, 'The Lord loveth the stranger in giving him food and raiment. The Rabbis identify the stranger with the proselyte... according to some "food" means the Torah and "raiment" the tallith'.[52] In biblical Hebrew the *ger* is the resident alien or stranger, but in rabbinic Hebrew the proselyte is called *ger*.[53] So, according to C.G. Montefiore and H. Loewe, 'All the laws in the Pentateuch enjoining kindness to the *ger* are by the Rabbis applied to the proselyte'.[54] In the case of the Canaanite

---

51. Anthony Saldarini, 'Delegitimation of Leaders in Matthew 23', *CBQ* 54 (1992), pp. 659-80 (661). So Celia M. Deutsch, 'Christians and Jews in the First Century: The Gospel of Matthew', *Thought* 67 (1992), pp. 399-408 (404).

52. David Daube, *The New Testament and Rabbinic Judaism* (Jordan Lectures, 1951; London: Athlone Press, 1956), p. 125. See also Jacob Neusner (*Eliezer ben Hyrcanus: The Tradition and The Man* [SJLA, 3; 2 vols.; Leiden: E.J. Brill, 1973], pp. 448-49) for R. Eliezer's discussion of the same text.

53. So also in the Qumran community, according to Lawrence H. Schiffman and James C. VanderKam (eds.), *Encyclopedia of the Dead Sea Scrolls* (2 vols.; Oxford: Oxford University Press, 2000), II, p. 700. However, proselytes were not accorded the same status as full Israelites at Qumran that they were in the rabbinic tradition (I, pp. 388-89).

54. C.G. Montefiore and H. Loewe, *A Rabbinic Anthology: Selected and Arranged with Comments and Introductions* (New York: Schocken Books, 1974), p. 566. Robert M. Seltzer ('Joining the Jewish People from Biblical to Modern Times', in Marty and Greenspahn [eds.], *Pushing the Faith*, pp. 41-63 [43-47]) and Solomon Zeitlin (*Studies in the Early History of Judaism* [2 vols.; New York: Ktav, 1973], II, pp. 409-17) discuss translations and interpretations of the Hebrew *ger*, types of proselytes and the absence and presence of proselyte rituals. See further Bernard Bamberger, *Proselytism in the Talmudic Period* (New York: Ktav, 1968), especially ch. 2, 'The Origins of Jewish Proselytism', pp. 13-24; John J. I. Dollinger, *The Gentile and the Jew in the Courts of the Temple of Christ: An Introduction in the History of Christianity* (2 vols.; London: Longman, Green, Longman, Roberts, and Green, 1962), II, p. 366; Sidney B. Hoenig, 'Conversion During the Talmudic Period', in David Max Eichhorn (ed.), *Conversion to Judaism: A History and Analysis* (New York: Ktav, 1965), pp. 33-66; Saul Lieberman, *Greek in Jewish Palestine: Studies in the Life and Manners of Jewish*

Woman, however, she is not, as depicted by Matthew, a 'resident stranger or sojourner'; she is an enemy of Israel and cannot, therefore, be called a 'proselyte'. Joshua makes that distinction with the aliens associated with Israel on the one hand:

> All Israel, alien as well as citizen, with their elders and officers and their judges, stood on opposite sides of the ark in front of the levitical priests who carried the ark of the covenant of the Lord... There was not a word of all that Moses commanded that Joshua did not read before all the assembly of Israel, and the women, and the little ones, and the aliens who resided among them. (Josh 8.33, 35)

On the other hand, the enemies of Israel are listed in the very next sentence:

> Now when all the kings who were beyond the Jordan in the hill country and in the lowland all along the coast of the Great Sea toward Lebanon—the Hittites, the Amorites, the Canaanites, the Perizzites, the Hivites, and the Jebusites—heard of this, they gathered together with one accord to fight Joshua and Israel. (Josh 9.1-2)

As will be shown, the story of the Canaanite Woman illustrates that an initial phase for any outsider desiring membership in the Matthean community of faith must initiate the proceedings; furthermore, it must be done properly. Jesus, therefore, responds to the woman from Tyre and Sidon in Matthew's Gospel as other Jewish leaders of the time would have. Accordingly, Lieberman states:

> The learned Rabbis were conscious of their great task of guarding the true faith, the high ethics and the pure family life of the Jews against any outside contamination; they made hedge upon hedge around the Law in order to protect it and to preserve it in its entire purity. But they were not blind, nay they refused to close their eyes to reality. They observed attentively and studied carefully the non-Jewish Hellenized world; they were quite conscious and well aware of it; they knew its shortcomings and failures. But they never denied the great virtue of the individual in that world.[55]

Palestine in the II–IV Centuries C. E. (New York: Jewish Theological Seminary of America, 1942), especially 'Gentiles and Semi-Proselytes', pp. 68-90; Hyam Maccoby, *Early Rabbinic Writings* (Cambridge Commentaries on Writings of the Jewish and Christian World 200 BC to AD 200; Cambridge: Cambridge University Press, 1988), pp. 163-65; Samuel Sandmel, *Judaism and Christian Beginnings* (New York: Oxford University Press, 1978), pp. 231-35.

55. Lieberman, *Greek in Jewish Palestine*, pp. 89-90.

Those who think that the status of Gentiles is left hanging in the air at the end of the story of the Canaanite Woman[56] are mistaken. The status of Gentiles is that they must become Jews in the community.[57]

5. *Matthew's Community*

This study does not attempt to historicize the Canaanite Woman herself, but to set the story told by the evangelist in the context of first-century communities that followed Jesus' teachings and actions.[58] Neither does this study attempt to historicize any of the Old Testament stories. It has yet to be determined what written or oral traditions the evangelist actually had in hand or head. Dependence on the Old Testament text is obvious; whether or not that text was believed to be historical is not an issue.[59] It was the text that counted, and the text that would determine the rules for living in community.

56. See, e.g., Donaldson, *Jesus on the Mountain: A Study in Matthean Theology* (JSNTSup, 8; Sheffield: JSOT, 1985), p. 134.

57. Against Davies and Allison, *Matthew*, II, p. 559.

58. In spite of the fact that Funk and The Jesus Seminar (*Acts of Jesus*, pp. 212-14) colors both the Markan and Matthean pericopes gray, they 'allowed that it had a pink core'; that is, 'that the story reflected a distant memory of an actual event, but were unable to identify precisely what that event was beyond the verbal battle between the woman and Jesus'. Meier (*Marginal Jew*, II, pp. 660-61) sees the story of the Syrophoenician Woman 'so shot through with Christian missionary theology and concerns that creation by first-generation Christians is the more likely conclusion'. See William Loader ('Challenged at the Boundaries: A Conservative Jesus in Mark's Tradition', *JSNT* 63 [1996], pp. 45-61) for the argument that the story told in Mark about the Syrophoenician Woman is an historical reminiscence of a Jewish Jesus struggling to cross frontiers. The Markan story may have an historical reminiscence, but, as will be shown, the story of the Canaanite Woman is a reflection of Matthew's preoccupation with Jewish Law. Sharon Ringe ('A Gentile Woman's Story', in Letty M. Russell [ed.], *Feminist Interpretation of the Bible*, [Philadelphia: Westminster Press, 1985], pp. 65-72 [69]) argues that 'the story could not have been invented by the church because of its shocking portrait of Jesus. Rather than inventing such a story, it is more likely that the early church tried to make the best out of a bizarre tradition which must have preserved the memory of an incident in the life of Jesus "when he was caught with his compassion down".' Marianne Sawicki (*Seeing the Lord: Resurrection and Early Christian Practices* [Minneapolis: Fortress Press, 1994], p. 155) audaciously recognizes the Syrophoenician/Canaanite Woman to be 'the bitch under the table'.

59. While it may not have mattered to Matthew whether or not the biblical stories were 'historical' or 'factual', the debate in contemporary scholarship cannot be ignored and will be discussed in Chapter 2.

Scholars who have established the importance of Matthew's use and interpretation of Old Testament passages include, among others, Ernst von Dobschütz, Krister Stendahl and Robert Horton Gundry.[60] Overman summarizes the connection:

> Jesus and the life of the Matthean community are in continuity with the traditions and promises of Israel's history. Indeed, as a result of this distinctive use of Scripture by Matthew, Jesus—and through him the Matthean community—is depicted as the fulfillment of that very history and tradition. This constitutes both a defense of Matthew's community and a challenge to the opposition.[61]

While modern writers disagree among themselves as to specific theories of use, as well as on the specific background of the evangelist, and most (Dobschütz excepted) do not explicitly discuss the story of the Canaanite Woman, this study will offer documentation in the pericope itself of the Matthean writer's molding of LXX passages for first-century purposes in that early first-century Jewish community. France makes a comment about Matthew 1–2 that can be applied to the entire Gospel:

60. Ernst von Dobschütz, 'Matthew as Rabbi and Catechist', *ZNW* 27 (1928), pp. 338-48 (reprinted in Graham Stanton [ed.], *The Interpretation of Matthew* [Studies in New Testament Interpretation; Edinburgh: T. & T. Clark, 2nd rev. edn, 1995], pp. 19-29; Krister Stendahl, *The School of St. Matthew and Its Use of the Old Testament* (Philadelphia: Fortress Press, 1968); Robert Horton Gundry, *The Use of the Old Testament in St. Matthew's Gospel* (NovTSup, 18; Leiden: E.J. Brill, 1967); William F. Albright and C.S. Mann, *Matthew* (AB, 26; Garden City, NY: Doubleday, 1971), pp. 54-73; Derrett, 'Law'; Eduard Schweizer, *The Good News According to Matthew* (Atlanta: John Knox Press, 1975), especially p. 330; G. Stanton, 'The Origin and Purpose of Matthew's Gospel: Matthean Scholarship from 1945-1980', in M. Temporini and W. Haase (eds.), *Aufstieg und Niedergang der Römischen Welt* II.25.3 (5 vols.; Berlin: W. de Gruyter, 1983), pp. 1889-951 (1930-34); O. Lamar Cope, *Matthew: A Scribe Trained for the Kingdom of Heaven* (CBQMS, 5; Washington: Catholic Biblical Society, 1976), especially ch. 1, 'The Working Hypothesis', p. 10.

61. J. Andrew Overman, *Matthew's Gospel and Formative Judaism: The Social World of the Matthean Community* (Minneapolis: Fortress Press, 1990), p. 78. William Richard Stegner ('Leadership and Governance in the Matthean Community', in Hills [ed.], *Common Life*, pp. 147-57) claims that certain usages of Old Testament passages 'point to scribal activity'. According to Bruce Chilton and Jacob Neusner (*Judaism in the New Testament: Practices and Beliefs* [London: Routledge, 1995] p. 118), 'the citation of passages verbatim [in Matthew more so than the other Gospel writers] is especially striking, and is somewhat reminiscent of the Essene technique of the Pesher'.

The deeper one digs into the language and conception of these chapters, the richer becomes the variety of scriptural material uncovered. Matthew did not just quote a few proof-texts; he delighted to weave scriptural themes into his narrative with an enthusiasm unmatched even at Qumran.[62]

Many contemporary scholars, for example, Ulrich Luz and David C. Sim, review the literature and define, expound and point out the problems with the choices for the background of the Matthean evangelist him/herself.[63] Of the choices (for example, Gentile Christian writing for a Gentile-Christian community, Jewish Christian, member of a mixed community or

62. R.T France, 'Scripture, Tradition and History in the Infancy Narratives of Matthew', in R.T. France, David Wenham and Craig Blomberg (eds.), *Gospel Perspectives: Studies of History and Tradition in the Four Gospels* (6 vols.; Sheffield: JSOT Press, 1980–86), II, pp. 239-66 (245). So also Kee, *Jesus in History: An Approach to the Study of the Gospels* (New York: Harcourt Brace Jovanovich, 2nd edn, 1977), especially in ch. 5, 'The Continuing Importance of Jewish Tradition', pp. 168-76.

63. Ulrich Luz, *The Theology of the Gospel of Matthew* (Cambridge: Cambridge University Press, 1995), pp. 11-21; Sim, *Gospel of Matthew*. The issues involved in the constituency of the Matthean community focus not only on the identity of the evangelist him/herself and the resulting community, but also self identity within and between both Judaism and early Christianity. See, for example, David L. Balch (ed.), *The Social History of the Matthean Community: Cross-Disciplinary Approaches* (Minneapolis: Fortress Press, 1991); James D.G. Dunn, *The Partings of the Ways between Christianity and Judaism and their Significance for the Character of Christianity* (London: SCM Press, 1991); *idem* (ed.), *Jews and Christians: The Parting of the Ways A.D. 70 to 135* (Tübingen: J.C.B. Mohr [Paul Siebeck], 1992), especially Philip S. Alexander, '"The Parting of the Ways" from the Perspective of Rabbinic Judaism', pp. 1-25; Sean Freyne, 'Vilifying the Other and Defining the Self: Matthew's and John's Anti-Jewish Polemic in Focus', in J. Neusner and E.S. Frerichs (eds.), *'To See Ourselves as Others See Us': Christians, Jews, 'Others' in Late Antiquity* (Chico, CA: Scholars Press, 1985), pp. 117-44; William Horbury, *Jews and Christians in Contact and Controversy* (Edinburgh: T. & T. Clark, 1998); Wayne A. Meeks, 'Breaking Away: Three New Testament Pictures of Christianity's Separation from the Jewish Communities', in Neusner and Frerichs (eds.), *'To See Ourselves'*, pp. 93-116; Overman, *Church and Community*; Saldarini, *Matthew's Christian–Jewish Community*; Jack T. Sanders, *Schismatics, Sectarians, Dissidents, Deviants: The First One Hundred Years of Jewish-Christian Relations* (Valley Forge, PA: Trinity Press International, 1993); Donald Senior, 'Between Two Worlds: Gentiles and Jewish Christians in Matthew's Gospel', *CBQ* 61 (1999), pp. 1-23; G. Stanton, 'Origin and Purpose', pp. 1889-951; *idem, A Gospel for a New People: Studies in Matthew* (Edinburgh: T. & T. Clark, 1992); *idem, Interpretation of Matthew*, pp. 17-19; Stephen G. Wilson, *Related Strangers: Jews and Christians, 70–170 C.E.* (Minneapolis: Fortress Press, 1995).

a sectarian Jew in competition with formative Judaism), I fall on the side of Matthew being a Jew whose community abided by the Torah, whether to the last 'tittle and jot' remains to be determined; I am reluctant to call Matthew's community a 'church'.[64] The group for whom Matthew was writing was undoubtedly one of many groups debating what it was to be Jewish or to follow Jewish law.

6. Method

This study employs the historical-critical method, concentrating on source, form and redaction criticisms. While the results intersect with several current issues in biblical studies (for example, Old Testament historicity, the historical Jesus, the historical Matthew and the identity of the Matthean community), special mention needs to be made of the issue of the status and role of women in first-century Judaism: a feminist critique is the underpinning to this study rather than a separate method; the assumption is that the story of the Canaanite Woman is feminine specific and could not be replaced by a story of a Canaanite Man.[65] It is of note that

---

64. Sim (*Gospel of Matthew*, p. 299) agrees that 'the Matthean community was first and foremost a Jewish group of believers in Jesus...but it is mistaken to label their religion "Christianity"'. Likewise, Saldarini (*Matthew's Christian–Jewish Community*, p. 193) insists that the label 'Christian' is anachronistic and an identity 'that most Christians created for themselves during the second century, often in contrast to Judaism'. In that light, it is difficult for me to conceive of Matthew's Gospel as a tool for 'anti-Jewish polemic'; see, for example, G. Stanton (*Gospel for a New People*, pp. 148-57) who understands Judaism as a whole to be rejected (p. 154). I like Overman's (*Church and Community in Crisis*, p. 19) description of Matthew's Gospel and community as a 'Jesus-centered Jewish community'. It would seem obvious that Jesus himself should not be called a 'Christian', but Allison (*The New Moses: A Matthean Typology* [Minneapolis: Fortress Press, 1993], pp. 97-106) includes Jesus as the first character under his chapter heading, 'Christian Figures'. Of the so-called Great Commission (Mt. 28.16-20), I wonder if the call was to re-unite all of the 'nations', the Nations of the Hebrew Bible, that is. It seems to me that one of Niels Peter Lemche's theses ('The Understanding of Community in the Old Testament and in the Dead Sea Scrolls', in Frederick H. Cryer and T.L. Thompson [eds.], *Qumran between the Old and New Testaments* [JSOTSup, 290; CIS, 6; Sheffield: Sheffield Academic Press, 1998], pp. 181-93), namely, that 'biblical Israel is founded on the Torah, the Law of Moses, presented to the Jews by God on Mount Sinai, as the basis of the covenant between Israel and God' (p. 188), is what Matthew's community is all about.

65. Contrary to the story of the Syrophoenician Woman, at least according to

Adolf Harnack includes a substantial subsection on 'the spread of Christianity among women'. Specific to this study is his observation that 'even within Judaism there were many women proselytes'.[66] If Matthew's narration reflects any kind of actual social setting in the late first century, then a study of the redactional purpose and technique in this text opens several windows into the reality of the status of women and converts and their role in church communities, and indeed contributes to the general social reconstruction of early Christianity.

Chapter 1 includes an investigation of the Gentile debate in Matthew's narration, and centers on the geographical setting of the Gentile cities of Tyre and Sidon. Chapter 2 continues the investigation of Matthew's sources, focusing on the change from 'Syrophoenician' in Mark's Gospel to 'Canaanite' in Matthew's. These sources help define the extended form the pericope takes in Matthew, which is the focal point of Chapter 3. The Conclusion emphasizes the fact that any study that ignores the proselyte dimension of the story of the Canaanite Woman is truncated.

Rhoads ('Jesus and the Syrophoenician Woman in Mark', p. 367): 'The story would have worked if a Gentile male had come on behalf of his daughter or son'. As will be shown, the story of the Canaanite Woman works only with a mother and a daughter and, as will become apparent, Neusner's (*Ruth Rabbah: An Analytic Translation* [Atlanta: Scholars Press, 1989], p. 149) assertion that the femininity of Ruth is 'critical to the whole' can be applied to the Canaanite Woman as well. Until recent times, women's roles in the gospel communities have been ignored, except as generic examples of subservient faith. In the 1800s, women such as Emily Grimke, Sarah Grimke and Elizabeth Cady Stanton attempted feminist interpretation of the Scriptures, but their work faded without major impacts during their lifetimes. Ninety years after *The Woman's Bible* (New York: European Publishing, 1898/Seattle: Coalition Task Force on Women and Religion, 1974) was first written by Cady Stanton, Fiorenza (*In Memory of Her*, especially pp. 68-95) wrote one of the first reconstructions of early Christian history as women's history; one of Fiorenza's 'mentors' was Cady Stanton. Fiorenza's 'hermeneutic of suspicion' continues to be the cornerstone of feminist biblical interpretation as it has been for the past decade. Her book, *But She Said*, is titled after the Syrophoenician//Canaanite Woman.

66. Adolf Harnack, *The Mission and Expansion of Christianity in the First Three Centuries* (2 vols.; New York: Putnam's Sons, 1908), II, p. 64 n. 2., Judith M. Lieu ('The "Attraction of Women" in/to Early Judaism and Christianity: Gender and the Politics of Conversion', *JSNT* 72 [1998], pp. 5-22 [6]) 'explore[s] the rhetoric that surrounds [such claims] and expose[s] the hazards of the naive use of sources that often accompanies it'.

Chapter 1

TYRE AND SIDON: A PARADIGMATIC SETTING

1. *Introduction*

Matthew 15.21	Mark 7.24
Καὶ ἐξελθὼν ἐκεῖθεν ὁ Ἰησοῦς ἀνεχώρησεν εἰς τὰ μέρη Τύρου καὶ Σιδῶνος.	Ἐκεῖθεν δὲ ἀναστὰς ἀπῆλθεν εἰς τὰ ὅρια Τύρου.
	Καὶ εἰσελθὼν εἰς οἰκίαν οὐδένα ἤθελεν γνῶναι, καὶ οὐκ ἠδυνήθη λαθεῖν.
And Jesus went away from there and withdrew to the district of Tyre and Sidon.	And from there he arose and went away to the region of Tyre.
	And he entered a house, and would not have any one know it; yet he could not be hid.

There are four principal investigations included in this chapter. The first is an examination of the development of the Gentile debate in Matthew's Gospel in order to measure the importance of the geographical setting of the Gentile cities of Tyre and Sidon in the story of the Canaanite Woman.[1] The second part of the investigation is an exploration of the reputation of the cities of Tyre and Sidon as presented in the Old Testament. Third, the setting of Tyre and Sidon in the story of the Canaanite Woman will be compared to Mark's designation of Tyre only. Fourth, the story of the Canaanite Woman as it relates to Matthew's Gentile context will be examined.

---

1. A complete listing of Matthew's geographical settings is supplied in Appendix 1.

2. Matthew's Development of the Gentile Debate

In an attempt to demonstrate the extreme peculiarity of the story of the Canaanite Woman in Mt. 15.21-28, it is necessary to see the story in its Gospel context.[2] Gentiles are included in Matthew's Gospel already in the first chapter.[3] The genealogy (1.1-16) begins with Abraham, traditionally a one-time pagan, and continues with four Gentile women, in fact, designated enemy[4] women: the Canaanites Tamar and Rahab (vv. 3, 5), the Moabite Ruth (v. 5), and the Hittite Bathsheba (according to the text, 'wife of Uriah', v. 6).[5] The relevance of these women to both the Gentile and gender issues in Matthew's Gospel will be discussed in the next chapter.

The inclusion of Gentiles remains obvious as the Gospel story immediately includes the wise men from the East worshipping the child Jesus,[6]

---

2.   The story of the Canaanite Woman has been placed in a number of Matthean structural outlines, some of which highlight it more than others. Jerome Murphy-O'Connor ('The Structure of Matthew XIV–XVII', *RB* 3 [1975], pp. 360-84), for example, cites P. Gaechter's 'two interlocking chiasms' in Matthew which places the Canaanite Woman in the center of the first chiasm (p. 362) and X. Leon-Dufour's 'three-part dynamic division' in the gospel which designates the story of the Canaanite Woman as the center of the 'Second Withdrawal' (p. 365). Murphy-O'Connor sees two '"withdrawal" blocks of material' with the Canaanite woman's confession in the second block being parallel (but out of order) to the disciples' confession (14.22-33) in the first block (p. 375).

3.   Matthew is the only one to include Gentiles in the very beginning of the Gospel; Luke introduces the issue in the story of Simeon (2.32).

4.   The enemies of Israel are listed in Exod. 23.23-24, 33.2 and Deut. 20.17 as six nations: Amorites, Hittites, Perizzites, Canaanites, Hivites and Jebusites. The Girgashites are added to the list in Deut. 7.1 and in 23.3 more prohibitions are included against certain other enemies: 'No Ammonites or Moabites shall enter the assembly of the Lord; even to the tenth generation none belonging to them shall enter the assembly of the Lord for ever'.

5.   Nancy de Chazal ('The Women in Jesus' Family Tree', *Theology* 97 [1994], pp. 413-19 [414]) introduces the women in this way: 'Tamar, from Genesis 38, who seduced her father-in-law Judah; Rahab, the prostitute from Jericho, who helped the Israelites to capture the city (Joshua 2); Ruth, a foreign woman from Moab who married Boaz, after some hanky-panky in a barn after heavy drinking at the harvest home (Ruth 3); the "wife of Uriah" the Hittite, Bathsheba, with whom David committed adultery (2 Sam. 11.2); and Mary, who became pregnant before her marriage to Joseph during their engagement'.

6.   David C. Sim ('The Magi: Gentiles or Jews?', *Hervormde Teologiese Studies* 55 [1999], pp. 980-1000) argues that the racial origins of the magi is nonspecific in Matthew and that it is plausible that they were Jews.

the family's departure for safety in Egypt, and John the Baptist's warning that God is not dependent upon the children of Abraham, but that 'God is able from these stones to raise up children to Abraham' (3.9b).[7] The story thus far is clearly inclusive of non-Jewish characters. The positive attitude toward Gentiles continues in spite of their status as outsiders to the Jewish faith:

> Now when he heard that John had been arrested, he withdrew into Galilee; and leaving Nazareth he went and dwelt in Capernaum by the sea, in the territory of Zebulun and Naphtali, so that what was spoken by the prophet Isaiah might be fulfilled: 'The land of Zebulun and the land of Naphtali, toward the sea, across the Jordan, Galilee of the Gentiles—the people who sat in darkness have seen a great light; and for those who sat in the region and shadow of death, light has dawned'. (4.12-16, quoting Isa. 9.1-2 [8.22b–9.2, LXX])[8]

The term 'Galilee' is derived from the Hebrew '*galil* (i.e., circuit) of the Gentiles' (Isa. 8.23, LXX).[9] In this fulfillment of the 'latter time', when all nations are illuminated, Galilee, the home of the Jews, will still be the beacon.[10]

The translations 'Gentiles' (Mt. 4.15) and 'nations' (Isa. 9.1) in the

---

7. Cf. Lk. 3.8. Jacobson (*First Gospel*, p. 83) points out that 'who these new children would be is not said. But, in the context of Q, we are bound to think of instances in which non-Israelites are used to put Israel to shame'. The point is not, however, that non-Israelites will put Israel to shame, but that non-Israelites who convert to Judaism may be included. Abraham's pagan background will be discussed in Chapter 2.

8. The parallel pericope in Mk 1.14b-15 does not contain the geographical references or saying regarding the fulfillment of the prophets. Luke has no corresponding passage.

9. Geoffrey Wigoder (ed.), *The New Standard Jewish Encyclopedia* (New York: Facts on File, 1992), p. 352.

10. According to Davies and Allison (*Matthew*, I, p. 383), Γαλιλαία τῶν ἐθνῶν 'is the key to and reason for the quotation of Isaiah's text', that is, the Isaian foreshadowing of the Messiah's work for the Gentiles has been made specific in the Matthean context, beginning with the genealogy and continuing through the foreign magi worshipping Jesus to John the Baptist's proclamation that God would raise up new sons to Abraham. Their statement can be clarified by Sean Freyne (*Galilee, Jesus and the Gospels: Literary Approaches and Historical Investigations* [Philadelphia: Fortress Press, 1988], p. 2) who agrees with Walter Bauer and Walter Grundmann that Galilee was a 'mixed population with a syncretistic religious mentality'. As for this text, he states that it is a 'proof-text for the legitimacy of Galilee as a place of messianic visitation' (p. 168).

translation presented above are both from the Greek ἔθνος,[11] a term that is rendered both ways in the NRSV and other translations. The term is used in four categories by Matthew:[12] (1) as examples of negative ethical behavior; (2) as outsiders to the Jewish faith; (3) as exemplars of the faith that Israel should have; and (4) as participants in the salvation of the Jews.

Examples of negative ethical behavior are common in Matthew:

> And if you salute your brethren, what more are you doing than others? Do not even the Gentiles do the same? (5.47)

> And in praying do not heap up empty phrases as the Gentiles do, for they think that they will be heard for their many words. (6.7)

> Therefore do not be anxious, saying, 'What shall we eat?' or 'What shall we drink?' or 'What shall we wear?' For the Gentiles seek all these things; and your heavenly Father knows that you need them all. (6.31-32)

> If the member refuses to listen to them, tell it to the church; and if the offender refuses to listen even to the church, let such a one be to you as a Gentile and a tax collector. (18.17)

In the only two officially recognized Gentile healings in the Gospel of Matthew,[13] the outsiders of the Jewish faith are not classified as ἔθνος, but by other clearly non-Jewish designations:[14] a Centurion's servant (8.5-13) and the daughter of a Canaanite woman. In the story of the Centurion's Servant, Jesus' eyes are opened to the fact that non-Jews are capable of a faith that has not been demonstrated by the Jews themselves (8.10). It is unclear at the narrative level whether the faith of the Centurion is based on

---

11. Cf. BAGD, *s.v.* ἔθνος, p. 218. See also Niels Peter Lemche (*The Israelites in History and Tradition* [Louisville, KY: Westminster John Knox Press, 1998], pp. 8-20) for a definition and history of the Greek term.

12. These are my categories based on the collection and examination of Matthew's usages of the term. While those examples from Category 1 could also be included in Category 2, they are nonetheless not identical and will be discussed separately. A complete listing is supplied in Appendix 2.

13. However, along with others such as Elizabeth Struthers Malbon ('Echoes and Foreshadowing in Mark 4–8: Reading and Rereading', *JBL* 112 [1993] pp. 211-30 [219]), I would add the story of the two demoniacs from Gadara (Mt. 8.28-34) to the list of Gentile healings. The Gadarenes as 'designated outsiders' in Matthew will be discussed in Chapter 2.

14. A slang expression for Gentile was κύων or κυνάριον (dog) and will be discussed later in this chapter. Since another metaphor for Gentiles is 'swine', there is additional reason for including the pericope of the Gadarene Demoniacs as a Gentile healing.

the person Jesus and his reputation or in the religion that Jesus espouses—
that is, Matthew has Jesus seeming to refer to the religion of the Jews
(8.11-12; cf. Luke 7.9).

The Centurion's exemplary faith fails to alter Jesus' religious isolation,
however, in his instructions to the disciples in 10.5. The mission of the
twelve is narrowly defined, not in scope (10.5-42 contains lengthy but
specific instructions and their impending consequences) but in religious
categories:

> Go nowhere among the Gentiles, and enter no town of the Samaritans, but
> go rather to the lost sheep of the house of Israel. (10.5-6)

The implication of the order to stay within Judaism continues in 10.23
after v. 18 includes the Gentiles with the rest of the wolves (v. 16):

> Behold, I send you out as sheep in the midst of wolves...and you will be
> dragged before governors and kings for my sake, to bear testimony before
> them and the Gentiles... When they persecute you in one town, flee to the
> next; for truly, I say to you, you will not have gone through all the towns of
> Israel, before the Son of Man comes. (10.16a, 18, 23)[15]

Not only is the single substance of Israel highlighted, but the reputation of
certain Gentile cities is also made clear:

> Woe to you, Chorazin! woe to you, Bethsaida! for if the mighty works done
> in you had been done in Tyre and Sidon, they would have repented long
> ago in sackcloth and ashes. (Mt. 11.21//Lk. 10.13)

However, the singleness of religious focus is immediately followed in
11.22 by an unusual softening, perhaps a literary presage of the story of
the Canaanite Woman:

> But I tell you, it shall be more tolerable on the day of judgment for Tyre
> and Sidon than for you. (cf. Lk. 10.14)

In this context, inhabitants of cities such as Tyre and Sidon are posed as
possible participants in the salvation of the Jews. This possibility will be
discussed later.

The evangelist, therefore, continues to make it paradoxically clear that in
spite of the words to the disciples in 10.5-6 a Gentile mission will ensue:

---

15. Neither Mark nor Luke contains the Gentile reference in the parallel passages
(Mk 6.8-11//Lk. 9.2-5).

This was to fulfill what was spoken by the prophet Isaiah:
'Behold, my servant whom I have chosen,
my beloved with whom my soul is well pleased.
I will put my Spirit upon him,
and he shall proclaim justice to the Gentiles.
He will not wrangle or cry aloud,
nor will anyone hear his voice in the streets;
he will not break a bruised reed
or quench a smoldering wick,
till he brings justice to victory;
and in his name will the Gentiles hope'. (12.17-21; cf. Isa. 42.1-4)

In fact, while the term ἔθνος is used ten more times in Matthew's Gospel, nine in a negative sense, the final time is a positive reference and found in the so-called Great Commission:

Go therefore and make disciples of all the Nations, baptizing them in the name of the Lord, who made heaven and earth. (Mt. 28.19)[16]

16. A.-J. Levine argues (*Social and Ethnic Dimensions*, p. 192) that ἔθνος should be translated as 'all the Gentiles' rather than 'all the nations' in 28.19. However, if 'nations' refers to the original natives of the land of Israel, that is, the 'Kenites, and the Kenizzites, and the Kadmonites, and the Hittites, and the Perizzites, and the Rephaims, and the Amorites, and the Canaanites, and the Girgashites, and the Jebusites' (Gen. 15.19-21), then the term ἔθνος can be translated as both 'Gentiles' and 'nations' and include the same population (see Lemche, *Israelites*, p. 126). Hengel (*Judaism and Hellenism*, p. 307) writes that to become a Jew was both a religious and political action: 'On his conversion the Gentile became a member of the Jewish "ethnos"'. This lends support to Levine's translation. While it is beyond the scope of this monograph to discuss the redaction of Mt. 28.19, I am suggesting that Ps. 123.8 (LXX) may have been an Old Testament source for Matthew, just as others, for example, Benjamin J. Hubbard (*The Matthean Redaction of a Primitive Apostolic Commissioning: An Exegesis of Mt 28.16-20* [SBLDS, 19; Missoula, MT: Scholars Press, 1974], p. 27) suggest Old Testament theophanies and commissionings as the sources of Matthew's Commission: 'God appeared to [Isaac] and said, "I am the God of your father Abraham; do not be afraid, for I am with you and will bless you and make your offspring numerous for my servant Abraham's sake"' (Gen. 26.23-24). Hubbard also cites the call of Moses, Gideon, Isaiah, Jeremiah, Ezekiel and Deutero-Isaiah. Jane Schaberg (*The Father, the Son and the Holy Spirit: The Triadic Phrase in Matthew 28.19b* [SBLDS, 61; Chico, CA: Scholars Press, 1982]) cites Dan. 7 as the source for the Matthean commission. Lachs (*Commentary*, p. 179) finds Mt. 28.19 ('Go therefore and make disciples of all nations, baptizing them in the name of the Father and of the Son and of the Holy Spirit...') irreconcilable with Mt. 10.5 or 15.24 because 'Jesus did minister only to Jews, and this was the attitude of the leaders of the early church in Palestine'.

For the story of the Canaanite Woman the Gentile debate[17] is not introduced with the term ἔθνος, but with a reference to the cities of Tyre and
Sidon. That reference will be discussed at length in the following section.
After the healing of the Canaanite Woman's daughter (15.28), crowds of
people with a variety of illnesses and impairments are healed by Jesus
(15.29-31). Their response is that 'they glorified the God of Israel' (v. 31).
It is probable that those who 'glorify the God of Israel' are Gentiles.[18]

The four key passages in Matthew's Gospel regarding the Gentiles are
1.1-17, 10.5-23, 15.21-28 and 28.16-20:[19]

17. Wainwright (*Matthew*, pp. 103-104) summarizes the Gentile issue from a narrative-critical perspective which includes the reader's 'conflicting expectations' as she
or he enters this story. For another narrative analysis of the pericope, see Jean-Yves
Thériault (ed.), 'Le Maitre Maitrisé! Mathieu 15, 21-28', in A.J. Greimas (ed.), *De
Jésus et des Femmes* (Montreal: Bellarmin, 1987), pp. 19-34.

18. So Alan Hugh McNeile (*The Gospel According to Matthew* [London: Macmillan, 1915], p. 233) and Francis Wright Beare (*The Gospel According to Matthew:
Translation, Introduction and Commentary* [San Francisco: Harper & Row, 1981],
p. 346). The people in the crowds are evidently a distance from their homes because
Jesus worries that they will 'faint on the way' (15.32) without first having something to
eat. Mark's narrative of the Syrophoenician Woman (7.24-30), the Healing of the
Hearing Impaired Man (7.31-37), and the Feeding of the Four Thousand (8.1-10)
contains three separate stories; those same stories in Matthew flow more smoothly as
one narrative. It is possible from Matthew's story to imagine that people were
following Jesus from the district of Tyre and Sidon to the Sea of Galilee as a result of
the healing of the Canaanite Woman's daughter (15.29). Daniel J. Harrington (*The
Gospel of Matthew* [Sacra Pagina, 1; Collegeville, MN: Liturgical Press, 1991], p. 237)
argues that 'Gentiles approach the God of Israel through Israel', i.e., Isa. 2.2-4; Zech.
8.20-23. According to Harrington, the latter reference ('In those days ten men from the
nations of every tongue shall take hold of the robe of the Jew, saying, "Let us go with
you, for we have heard that God is with you"', Zech. 8.23) is the 'kind of dynamic
[that] is played out in Matthew's version of the conversation between Jesus and the
Canaanite woman'. Although the hemorrhaging woman (Mt. 9.18-22) is not classified
as a Gentile, she is like one because she is unclean. By touching Jesus' robe (v. 20),
she will become clean, and, therefore, a Jew in good standing again. See Jackson
('Jesus as First-Century Feminist') for an analysis of this pericope.

19. A.-J. Levine ('Anti-Judaism and the Gospel of Matthew', pp. 9-36) includes
the following pericopes as examples of 'Gentilizing Anti-Judaism (abrogating anti-
Judaism)': Herod and the Magi (Mt. 2), Who's Coming to Dinner? (Mt. 8.10-12),
Exclusivity Logia and the Great Commission (Mt. 10.5-6; 15.24; 28.18-20), Sour
Grapes (Mt. 21.33-43), Jewish Leaders (Mt. 23), and The Death of Jesus (Mt. 27).
Senior ('Between Two Worlds', pp. 14-16) lists 18 pericopes that refer to Jesus' in-
volvement with Gentiles.

The book of the genealogy of Jesus Christ, the son of David, the son of Abraham [a pagan who turned to monotheism]. Abraham was the [progenitor of many nations and peoples, including] Jacob…Judah…Perez and Zerah by [the Canaanite] Tamar…Salmon the father of Boaz by [the Canaanite] Rahab, and Boaz the father of Obed by [the Moabite] Ruth, and Obed the father of Jesse, and Jesse the father of David the king. And David was the father of Solomon by [the Hittite Bathsheba,] the wife of Uriah… and Jacob the father of Joseph the husband of Mary, of whom Jesus was born, who is called Christ.

[People began to follow Jesus and he gathered together a few of them to help with a specific mission.]'These twelve Jesus sent out, charging them, 'Go nowhere among the Gentiles, and enter no town of the Samaritans, but go rather to the lost sheep of the house of Israel'.

[As time went on] Jesus [and some of his followers]…withdrew to the district of Tyre and Sidon. And behold, a Canaanite woman from that region came out and cried,[20] 'Have mercy on me, Lord, Son of David; my daughter is badly demonized'. He answered, 'I was sent only to the lost sheep of the house of Israel; it is not fair to take the children's bread and throw it to the dogs'. She said, 'Yes, Lord, yet even the dogs eat the crumbs that fall from their masters' table'. Then Jesus answered her, 'Be it done for you as you will [because you have fulfilled the requirements of the Law]'.[21]

[And so when] the eleven disciples went to Galilee, to the mountain to which Jesus had directed them, he said to them, 'Go therefore and make disciples of all Gentiles, baptizing them in the name of the [Lord, who made heaven and earth]'.[22]

While older scholars conclude that the Gospel of Matthew is pro-Gentile,[23] even to the extent of being anti-Jewish, I concur with the growing number of contemporary scholars who maintain that Matthew's community still identified itself as Jewish.[24] I argue even further that the story of the Canaanite Woman is evidence not so much of an *anti*-Gentile attitude, but of a *pro*-Jewish one.[25]

20. There are several women who speak in Matthew's Gospel; see Appendix 3 for a complete listing of women's direct speech in the Gospel narratives. Further on this topic, see Chapter 3.

21. For an explanation of this addition, see Chapter 3.

22. For an explanation of this addition, see Chapter 3.

23. David C. Sim lists those scholars in 'The Gospel of Matthew and the Gentiles', *JSNT* 57 (1995), pp. 19-48 (19-20), with special mention of Kenneth Willis Clark, 'The Gentile Bias in Matthew', *JBL* 66 (1947), pp. 165-72. See also Davies and Allison, *Matthew*, I, pp. 10-11.

24. See, for example, Farmer (ed.), *Anti-Judaism and the Gospels*, especially A.-J. Levine, 'Anti-Judaism and the Gospel of Matthew'; Senior, 'Between Two Worlds'.

25. While Sim ('Gospel of Matthew and the Gentiles', p. 45) does not expound on

3. *Tyre and Sidon in the Old Testament*

Two different themes from an Old Testament tradition are evident in the names of the cities Tyre and Sidon.[26] On the positive side, the inhabitants of Tyre and Sidon are an intelligent, skilled people who give generously to the kings of Israel, and are used by God to offer help in time of need. On the negative side, they are often described as enemies of Israel, primarily because of their foreign gods, and consequently serve as the victims of God's wrath on many occasions. Even in those particularly negative passages, however, stories of their competence as merchants and traders, as well as their wealth, are told in the Old Testament tradition.[27] According to

the story of the Canaanite Woman, it in fact fits in with one of his conclusions: 'We can hardly suppose that the Gentiles in Matthew's church were excluded from this command to keep the Torah in its entirety. This means that those Gentiles who became Matthaean Christians became Jews in the process.'

26. T.L. Thompson (*Early History*, p. 128) distinguishes between 'reality' and 'tradition' in Old Testament accounts, distinctions that are appropriate in New Testament writings as well. Of the questions that Thompson asks of 'reality', the important application for this study is that, 'the traditions of the past [are] made present for present ideological purposes'; that is, Matthew uses Old Testament 'tradition' without addressing its 'reality'.

27. See, for example, Isa. 23. Since this study is concerned exclusively with Matthew's use of the tradition, that is, not how the tradition was originally formulated in the Old Testament text, I am working only marginally with data on the geography, language, politics and economics of the cities. However, important findings on these matters can be found in a variety of recent studies, for example, Michael D. Coogan, 'Canaanites: Who Were They and Where Did They Live?', *BR* 9 (1993), pp. 44-45; Baruch Halpern, 'Dialect Distribution in Canaan and the Deir Alla Inscriptions', in D.M. Golomb (ed.), *Working With No Data: Semitic and Egyptian Studies Presented to Thomas O. Lambdin* (Winona Lake, IN: Eisenbrauns, 1988), pp. 119-39; Lemche, *Israelites*, especially pp. 24-30; *idem, Prelude to Israel's Past* (Peabody, MA: Hendrickson, 1998), especially pp. 214-19; S. Moscati (ed.), *The Phoenicians* (New York: Abbeville, 1988); David Neiman, 'Phoenician Place-Names', *JNES* 24 (1965), pp. 113-15; M. O'Connor, 'The Rhetoric of the Kilamuwa Inscription', *BASOR* 226 (1977), pp. 15-29; T.L. Thompson, *Early History*, especially pp. 262, 306-307, 317-18; I. Irving Ziderman, 'Seashells and Ancient Purple Dyeing', *BA* 53 (1990), pp. 98-101. See also Feldman (*Jew and Gentile*, p. 4) where mention is made of the commercial contacts between the Athenians who inhabited the coast of the Land of Israel at Acre and the Sidonians. Decent relations between the Sidonians and the Jews are alluded to by Feldman (p. 120) through the claim by Josephus (*War* 2.479) that the 'only cities in Syria where there were not massacres [of Jews] were Antioch, Sidon, and Apamea'.

Carol Newsom, Tyre's location in Phoenician lore is significant because
Tyre was founded on two floating rocks anchored to the bottom of the
sea: 'To call the physical location "rock" would be to make a fairly
literal description. But to call the city "rock" is to speak metaphorically,
to claim for the identity of the city the qualities of the ground on which it
was built.'[28]

The cities and inhabitants of Tyre and Sidon function in four categories
in the Old Testament:[29] (1) as examples of negative ethical behavior; (2) as
outsiders to the Jewish faith; (3) as friends of Israel; and (4) as participants
in the same salvation as the Jews. Each category will be looked at briefly;
a complete listing appears in Appendix 4.

The prophetic oracles that order the destruction of Tyre and Sidon are
the most conspicuous examples of negative ethical behavior. Isaiah 23
likens the city of Tyre to a harlot, where she will be used and abused gro-
tesquely by the righteous:[30]

> And thy hand prevails no more by sea, which troubled kings: the Lord of
> hosts has given a command concerning Canaan, to destroy the strength
> thereof...
>
> And it shall come to pass in that day, that Tyre shall be left seventy
> years, as the time of a king, as the time of a human being: and it shall come
> to pass after seventy years, that Tyre shall be as the song of a harlot.
>
> 'Take a harp, go about, O city,
>   harlot that has been forgotten;
> Play well on the harp,
>   sing many songs,
>   that you may be remembered'.
>
> And it shall come to pass after the seventy years, that God will visit Tyre,
> and she shall again be restored to her primitive state, and she shall be a
> market house for all the kingdoms of the world on the face of the earth.
> (Isa. 23.11, 15-17, LXX)

28. Carol A. Newsom, 'A Maker of Metaphors: Ezekiel's Oracles against Tyre', in
Robert P. Gordon (ed.), *'The Place Is Too Small for Us': The Israelite Prophets in
Recent Scholarship* (Winona Lake, IN: Eisenbrauns, 1995), pp. 191-204 (195).

29. As in my categorization of Matthew's use of the term ἔθνος, these are also my
categories.

30. Selvidge (*Woman, Cult, and Miracle Recital: A Redactional Critical Investigation on Mark 5.24-34* [London: Associated University Presses; Lewisburg, PA:
Bucknell University Press, 1990], p. 78) includes a discussion of the role of pagan
women in oracles which brings to the forefront the most extreme negativity surrounding women's roles in some Old Testament writings.

Zechariah also pictures Tyre as though he were speaking of a woman:

> Thus says the Lord Almighty: In those days my word shall be fulfilled if ten
> men of all the languages of the nations should take hold—even take hold of
> the hem of a Jew, saying, 'We will go with you; for we have heard that God
> is with you'... And in Emath, even in her coasts, are Tyre and Sidon,
> because they were very wise. And Tyre built strongholds for herself, and
> heaped up silver as dust, and gathered gold as the mire of the ways. And
> therefore the Lord will take them for a possession, and will smite her power
> in the sea; and she shall be consumed with fire. (Zech. 8.23; 9.2-4, LXX)

Prophecies against both Tyre and Sidon, which are numerous, can be
found, for example, in Ezekiel 26–28, Amos 1[31] and Joel 3.2-6.

Foreign gods mark the people of Tyre and Sidon as outsiders to the
Israelite faith:

> And the children of Israel did evil again in the sight of the Lord, and served
> the Baals, and Astartes, the gods of Aram, and the gods of *Sidon*, and the
> gods of Moab, and the gods of the children of the Ammonites, and the gods
> of the Philistines; and they forsook the Lord, and did not serve him. (Judg.
> 10.6, LXX)

Ahab sins three times before the Lord (1 Kgs 16): once by following in the
steps of Jeroboam, a second time by marrying Jezebel, the daughter of
Ethbaal, king of the Sidonians, and a third time by worshipping Baal.[32]

Psalm 82 (LXX) also lists the inhabitants of Tyre, along with nine other
nations, as conspirators against Israel:

> O God, who shall be compared to thee?
> be not silent, neither be still, O God.
> For behold, thine enemies have made a noise;
> and they that hate thee have lifted up the head...
> they have said, Come, and let us utterly destroy them out of the nation;
> and let the name of Israel be remembered no more at all.
> For they have taken counsel together with one consent:
> they have made a confederacy against thee;
> even the tents of Edam and the Ishmaelites;
> Moab, and the Hagrites; Gebal, and Ammon, and Amalek;

---

31. See Newsom ('Maker of Metaphors', pp. 191-204) for a detailed study of the
use of metaphors in Ezekiel's tirade against Tyre. See John T. Strong ('Tyre's
Isolationist Policies in the Early Sixth Century BCE: Evidence from the Prophets', *VT*
47 [1997], pp. 207-19) for a literary analysis of oracles against the nations, including
Tyre, in the book of Amos.

32. Josephus (*Ant.* 9.6.6) discusses the same story.

the Philistines also, with them that dwell at Tyre.
Yea, Assyria too is come with them:
they have become a help to the children of Lot. (Ps. 82.1-2, 4-8, LXX)

While the above examples show that the people of Tyre and Sidon are often considered by Old Testament writers to be targets of God's wrath because of their supposed heathen ways and bad influence on the Israelites, another perspective is that individuals of the cities are often pictured on friendly terms with the leaders of Israel.[33]

For example, Hiram, the king of Tyre, plays a major role in the traditions about both David and Solomon. According to the story, the Sidonians have a reputation for being good craftworkers in wood and stone, and so the wealthy Hiram is responsible for building both David's and Solomon's houses, as well as the temple (2 Sam. 5.11-12; 1 Chron. 14.1-2; 22.4; 2 Chron. 2; 1 Kgs 5; 10.11-12).[34]

Another Sidonian who is used by God to help the Israelites is the widow from Sidon (1 Kgs 17). She saves Elijah from starvation during the famine and he in turn revives her son from death. This takes place in the context of Elijah trying to prove that 'the Lord the God of Israel' controls the rain, not the Canaanite god Baal. This pericope would seem to be an obvious source for either of the authors of Mark or Matthew to have drawn from for the story of the Syrophoenician/Canaanite Woman—that is, the story in 1 Kings includes Canaanite Baal and the God of Israel in competition (in fact, the Lord prevails on Phoenician soil), a miracle performed on a Sidonian woman's sick child, and the central figure, Elijah. The writers of Matthew and Mark do refer to Elijah in other prominent contexts (Mt. 16.14//Mk 8.28; Mt. 17.3, 4, 10-12//Mk 9.4-13; Mt. 27.47, 49//Mk 15.35-36).

Some scholars claim that the Old Testament story of Elijah is indeed a precedent for the story of the Syrophoenician Woman in Mark, that is, that the Markan story is a midrash on the Elijah story.[35] The fact remains,

33. There are also several references to the greatness of Sidon as a city and to the fortified city of Tyre, for example, Josh. 11.8; 19.28-29; Judg. 18.7.

34. Josephus (*Ant.* 7.2.6-9) also discusses the relationship that Hiram, king of Tyre, had with David and Solomon. Another Hiram of Tyre did all of the bronze work for Solomon (1 Kgs 7.13-47; 2 Chron. 2.13-16); Josephus (*Ant.* 7.3.4) credits the same man with being skillful in gold, silver and brass.

35. See, e.g., Derrett, 'Law', pp. 161-83, especially pp. 162-74. Derrett's definition of midrash (p. 163) is 'the interaction of Old Testament text and first-century event, so that the former seems to be illustrated or revivified by the latter, and the former

however, that the writer of Luke is the only one to refer directly to the story of the Sidonian Widow (Lk. 4.25-27).[36]

Other Old Testament passages involving the cities of Tyre and Sidon include their citizens as God's people and, therefore, recipients of salvation. One such passage is found in 2 Samuel 24. It concerns the citizens of Tyre and Sidon in the census taking of Israel and Judah:

> And the Lord caused his anger to burn forth again in Israel, and Satan stirred up David against them, saying, 'Go, number Israel and Judah'…and they came to Gilead, and into the land of Thabason, which is Adasai, and they came to Dan and Udan, and compassed Sidon. And they came to Mapsar of Tyre, and to all the cities of the Hivites and the Canaanites: … And Joab gave in the number of the census of the people to the king: and Israel consisted of eight hundred thousand men of might that drew sword: and the men of Judah, five hundred thousand fighting men. (2 Kgdms 24.1, 6-7, 9, LXX)[37]

Psalm 86 (LXX) also states that the citizens of Tyre are claimed by God:

> I will make mention of Rahab and Babylon to them that know me; behold also the Philistines, and Tyre, and the people of the Ethiopians: these were born there… The Lord shall recount it in the writing of the people, and of these princes that were born in her. (Ps. 86.4,6, LXX)[38]

explains and illuminates the latter: the duty of the evangelist is not merely to tell a tale, but also to develop its contextuality with the Hebrew Bible. To him Jesus's life was a representation of familiar Old Testament narratives.'

36. Davies and Allison (*Matthew*, I, p. 545) agree: 'The relationship (if any) between Mt 15.21-28 par. and the tale about Elijah remains obscure'. Perhaps the evangelist wanted to assume God's power, rather than get into a contest between God and a god from the Sidonian woman's original religious background. See further L.C. Crockett, 'Luke 4.25-27 and Jewish–Gentile Relations in Luke–Acts', *JBL* 88 (1969), pp. 177-83; Joseph A. Fitzmyer, *The Gospel According to Luke I–IX* (AB, 28; New York: Doubleday, 1981), p. 537; Robert C. Tannehill, 'The Mission of Jesus According to Luke ix 16-30', in W. Eltester (ed.), *Jesus in Nazareth* (BZNW, 40; Berlin: W. de Gruyter, 1972), pp. 51-75.

37. Niels Peter Lemche (*Early Israel: Anthropological and Historical Studies on the Israelite Society Before the Monarchy* [Leiden: E.J. Brill, 1985], p. 266) points out the unusual nature of the census 'since Oriental traditional societies are virtually notorious for their aversion to censuses'.

38. A similar understanding of the traditional enemy Moab, as one to whom the God of Israel lays claim, can be found in Ps. 60.6. Matthew's familiarity with the Psalms can be found, for example, in Mt. 4.6//Ps. 91.11; Mt. 13.35b//Ps. 78.2. See further, Roger Beckwith, *The Old Testament Canon of the New Testament Church and its Background in Early Judaism* (Grand Rapids: Eerdmans, 1985), p. 80.

A.A. Anderson suggests that the five countries mentioned in this Psalm 'probably represent *all* the Jews and proselytes of the *Diaspora*, or Dispersion, unless the author envisages a world-wide turning to Yahweh at the end-time'.[39] Anderson acknowledges that the mention of the foreign countries is a problem, and suggests that 'the allusion is to the proselytes from various lands, who had come to Jerusalem for the particular festival... The presence of the comparatively few foreign converts could be taken symbolically of the universal worship of Yahweh, in the time to come.'[40] Artur Weiser does not equivocate on the issue of universal worship as Anderson does:

> The divine utterance for the first time makes clear to the poet the full significance for the comprehensive range of the Kingdom of God of what he himself sees with his own eyes when he looks at the proselytes, who have gathered at the Temple feast from the most diverse countries: the universal Kingdom of his God and the dawn of the age of salvation linked up with it have become a living reality![41]

Psalm 45 (44, LXX) also includes a most impressive reference to Tyre. This Psalm, sometimes regarded as a marriage song,[42] is troublesome because of its ambiguous reading of the description of the bride:

> Hear, O daughter, and see, and incline your ear;
> forget also your people, and your father's house.
> Because the king has desired your beauty;
> for he is your lord.
> And the daughter of Tyre will adore him with gifts;
> the rich of the people of the land will supplicate your favour.
> (Ps. 44.10-12, LXX)

---

39. A.A. Anderson, *Psalms* (NCB; 2 vols.; Grand Rapids: Eerdmans, 1985), II, p. 621.

40. A.A. Anderson, *Psalms*, II, p. 619.

41. Artur Weiser, *The Psalms* (Philadelphia: Westminster Press, 1959] pp. 582-83. T. Booij ('Some Observations on Psalm LXXXVII', *VT* 37 [1987], pp. 16-24 [24]) makes a comparison of the attitude of God's former enemies in this Psalm to that of other Psalms. The midrashim (William G. Braude, *The Midrash on Psalms* [2 vols.; New Haven: Yale University Press, 1959], II, pp. 77-79) indicate that the meaning of Psalm 87 is that the exiled Jews will be given back to God by the Gentile nations, and those nations who return the children of Israel will also be considered for priests and Levites.

42. A.A. Anderson, *Psalms*, I, p. 352.

The literal translation, 'daughter', could refer 'to a princess from Tyre or, more likely, to the people of this great trading centre'.[43] The phrase, 'daughter...forget your people', implies to Anderson 'that she was a foreigner (cf. Dt. 21.13)...[and] her rule of conduct should be the same as the sentiment expressed by Ruth (Ru. 1.16): "Your people shall be my people, and your God my God".'[44] Weiser points out the benediction addressed to the king in v. 17 of the Psalm ('I will cause your name to be celebrated in all generations; therefore the peoples will praise you for ever and ever') and also sees a link with the book of Ruth.[45]

> And all the people who were in the gate said, 'We are witnesses': and the elders said, 'The Lord make your wife who goes into your house, as Rachel and as Leah, who both together built the house of Israel, and wrought mightily in Ephratha, and there shall be a name to you in Bethlehem. And let your house be as the house of Perez, whom Tamar bore to Judah, of the seed which the Lord shall give you of this handmaid'. (Ruth 4.11-12, LXX)

Ruth and Boaz do prosper; they are the ancestors of King David and of Jesus who was born in Bethlehem. Their story will be discussed further in Chapter 3.

4. *Tyre and Sidon in Matthew*[46]

Matthew states that Jesus has left Gennesaret, where he has been besieged not only with ill people in need of a cure (14.35-36) but also with chiding Pharisees and scribes from Jerusalem (15.1-2).[47] Throughout chs. 4–15, therefore, Matthew engages Jesus in a frantic agenda with the needs of the

43. A.A. Anderson, *Psalms*, II, p. 353. Anderson correlates 'daughter of Tyre' with 'daughter of Zion' (Ps. 9.14) or 'daughter of Babylon' (Ps. 137.8). Therefore, he argues that the meaning of v. 12 may be that envoys will come from the various neighbouring countries bringing their gifts for the royal bride.

44. A.A. Anderson, *Psalms*, II, p. 352.

45. Weiser, *Psalms*, p. 364. Beckwith (*Canon*, p. 101), writes: 'And since [the book of Ruth] ends with the genealogy of the psalmist David, it can naturally be prefixed to Psalms'. See his discussion (pp. 304-306) on 'A rabbinical dispute about Ruth?'

46. One can also find Tyre in early Christian history where it enjoyed pre-eminence as a Christian center. See Harnack, *Mission*, I, p. 502; II, pp. 121-22; Horsley and Llewelyn (eds.), *New Documents*, II, pp. 26, 94.

47. See Jack Dean Kingsbury, 'The Developing Conflict between Jesus and the Jewish Leaders in Matthew's Gospel: A Literary-Critical Study', *CBQ* 49 (1987), pp. 57-73; *idem*, 'Reflections on "The Reader" of Matthew's Gospel', *NTS* 34 (1988), pp. 442-60 (448-54).

people on one hand and the hostile attitude of some of the scribes and Pharisees escalating on the other. It therefore comes as no surprise that Jesus once again attempts to 'withdraw' in 15.21. In fact, Matthew exchanges Mark's εἰς τὰ ὅρια Τύρου for εἰς τὰ μέρη Τύρου Mk 7.24 in order to 'forestall an inference that Jesus went up to the borders of Gentile territory but did not enter'.[48]

Matthew's redactional use of the verb ἀναχωρέω (15.21) in place of Mark's ἀνέρχομαι (7.24) is an indication of the growing hostility towards Jesus.[49] An implication of Gentile environs is present, and so according to

48. Gundry, *Matthew: A Commentary On His Handbook for a Mixed Church Under Persecution* (Grand Rapids: Eerdmans, 1994), p. 310, against John Lightfoot, *A Commentary on the New Testament from the Talmud and Hebraica* (4 vols.; Grand Rapids: Baker Book House, 1979), II, p. 245, and Donaldson, *Jesus on the Mountain*, p. 132. A.-J. Levine ('Matthew', in Carol A. Newsom and Sharon H. Ringe [eds.], *The Women's Bible Commentary* [Louisville, KY: Westminster John Knox Press, 1992], pp. 252-62 [259]) also writes that 'Matthew's [account] does not present Jesus entering Tyre and Sidon; rather, the woman leaves her native land to meet Jesus… By meeting Jesus both on his own turf and on his own terms, the Canaanite woman acknowledges the priority of the Jews in the divine plan of salvation.' While it is true that the woman understands the priority of the Jews, it is not evidenced by her going to Jesus' 'own turf', because he goes to hers. Saldarini (*Matthew's Christian–Jewish Community*, p. 76) and Senior ('Between Two Worlds', p. 13) agree with Lightfoot and A.-J. Levine. Meier (*Marginal Jew*, II, pp. 659, 719) seems to be saying that both Mark's and Matthew's accounts take place on non-Jewish territory. See further, Wainwright, *Matthew*, p. 103 n. 120. Luz (*Theology of the Gospel of Matthew*, p. 82) agrees that Jesus probably withdrew to the Canaanite Woman's territory in Tyre and Sidon. For the composition of Mark's audience, see Howard Clark Kee (*Community of the New Age* [Philadelphia: Westminster Press, 1977], especially pp. 93-97) and Selvidge (*Woman, Cult, and Miracle Recital*, pp. 31-46, esp. pp. 35-37, 44-46) for the Gentile community. For a discussion on the mixed evidence of the impurity of Gentiles, see E.P. Sanders, *Judaism: Practice and Belief 63 BCE–66 CE* (Philadelphia: Trinity Press International, 1992), pp. 72-76.

49. Alice Dermience, 'La péricope de la Cananéenne (Mt 15, 21-28): Rédaction et théologie', *ETL* 58 (1982), pp. 25-49 (27). She cites the 14 instances from the LXX in which ἀναχωρέω is used, e.g., Exod. 2.15 (Moses fled from Pharoah); Josh. 8.15 (Joshua and Israel fled in the direction of the wilderness); Judg. 4.17 (Sisera fled away on foot to the tent of Jael). See further, David R. Bauer, *The Structure of Matthew's Gospel: A Study in Literary Design* (Bible & Literature Series, 15; Sheffield: Almond Press, 1988) p. 93; Gundry, *Matthew*, p. 310. For the importance of 'withdrawal' as a literary device for the purpose of 'punctuating a studied oscillation between the hostile reaction to Jesus and his ongoing authoritative ministry' in Matthew's Gospel, see Donald J. Verseput, 'The Faith of the Reader and the Narrative of Matthew 13.53–16.20', *JSNT* 46 (1992), pp. 3-24 (7).

A.-J. Levine, the technical expression 'to withdraw' becomes both ethnic and political.[50] It is also religious. Of the six times that Matthew uses the term,[51] four are political, while two of the incidents indicate withdrawal from some of the Jewish religious leaders:

> But the Pharisees went out and took counsel against him, how to destroy him. Jesus, aware of this, withdrew from there. (12.14-15a)

> And Jesus went away from there [where he had been arguing with the Pharisees about defilement] and withdrew to the district of Tyre and Sidon. (15.21)

Mark introduces the story of the Syrophoenician Woman with Jesus going to the district of Tyre;[52] Matthew adds 'and Sidon'.[53] Matthew then

---

50. A.-J. Levine, *Social and Ethnic Dimensions*, pp. 133-34.

51. Matthew 2.14; 2.22; 4.12; 12.15; 14.13; 15.21. Wainwright (*Matthew*, p. 223) also cites the pertinent withdrawals. Her first discussion centers on Mt. 12.15, which 'is followed by the prediction of a mission to the Gentiles according to the vision of Isaiah (Isa. 42.1-4, 9; 11.10 LXX)'. The scant history of interpretation regarding ἀνεχώρησεν is reviewed by Deirdre Good ('The Verb ΑΝΑΧΩΡΕΟ in Matthew's Gospel', *NovT* 32 [1990], pp. 1-12 [12]). She looks to Israelite Wisdom Literature for theological uses of the term: 'This wider context ensures that the reader understands the withdrawal of Jesus as Wisdom to be part of the larger pattern of God's design. After all, those who oppose Jesus participate in salvation-history. So it is not *retreat from* hostility but rather *withdrawal for* the fulfillment of prophecy that demonstrates Matthew's intention in his creation of this pattern.' Murphy-O'Connor ('Structure', p. 375) also discusses the role of 'withdrawal' in a structural understanding of Matthew.

52. Coincidentally, the city of Tyre is one of the few places in which the professional lives of women are known. Horsley and Llewelyn (*New Documents*, III, pp. 53-55, 157) document the role of women in the purple trade in the city of Tyre.

53. The Markan setting of 'and Sidon' is an appendage or an assimilation. See Reuben Swanson (ed.), *New Testament Greek Manuscripts: Variant Readings Arranged in Horizontal Lines Against Codex Vaticanus*, II, *Mark* (4 vols.; Sheffield: Sheffield Academic Press, 1995), p. 112. Bruce A. Metzger (*A Textual Commentary on the Greek New Testament* [New York: United Bible Societies, 2nd edn, 1971], p. 95) argues that 'καὶ Σιδῶνος seems to be an assimilation to Mt 15.21 and Mk 7.31'. So Morna Hooker, *The Gospel According to Saint Mark* (BNTC; Peabody, MA: Hendrickson, 1991), p. 183. Burkill (*New Light*, p. 71) agrees: '[the words] 'and Sidon' are omitted by D and other authorities; probably they were brought into the text through the influence of Matt. 15.21 and Mark 7.31; cf. Mark 3.8'. See further Clark's discussion of Mark 7.24 in *Gentile Bias*, pp. 72, 78; Derrett, 'Law', p. 163; Lightfoot, *Commentary*, II, pp. 174-75, 308-309; Theissen, *Gospels*, especially ch. 2, 'Crossing Boundaries in the Narrative Tradition', pp. 60-80; *idem*, 'Lokal- und Sozialkolorit in der Geschichte von der syrophönikischen Frau (Mk 7.24-30)', *ZNW* 75 (1984), pp. 202-25; *idem*, *Sociology*,

changes the Markan term 'Syrophoenician' to 'Canaanite' (Mk 7.26//Mt. 15.22). While there is some debate over the meaning of the eponym Sidon in Genesis 10,[54] the importance of the term for this study is that the terms 'Canaan' and 'Sidon' are introduced in the same setting in Genesis:

> Canaan became the father of Sidon, his first-born... And the territory of the Canaanites extended from Sidon, in the direction of Gerar. (Gen. 10.15, 19)

Since the terms 'Canaan' and 'Sidon' are introduced together in Genesis, it would not be unusual for Matthew to think in terms of 'Canaanite' rather than 'Syrophoenician' as well as adding 'Sidon' to Mark's original 'Tyre'.[55]

Mark	Old Testament Influence	Matthew
Tyre	Tyre and Sidon	Tyre and Sidon[56]
Syrophoenician	Sidon and Canaan	Canaanite

Matthew has made it clear in the genealogy that 'Canaanites' are included in the Gospel story (Tamar and Rahab, 1.3, 5). The extra 'and Sidon' attached to 'Tyre' in 15.21 strengthens the inclusion since the cities and the Canaanites are so closely linked together in the Old Testament.[57]

p. 47. Willi Marxsen (*Mark the Evangelist: Studies on the Redaction History of the Gospel* [Nashville: Abingdon Press, 1969], p. 69) agrees that 'Sidon' is added. See Appendix 4 of this study for a comparison of the geographical settings of the miracle stories that Matthew and Mark have in common.

54. According to Niels Peter Lemche (*The Canaanites and Their Land* [JSOTSup, 110; Sheffield: JSOT Press, 1991], p. 77), 'In this text [Gen. 10] Sidon is obviously understood to be the *heros eponymos* of the city called Sidon and the city itself. The eponymous quality of Sidon is here meant to designate the Phoenicians, or at least the Phoenicians who lived in southern Lebanon.' So Elias J. Bickerman, *The Jews in the Greek Age* (Cambridge, MA: Harvard University Press, 1988), p. 11.

55. A precedent for Matthew's style might be the reference to 'Zebulun and Naphtali' in 4.13 as a set-up for quoting Old Testament (Isa. 9.1-2) in what follows (4.14-16) in order to establish Capernaum as scriptural.

56. Matthew always includes the cities as pairs; for example, 11.21, 22; 15.21. Mark is inconsistent: 3.8 = Tyre and Sidon; 7.24 = Tyre; 7.31 = 'Tyre, and went through Sidon'. Luke is consistent with the pairing in the Gospel, for example, 6.17; 10.13, 14, and again in Acts 12.20, where mention is made of the people in general. The cities are listed separately in Acts 21.3, 7, and 27.3, where they are mentioned as specific port cities.

57. Matthew includes other word associations from the Old Testament. In this example, the evangelist goes full circle: Jesus is born in Bethlehem (2.1), the burial place of Rachel (Gen. 35.19); Matthew reminisces about Rachel weeping for her children in Ramah (2.18//Jer. 31.15), where the elders meet with Samuel because they

Other scholars, such as Gundry, also see the geographical setting as important to the traditionally understood purpose of this story:

> The concern to make the story a dominical example of ministry to Gentiles also leads Matthew to add 'and Sidon' to 'Tyre'. The stereotyped pairing of the cities conforms to the language of the Old Testament…and makes them typical of the whole world of Gentiles.[58]

Derrett capitalizes on Pss. 45.10-13 and 87.4:

> 'Tyre' may be stimulated by the identification of the woman as Syro-Phoenician [in Mark] in the nucleus of the tradition. Such women must have been known in Jewish districts; but Mark wishes to show the Messiah visiting Tyre, for the daughter of Tyre would sue for the Lord's favour (Ps. xlv 12; cf. Ps. lxxxvii 4)…the mention of Tyre automatically recalls Sidon (Is. xxiii; Jer. xlvii 4; Jl. iii 4-8; Zech. ix 2).[59]

Tyre and Sidon are mentioned earlier in both Matthew's and Mark's Gospels, but are not specifically cited as Canaanite or Gentile cities. Mark's first reference is in 3.7-8, where we are told that Jesus has a following from that area:

> Jesus withdrew with his disciples to the sea, and a great multitude from Galilee followed; also from Judea and Jerusalem and Idumea and from beyond the Jordan and from about *Tyre* and *Sidon* a great multitude, hearing all that he did, came to him.[60]

want Israel to be like all the nations (ἔθνη) in selecting a leader (1 Sam. 8.4-5); finally, Jesus instructs his followers to make disciples of all the nations:

Bethlehem (Mt. 2.1//Gen. 35.19)—
Rachel (Gen. 35.19//Mt. 2.18)—
weeping in Ramah (Mt. 2.18//Jer. 31.15)—
   Ramah (Jer. 31.15//1 Sam. 8.4-5)—
   all the nations (1 Sam. 8.4-5//Mt. 28.19)

58. Gundry, *Matthew*, p. 310. So Joachim Jeremias, *Jesus' Promise to the Nations* (SBT, 1/24; London: SCM Press, 1958), pp. 32-33 n. 3, 35-36.

59. Derrett, 'Law', p. 164.

60. The mention of these particular cities, according to Malbon (*Narrative Space and Mythic Meaning in Mark* [San Francisco: Harper & Row, 1986], p. 42), indicates the wider geographical area in which Jesus has become known and is gaining popularity. She states (*idem*, 'The Jesus of Mark and the Sea of Galilee', *JBL* 103 [1984] pp. 363-77 [370, 372]) that 'the land journeys of 7.24 and 7.31…appear to take the group from the west side to the east side of the lake by a northerly, overland route…[they] travel to the most distant foreign (Gentile) cities of Mark, Tyre and Sidon, where he confirms the faith of the Gentile woman that even dogs (Gentiles)

The parallel pericope in Mt. 4.25 omits the names of Tyre and Sidon:

> And great crowds followed him from Galilee and the Decapolis and
> Jerusalem and Judea and from beyond the Jordan.[61]

While one can only note their absence, Montague includes v. 24 with his
discussion of Mt. 4.25 ('So his fame spread throughout all Syria, and they
brought him all the sick, those afflicted with various diseases and pains,
demoniacs, epileptics and paralytics, and he healed them'), and calls the
singling out of 'Syria' 'a fascinating question', and the inclusion of the
term as 'another forecast of the Gentile mission and the mixed composition of Matthew's community'.[62] The story of the Canaanite Woman is
cited as an example of the Gentile mission to come. If Montague is correct, then it becomes even more fascinating that the writer of Matthew opts
for the term 'Canaanite' rather than keeping Mark's term '*Syro*phoenician'.

Matthew's introduction to the cities is taken from Q, in which the expected righteousness of two Israelite cities is compared with the assumed
impossibility of righteousness in two notoriously evil Gentile cities:

> Then he began to upbraid the cities where most of his mighty works had
> been done, because they did not repent. 'Woe to you, Chorazin! Woe to
> you, Bethsaida! For if the mighty works done in you had been done in *Tyre*
> and *Sidon*, they would have repented long ago in sackcloth and ashes. But I
> tell you, it shall be more tolerable on the day of judgment for *Tyre* and
> *Sidon* than for you'. (Mt. 11.20-22; cf. Lk. 10.12-15)

While the mention of the cities by the evangelists seems to be for the
purpose of 'guilt tripping' the reader by comparing the righteous cities of
Chorazin and Bethsaida with the evil cities of Tyre and Sidon,[63] thus

---

deserve the children's (Jews') crumbs...there is bread for the people on the east as well
as on the west of the sea.' The story thus serves as a theological statement of inclusivity for Mark. See further, *idem*, 'Mythic Structure and Meaning in Mark: Elements
of a Levi-Straussian Analysis', *Semeia* 16 (1979), pp. 97-132; *idem*, 'Galilee and Jerusalem: History and Literature in Marcan Interpretation', *CBQ* 44 (1982), pp. 242-55.

61. Luke's parallel includes the names of the cities Tyre and Sidon (6.17).
According to Ulrich Luz (*Matthew 1–7: A Commentary* [Minneapolis: Augsburg,
1989], p. 206), Matthew 'wanted to speak of the ministry and the success of Jesus in
Israel [only]'.

62. Montague, *Companion God*, p. 46. See further, Eduard Schweizer, 'Matthew's
Church', in G. Stanton (ed.), *Interpretation*, pp. 129-55; Gundry, *Matthew*, p. 64.

63. Arland D. Jacobson ('Wisdom Christology in Q' [unpublished Doctoral
dissertation, Claremont Graduate School, 1978], p. 135) writes that 'the intent of the
account is not to provide information about a past mission or instructions for an

letting the disapproving stance toward the cities be the accepted bias and a woman coming from that district in 15.21 even more conspicuous,[64] a more positive reading of that passage is possible. According to Matthew, Tyre and Sidon are not only open to God, but in fact are more so than the Israelite cities of Chorazin and Bethsaida. L. Michael White compares the two texts and concludes that the difference is dependent on the use of the Q unit—that is, Luke followed the original form which legitimated an existing Gentile mission. Matthew, however, used the unit to demonstrate that the lost sheep of the house of Israel had failed to respond. Therefore, according to White, Matthew foreshadows a turn toward a broader audience without necessarily abandoning his primary mission to the Jews. In fact, 'Jesus is still resisting a mission to Gentiles, until the "faith" demonstrated by the Syro-Phoenician [*sic*] woman begins to show that non-Jews also could demonstrate appropriate signs of true discipleship'.[65] White assumes that 'faith' alone leads to discipleship, thereby allowing the proselyte to skip the steps necessary to become a member of a Jewish community.

A.-J. Levine, looking at the text as a traditionally interpreted anti-Jewish polemic, offers an alternative interpretation:

> Matthew 11.22…is a lesson about the failings of the Jewish cities, not about the righteousness of the Gentile ones. The parallel associations of Capernaum with Chorazin and Bethsaida on the one hand and Tyre and Sidon with Sodom on the other confirm the negative valuation of all the cities, both Jewish and Gentile.[66]

ongoing mission but to make a theological point about the unbelief encountered in Israel'. He also suggests (*First Gospel*, pp. 65, 73) that the positive response of Gentiles is for the purpose of putting Israel to shame. He introduces this work by saying that Q is not a Christian document: 'it became a part of the tradition of the church, but only as recontextualized by Matthew and Luke' (p. 2). See further his conclusions, pp. 255-59.

64. Derrett, 'Law', p. 164; Jack Dean Kingsbury, *Matthew* (Proclamation Commentaries; Philadelphia: Fortress Press, 1977), p. 73; Montague, *Companion God*, p. 139; Daniel Patte, *The Gospel According to Matthew: A Structural Commentary on Matthew's Faith* (Philadelphia: Fortress Press, 1987), pp. 162-63, 202 n. 41.

65. L. Michael White, 'Crisis Management and Boundary Maintenance' in Balch (ed.), *Social History*, pp. 211-47 (240 n. 98). White also notes other redactional differences between Luke and Matthew in the placing of the Chorazin–Bethsaida/Tyre–Sidon pericope. See further, Gerhard Lohfink, *Jesus and Community* (Philadelphia: Fortress Press, 2nd edn, 1989), pp. 20-23.

66. A.-J. Levine, *Social and Ethnic Dimensions*, p. 135.

Her point is that 'the evangelist undercuts the simplistic division between good Gentiles and evil Jews'.[67] No matter how the text is used, if Matthew is a Jew, and his congregation is Jewish, then this is an in-house argument, not a condemnation of an entire people.

5. The Gentile Debate in the Story of the Canaanite Woman

There are two particularly difficult sayings in the story of the Canaanite Woman. The first is the exclusivity logion in 15.24 and the second is the reference to dogs in 15.26. They can both be tied to the Gentile issue presented in the story.

Matthew 15.24

ὁ δὲ ἀποκριθεὶς εἶπεν	But he answered, saying,
οὐκ ἀπεστάλην εἰ μὴ εἰς	I was sent only to the
τὰ πρόβατα τὰ ἀπολωλότα	lost sheep of the
οἴκου Ἰσραήλ.	house of Israel.

The exclusivity logion, as 15.24 has come to be known,[68] has caused great consternation among scholars. When the woman begs Jesus this second time (the first is in v. 22), his response is, 'I was sent only to the lost sheep of the house of Israel'.[69] The statement first appears in Matthew in 10.6:

67. A.-J. Levine, *Social and Ethnic Dimensions*, p. 135.

68. 'Exclusivity logion' derives its name from the transmitting of a saying that limits Jesus' mission to the Jews only (10.6; 15.24). For a thorough discussion on the topic, see A.-J. Levine, *Social and Ethnic Dimensions*, pp. 13-57; Matthew Black, *The Gospel of Matthew* (NCB; London: Marshall, Morgan & Scott, 1972), p. 254; Gunther Bornkamm, *Jesus of Nazareth* (New York: Harper & Row, 1960), especially pp. 76-80; Franz-Josef Steinmetz, 'Jesus bei den Heiden: Aktuelle Überlegungen zur Heilung der Syrophönizierin', *GuL* 55 (1982), pp. 177-84; Georg Strecker, 'The Concept of History in Matthew', in G. Stanton (ed.), *Interpretation*, pp. 67-84, especially p. 72. According to Jeremias (*Promise*, p. 26), the isolated logion 'goes back to an early Aramaic tradition'.

69. According to France (*Matthew*, p. 135), the saying in 15.24 is the difference between Matthew's account and Mark's 'simple exorcism story'. Others, such as J.C. Fenton (*Saint Matthew* [Westminster Pelican Commentaries; Philadelphia: Westminster Press, 1963], p. 255) treat the logion and the extended dialogue allegorically, claiming that the 'delay corresponds to the interval between the ministry of Jesus and the time when Gentiles were admitted to the Church'. So Neenanya Onwu, 'Jesus and the Canaanite Woman (Mt. 15.21-28)', *Bible Bhashyam* 11 (1985), pp. 130-43 (140).

> These twelve Jesus sent out, charging them, 'Go nowhere among the Gentiles, and enter no town of the Samaritans, but go rather to the lost sheep of the house of Israel...' (Mt. 10.5-6; see also 9.36.)

There are many Old Testament references to the lost sheep image that were undoubtedly familiar to Matthew:

> My people have been lost sheep; their shepherds thrust them out, they caused them to wander on the mountains: they went from mountain to hill, they forgot their resting place. (Jer. 27.6, LXX)

Ezekiel may have been especially appropriate for Matthew's use because he portrays the Lord as the good shepherd, predicts David to be the shepherd, and refers to the 'house of Israel':

> And I will raise up one shepherd over them, and he shall tend them, even my servant David, and he shall be their shepherd; and I the Lord will be to them a God, and David a prince in the midst of them; I the Lord have spoken it... And they shall know that I am the Lord their God, and they my people. O house of Israel, saith the Lord God, ye are my sheep, even the sheep of my flock, and I am the Lord your God, saith the Lord God. (Ezek. 34.23-24, 30-31, LXX)[70]

Isaiah 11 may also have been an important reference for the image in Matthew for at least three reasons: the prediction that a 'root of Jesse' will rule, that a Gentile mission will occur, and the reference to the 'lost ones of Israel':

According to Georgi (*Opponents*, pp. 165-66), the saying in Matthew 'still reflects an immediate expectation of the parousia'. Gerd Theissen (*Social Reality and the Early Christians: Theology, Ethics and the World of the New Testament* [Minneapolis: Fortress Press, 1992], p. 55) takes a pragmatic stance with the assumption that 'the wandering radicals had made their way from Palestine into other areas as well' and simply needed to be corrected. Richard A. Horsley (*Jesus and the Spiral of Violence: Popular Jewish Resistance in Roman Palestine* [Minneapolis: Fortress Press, 1993], pp. 194-95) argues that since the early churches were already engaged in a mission to the Gentiles, the saying must have originated with Jesus himself. According to Jacobson (*Gospel*, p. 137), Matthew solved the problem of the antiquated mission statement 'with his post-resurrection extension of the mission'. Funk, Hoover and The Jesus Seminar (*Five Gospels*, p. 270) determine that because each of the commissions in Matthew, Luke and John have little in common, they were created by the individual evangelists and cannot be traced back to Jesus.

70. Jacobson (*Gospel*, p. 225) cites Ezek. 34.16 as a possible influence: 'I will seek the lost, and I will bring back the strayed'.

> And in that day there shall be a root of Jesse, and he that shall arise to rule
> over the Gentiles; in him shall the Gentiles trust, and his rest shall be
> glorious... And he shall lift up a standard for the nations, and he shall
> gather the lost ones of Israel, and he shall gather the dispersed of Judah
> from the four corners of the earth. (Isa. 11.10, 12, LXX)

Matthew likes 'echoes' and often uses the same idea twice, as in the
example of 10.6 and 15.24. Matthew's source for the mission discourse in
10.6 may have contained the lost sheep image, but, according to Dobschütz, Matthew 'inserted it himself into the Marcan tradition'.[71] However,
Dobschütz does not solve the redactional problem as to why the phrase
gets used at all. In fact, Matthew is obviously familiar with Isaiah, and so
the exclusivity logion makes no sense *unless* it is assumed that the Gentiles will not remain Gentiles, that is, they will need to convert to Judaism.
Isaiah's prediction leaves that question open.

Some scholars historicize the situation in the Gospels, and conclude that
'the synoptic tradition records miracles performed by Jesus for the benefit
of Gentiles [and] such instances indicate a certain openness towards non-
Jews on Jesus' part'.[72] Others have included this text as a 'seal of guilt' for
Israel.[73] A.-J. Levine responds differently:

71. Dobschütz, 'Matthew', p. 20. Marshall D. Johnson (*The Purpose of the Biblical
Genealogies* [Cambridge: Cambridge University Press, 1988], p. 211) also cites
Dobschütz and includes a list of repeated words or phrases from Matthew which, of
course, includes 10.6 and 15.24. Other examples include 'I desire mercy, and not sacrifice' (9.13//12.7 [Hos 6.6]); 'But many that are first will be last, and the last first'
(19.30//20.16). See further Georg Strecker, *Der Weg der Gerechtigkeit: Untersuchung
zur Theologie des Matthäus* (FRLANT, 82; Göttingen: Vandenhoeck & Ruprecht,
1966), p. 107. David Weber ('Jesus' Use of Echoic Utterance', *Notes on Translation*
12.2 [1998], pp. 1-10 [3-7]) discusses two cases of echoes in the pericope of
the Canaanite woman, but with many unargued inferences and twentieth-century
sensitivities.

72. Schuyler Brown, 'The Matthean Community and the Gentile Mission', *NovT*
22 (1980), pp. 193-221 (194). Brown historicizes the story of the Gentile woman: 'At
the same time Jesus is represented as addressing a pagan woman with a contemptuous
epithet (Mk vii 27 par)...and one wonders whether the author may not, perhaps
unconsciously, have been moved by a desire not to attribute to Jesus a statement which
suggests that he was not exempt from the tribal prejudices of his nation and age' (pp.
194-95 n. 7).

73. Davies and Allison (*Matthew*, pp. 550-51) discuss other possible interpretations. France (*Matthew*, p. 162) contradicts himself by saying at one point that this
text has an 'almost offensively "Jewish chauvinist" tone' and at another, 'It is remarkable how often this verse is quoted out of context as a proof-text for the

It is not likely that either Jesus or his disciples would have thought to restrict
the mission: the outreach to the Gentiles was not part of Jesus' plan, and
the question of a mission beyond the people Israel would consequently not
have arisen.[74]

For Levine, 15.24 'summarizes and secures the gospel's temporal axis. As
a reexpression of 10.6, the restriction is now specifically related to Jesus'
own mission rather than cast as instructions to the disciples. Further, it is
now addressed to a Gentile rather than to Jews.'[75] Levine is correct in
stating that 'Mt. 15.21-28 clearly indicates that the logion is consistent
with themes established in the Hebrew scriptures: it confirms the doctrine
of election and the supercession of Israel over Canaan'.[76] And here is the
crux to her argument: 'Nor are these concepts incompatible with universal
salvation. For example, while Israel may be the "chosen people", conversion into this nation had become both possible and not infrequent.'[77] She,

"parochialism" of Matthew, but it is nothing of the sort' (p. 234). In an attempt to
highlight the complexities of the issue of universalism in Jewish writings, Terence L.
Donaldson ('Proselytes or "Righteous Gentiles?" The Status of Gentiles in Eschatological Pilgrimage Patterns of Thought', *JSP* 7 [1990], pp. 3-27 [3]) identifies proselytism as one of the 'three distinct ways in which hope for the 'salvation' of the Gentiles
was entertained'.

74. A.-J. Levine, *Social and Ethnic Dimensions*, p. 20. So Meier, *Marginal Jew*, I,
p. 64.

75. A.-J. Levine (*Social and Ethnic Dimensions*, p. 141), against Gundry and others
who claim that Jesus is talking to the disciples, *not* to the Canaanite Woman. The
argument that Jesus is talking to the disciples is attractive because one could
conceivably come up with the explanation that Jesus is including her as one of the lost
sheep of the house of Israel. If that were the case, however, then v. 26 ('It is not fair to
take the children's bread and throw it to the dogs') does not fit. See further Levine's
discussion on the 'gospel's ultimate cross-ethnic, social concern' as it relates to
'Christian apologetic' which can make texts sound like 'repellent exclusivity' (pp. 142-
45). Wolfgang Trilling (*The Gospel According to Matthew* [New Testament for
Spiritual Reading, 2; London: Burns & Oates, 1981], p. 51) also espouses the view that
Jesus was talking to the disciples, not to the woman, in the story.

76. A.-J. Levine, *Social and Ethnic Dimensions*, p. 143. See also, *idem*, 'Anti-
Judaism', pp. 29-30.

77. A.-J. Levine, *Social and Ethnic Dimensions*, p. 143. According to Gabriele
Boccaccini (*Middle Judaism: Jewish Thought 300 B.C.E. to 200 C.E.* [Minneapolis:
Fortress Press, 1991], p. 251), 'one of the worst stereotypes of the Christian theological
tradition is that of a "universalistic" Christianity emerging from a "particularistic"
Judaism. History instead reveals a great variety of attitudes of middle Judaisms
towards Gentiles as well as divisions among and within these Judaisms on the question
of the possible salvation of Gentiles.'

in a later work, states that the term 'Israel' can itself refer to proselytes.[78]

Overman does not include the story of the Canaanite Woman in his discussion, but his insight on the Matthean community and its view of outsiders is relevant for this study in that Matthew was apprehensive toward the outside world and required an allegiance not found in the other gospel communities: 'Membership in the Matthean community is critical. In Matthew's view, one is required to make a conscious decision to become a disciple and join the community'.[79]

Matthew 15.26	Mark 7.27
ὁ δὲ ἀποκριθεὶς εἶπεν	Καὶ ἔλεγεν αὐτῇ ἄφες πρῶτον χορτασθῆναι τὰ τέκνα,
οὐκ ἔστιν καλὸν λαβεῖν τὸν ἄρτον τῶν τέκνων καὶ βαλεῖν τοῖς κυναρίοις.	οὐ γάρ ἐστιν λαλὸν λαβεῖν τὸν ἄρτον τῶν τέκνων καὶ τοῖς κυναρίοις βαλεῖν.
But he answered, saying	And he said to her, 'Let the children first be
'It is not pleasing to God[80] to take the bread of the children and throw it to the dogs'.	fed, for it is not pleasing to God to take the children's bread and throw it to the dogs'.

Matthew's version of Jesus' answer to the woman's third request (Mark's second) has been a puzzle to scholars;[81] many have tried to explain the saying in ways that dispel Jesus' seeming meanness.[82] And

78. A.-J. Levine, 'Anti-Judaism', p. 29.

79. Overman, *Matthew's Gospel*, pp. 109-10. The community, for Overman, resembles a sectarian community in that it has rejected the existing civil authorities.

80. Cf. BAGD, καλόν, p. 400, for this translation. Also see Kilpatrick, *Origins*, p. 19, for the variants.

81. McNeile (*Matthew*, p. 231) disagrees. He claims (that is, historicizes) that 'if the woman was actually within ear shot, we may be sure that a half-humorous tenderness of manner would deprive them of all their sting'. See further Alfred Plummer, *An Exegetical Commentary on the Gospel According to Saint Matthew* (London: Scott, 1915), p. 216; Jeremias, *Promise*, p. 29; E.A. Russell, 'The Canaanite Woman', pp. 281-82. According to Vincent Taylor (*The Gospel According to St. Mark* [London: Macmillan, 2nd edn, 1966], p. 350), 'internal consistency' supports Mark's originality in the saying.

82. For example, Gundry (*Matthew*, p. 314) and Harrington (*Matthew*, p. 235) excuse Jesus' lack of consideration for the woman. Theissen (*Gospels*, pp. 62-66) includes a summary of the three types of interpretation of this 'offensive saying':

while Matthew shortens Mark's version of the logion, the sting does not get removed.

The absence of Mark's temporal indicator πρῶτον in Matthew's version is conspicuous. A.-J. Levine claims against most scholars that 'Matthew shifts Mark's emphasis on the Gentile mission to a focus on the present priority of the Jews'.[83] As such, πρῶτον for Mark implies a distinction rather than a continuation... Matthew, however, explicitly indicates that Jesus' mission is to the Jews alone; there is no need for a "first" since for Jesus' earthly charge there can be no "next".'[84] As will be shown in Chapter 3, Levine's conclusion is supported by the particular shape that the pericope takes.

One of the stumbling blocks for scholars has been the term κυνάριον.[85]

---

biographical, paradigmatic and salvation-historical. Beare (*Matthew*, pp. 343-44) regards the 'atrocious saying' as a reflection on early church attitude toward the Gentiles. The evangelists then 'denature[d] it by diverting attention to the significant outcome—that Jesus actually granted the request of the woman and healed her daughter'. Luz (*Theology*, p. 72 n. 12), convinced that the term refers to domesticated housedogs rather than stray mongrels, argues that this is not a display of contempt felt by a pious Jew toward Gentiles, but that 'Matthew makes clear that...there is a *difference in kind* between Israelites and Gentiles, with the former having not just an initial but an exclusive claim to God's salvation'. All of these explanations are the result of wishful thinking: the points of apparent rudeness do not disappear. Although Sim (*Gospel of Matthew*, p. 255) argues with Overman (*Church and Community*, p. 229), who guesses that the Canaanite Woman is a Matthean Jew in good standing, he makes a wry observation: 'If the evangelist had intended to portray this woman as a role model for the Gentiles in his community, as many scholars argue, then he has done a remarkably poor job in the initial section of this passage' (p. 223).

83. A.-J. Levine, *Social and Ethnic Dimensions*, p. 145; also, Jeremias, *Promise*, p. 29 n. 2. Against Harnack, *Mission*, I, p. 39.

84. A.-J. Levine, *Social and Ethnic Dimensions*, pp. 146-47. Huub van de Sandt ('An Explanation of Acts 15.6-21 in the Light of Deuteronomy 4.29-35 (LXX)', *JSNT* 46 [1992], pp. 73-97 [97]) judges πρῶτον in the same light as Levine in Acts 15. He concludes that the temporal indications in Acts 15.7, 14, help to show that for Luke, the unique experiences of Israel are linked to events in the recent past of believing Gentiles as well.

85. According to A.L. Connolly ('κυνάριον', in Horsley and Llewelyn [eds.], *Documents*, IV, pp. 158-59), the term ranges in meaning from puppies, small dogs and affectionate dogs to model dogs fashioned from dough or wax, house dogs, hunting dogs gardener's dogs, and pet dogs. His suggestion that the diminutive form in Mt. 15.26 may have been inserted to soften the saying, or may have been a 'lexical choice when describing dogs that could be present at a home meal', makes sense only if a post-Easter interpretation is placed on the pericope, thus indicating a eucharistic theme.

The fact that the diminutive is used rather than κύων has led many scholars to argue against 'little dogs, puppies' containing a slurring reference to Gentiles.[86] Several different sources will be listed briefly to gain a broader representation of the dog image.

a. New Testament

There is no mistaking the negative connotation of 'dogs' in Mt. 7.6:

> Do not give dogs (κυσὶν) what is holy; and do not throw your pearls before swine, lest they trample them under foot and turn to attack you.[87]

Dogs and swine are metaphors for outcasts:

> The demons begged him, 'If you cast us out, send us into the herd of swine'. And he said to them, 'Go!' So they came out and entered the swine; and suddenly, the whole herd rushed down the steep bank into the sea and perished in the water. (Mt. 8.31-32)[88]

> It has happened to them according to the true proverb, the dog (κύων) turns back to his own vomit, and the sow is washed only to wallow in the mire. (2 Pet. 2.22; cf Prov. 26.11)

b. Old Testament

'Dogs and swine' as well as 'dogs and harlots' are also common metaphors for outcasts in the Old Testament:[89]

> And they washed the chariot at the fountain of Samaria; and the swine and the dogs (κύνες) licked up the blood [of King Ahab], and the harlots washed themselves in the blood, according to the word of the Lord which he spoke. (3 Kgdms 22.38, LXX)[90]

---

86. Gundry, *Matthew*, p. 314; Plummer, *Matthew*, pp. 217-18; Kenza Tagawa, *Miracles et Evangile: La Pensée Personnelle de L'Evangéliste Marc* (Paris: Presses Universitaires de France, 1966), pp. 118-19.

87. Cf. *Gos. Thom.* 93.

88. This pericope will be discussed in Chapter 2.

89. Gary G. Porton (*Gentiles and Israelites in Mishnah-Tosefta* [BJS, 155; Atlanta: Scholars Press, 1988], p. 95) cites Mishna-Tosefta in which 'one may not prepare food for Gentiles or dogs on a festival' (ṭ. Ṭeb. Y. 2.6). However, there is also a commonly reported tradition that states: 'There are three obstinate things: among animals the dog, among birds the cock, and among the nations Israel. This is not told in disparagement, but in praise, of Israel (b.Beca, 25b and par.; Str-B., I, 723)'. See also Otto Michel, 'κύων', in *TDNT*, III, pp. 1101-04 (1101).

90. In this same context, Asphodel P. Long ('Book Review: Schüssler Fiorenza, Elisabeth, *But She Said: Feminist Practices of Biblical Interpretation*' *FemTh*, 7

They shall return at evening,
  and hunger like a dog (κύων) and go round about the city.
Behold, they shall utter a voice with their mouth,
  and a sword is in their lips;
  for who, say they, has heard?
But thou, Lord, will laugh them to scorn;
  thou wilt utterly set at nought all the heathen.
  (Ps 58.7-9, LXX)[91]

See how they are all blinded:
  they have not known;
they are dumb dogs that will not bark;
dreaming of rest, loving to slumber.
Yea, they are insatiable dogs,
  that know not what it is to be filled,
  and they are wicked,
  having no understanding:
all have followed their own ways,
  each according to his own will. (Isa. 56.10-11, LXX)[92]

D. Winton Thomas shows a spectrum of possible meanings for the Hebrew term *keleb*, 'dog'. The meanings range from 'slave' and 'term of abuse'[93] to 'faithful servant' as in 'man's address to God', particularly David's address to God:

David can thus refer to himself as Yahweh's dog, as the suppliant to Marduk refers to himself as a little dog. The most ignoble and contemptible of

[1994], pp. 135-39) brings attention to 1 Kgs 11.5, 18.2-40 and 2 Kgs 23.13 where goddess worship is an issue for the Israelites and Deut. 23.18 where temple prostitutes (male and female) are called dogs, that is, unclean and defiling. She, therefore, concludes that a possible scenario of the story of the Syro-Phoenician/Canaanite Woman could include a self designation as temple servant, priestess or holy woman, thus giving Jesus cause to pause, change his mind and take up her challenge. I have no problem with this scenario except that Jesus is not changing his mind, but, according to Matthew, putting the woman through her paces to become a member of his Jewish community.

91. Cf. Ps. 22.16.

92. The NRSV (MT) renders v. 11 as follows: 'The dogs have a mighty appetite; they never have enough. The shepherds also have no understanding; they have all turned to their own way, to their own gain, one and all.' In this case, it is just as judgment day will be better for Tyre and Sidon than for Chorazin and Bethsaida (Mt. 11.21-22), so the dogs will be on equal footing with the shepherds.

93. D. Winton Thomas, 'KELEBH "Dog": Its Origin and Some Usages of It in the Old Testament', *VT* 10 (1960), pp. 410-27 (414-15).

animals is thus made the comparison of David's sense of humility before, and fidelity to, Yahweh.[94]

Since it is a term used in temple cults, and among certain of today's Muslims, Thomas concludes that:

> *keleb*, when it refers to temple servants, while it has the normal meaning 'dog', has attained the idea of the faithful dog of god, his humble slave and devotee... We see how a term which in the secular world signifies a contemptible animal has been raised into the sphere where God and man are in near relationship to each other, in the cultus.[95]

c. *Targums*

> You shall not eat flesh torn by a wild beast... You shall throw it to the dogs, or you shall throw it to the Gentile stranger, who is likened to the dog. (Exod. 29.33//Lev. 22.6-8, 10//*Codex Neofiti* 1)

Roger Le Déaut writes that this passage gives 'the proper dimension of Jesus' answer to the Canaanite woman...he only repeats, without sanctioning it, a traditional expression of the contempt with which in the Jewish ambient the pagans were looked upon'.[96] This so-called contempt is integral to the rabbinic form that the pericope of the Canaanite Woman takes and will be discussed in Chapter 3. Suffice it to say for now that the words of contempt have a deeper and clearer purpose than that of simply echoing Jewish prejudice.

d. *Rabbinic Writings*

An example of the contempt that 'dogs' connote from rabbinic writings includes:

> What is holy is not to be released to be eaten by dogs. (*b. Bek.*, 15a on Deut. 12.15; Tem. 5; 6; cf. *b. Tem.*, 130b [or 30b]; 1171; b. Šebu. 11b [in the form of a question]; *b. Pes.* 29a.)[97]

e. *Contemporary Texts*

Dogs, according to Philo (*Dec.* 23.115), are 'the most audacious of beasts'. In Josephus (*Ant.* 12.4.9), Hyrcanus cleverly turns around a joke

---

94. Thomas, 'KELEBH', p. 424 nn. 3, 4. See 2 Sam. 7.21; 1 Chron. 17.19.

95. Thomas, 'KELEBH', p. 426. See 2 Kgs 8.13.

96. Roger Le Déaut, 'Targumic Literature and New Testament Interpretation', *BTB* 4 (1974), pp. 243-89 (247). Derrett ('Law', p. 170) also acknowledges the simile between Gentile and dog.

97. Michel, 'κύων', pp. 1101-1102.

played on him by referring to the other guests as dogs who eat flesh and bones together. And, according to the *Didache*, only baptized persons can partake of the Eucharist: 'Give not that which is holy to the dogs' (9.5).

f. *Ugaritic Texts*
In Ugaritic texts, some of the lower deities must cower like dogs under the table while the more important deities are dining. In one particular story, one of the dogs approaches Anatu and Athtartu to beg for food; they are given the best pieces of meat, but the gatekeeper of Ilu's house chastises them because 'one does not put down meat for a dog or a puppy'.[98]

g. *Archaeology*
Excavators have unearthed dog cemeteries with possibly thousands of partial or complete dog and puppy carcasses in an ancient area known as Ashkelon, a '"city of the Tyrians" and headquarters of a Tyrian governor'.[99] The cemeteries indicate that the Ashkelon dogs were thought to be sacred animals and associated with healing. One neo-Assyrian text in cuneiform reads, 'If a man goes to the temple of his god, and if he touches...(?), he is clean (again?): likewise if he touches the dog of Gula [the goddess of healing], he is clean (again?)'.[100] While the connection is inconclusive at this point, one cannot help but be intrigued by the link between Tyre, dogs and healing.

h. *Assessment*
The net result of this brief review of κύων and *keleb* in the literature demonstrates that the term is clearly a literary metaphor fashioned from common sources to distinguish persons outside the Jewish faith or the established in-group (see *Did*. 9.5). Matthew maximizes the term rather than diminishes it by appealing to its double entendre. Just as 'Tyre and Sidon' brings a mixed message, so does 'dog'—is it 'scavenger', 'servant of God', or lesser deity?[101] Archaeological discoveries reinforce the

98. Marjo Christina Annette Korpel, *A Rift in the Clouds: Ugaritic and Hebrew Descriptions of the Divine* (Münster: Ugarit-Verlag, 1990), p. 529; see KTU 1.114.12-13.

99. Lawrance E. Stager, 'Why Were Hundreds of Dogs Buried at Ashkelon?' *BARev* 17 (1991), pp. 26-42, 34-53, 72 (28).

100. Stager, 'Hundreds of Dogs', p. 39.

101. See also Donaldson's discussion of 1 En. 90.18-33 ('Proselytes', pp. 3-27 [20-22]), in which the animals (including dogs in v. 4) and birds move from oppressors of

connection between the people of Tyre, dogs and puppies, and healing.

Burkill and Bundy object to softening the impact of Jesus' words,[102] while Burkill, at least for Matthew's community, suggests that there were those in Jewish-Christian groups who had come to the conclusion that 'a belief in the Messiahship of Jesus was in itself a sufficient qualification for church membership'.[103] It will be shown that Matthew argues *against* a requisite one-step confession of faith for entry into the community.

6. *Summary*

Matthew's Gospel begins and ends with the Jewish–Gentile debate, and at the heart of both the issue and the Gospel is the story of the Canaanite Woman. The cities of Tyre and Sidon are used by Matthew much as they are used in Old Testament stories: on the one hand, their inhabitants are idolaters who represent a threat to the monotheism of Israel; on the other hand, under certain conditions they are capable of becoming more righteous than even the Israelites. It is no accident that the categories for Matthew's use of ἔθνος and the entire Gentile issue follow that of the categories for the portrayal of Tyre and Sidon in the Old Testament. Tyre and Sidon are appropriate cities for any gospel writer to use as a setting for a Gentile–Jewish dispute. The debate is settled in the story of the Canaanite Woman through two difficult sayings, one of which is unique to Matthew—namely, the exclusivity logion and the other of which was taken from Mark—namely, the dog metaphor.

Israel to seemingly full participants in the final gathering in Jerusalem. He argues, however, that instead of actually becoming Jews, the proselytes are still categorized as 'righteous Gentiles' (p. 27).

102. Burkill, 'Historical Development', p. 171; Walter E. Bundy (*Jesus and the First Three Gospels: An Introduction to the Synoptic Tradition* [Cambridge, MA: Harvard University Press, 1955], p. 280) against, for example, Ernest Lohmeyer, *Das Evangelium des Markus* (Meyer's Kommentar zum Neue Testament, 2; Göttingen: Vandenhoeck & Ruprecht, 1963), p. 148; C.E.B. Cranfield, *The Gospel According to Saint Mark* (CGTC; Cambridge: Cambridge University Press, rev. edn, 1977), p. 248; Floyd V. Filson, *A Commentary on the Gospel According to St. Matthew* (BNTC; London: A. & C. Black, 1960), p. 180; V. Taylor, *Mark*, p. 350.

103. Burkill, 'Historical Development', p. 176. He contends that those in Matthew's community 'elaborate the anecdote of the Syrophoenician woman in the interest of their own theological interpretation', that is, that a belief in Jesus' messiahship like that of the Syrophoenician and Canaanite Woman is the only requirement for church membership.

Consideration of the setting of Tyre and Sidon along with the two sayings has shown that Matthew is pursuing a solution for the debate between Jews and Gentiles. While this demonstration is a crucial first step, it is now necessary to determine the reason for Matthew's designation of the woman as a Canaanite rather than a Syrophoenician.

Chapter 2

The Canaanites in Matthew's Gospel

1. *Introduction*

Matthew 15.22	Mark 7.26a
Καὶ ἰδοὺ γυνὴ Χαναναία ἀπὸ τῶν ὁρίων ἐκείνων ἐξελθοῦσα...	ἡ δὲ γυνὴ Ἑλληνίς, Συροφοινίκισσα τῷ γένει.
And behold, a Canaanite woman from that region came out....	Now the woman was a Greek, a Syrophoenician by birth.

The significance of the reputation of the Gentile cities of Tyre and Sidon as Matthew would have known them has been demonstrated. It is now necessary to consider the evangelist's use of the term 'Canaanite' as it applies to the woman from that region. Matthew not only adds 'and Sidon' to Mark's geographical setting, but also changes 'the woman was a Greek, a Syrophoenician by birth' (Mk 7.26) to 'a Canaanite woman' (Mt. 15.22). As will be shown, the term 'Canaanite' is the key to understanding the woman's activity as representing that of a female proselyte in Matthew's religious community.

A survey of persons identified specifically by geographical titles in the Matthean Gospel will serve as a preface to an investigation of Matthew's concept of 'outsiders'. Since 'Canaanites' were often identified as the most extreme outsiders or as Israel's enemies in the Old Testament, a discussion of Old Testament views on the Canaanites will follow. Then it will be shown that in Matthew's genealogy the deliberate inclusion of foreign women, especially Canaanites who are stereotyped enemies of Israel,[1] is a backdrop for the designation of the woman in 15.21-28 as a Canaanite rather than a Syrophoenician. While Benjamin W. Bacon may be correct in saying that 'a resident [of Matthew's community] would hardly be apt

---

1. According to Dobschütz ('Matthew', p. 23), Matthew 'delight[s] in stereotypes'.

to speak of the Syrophoenician as a "Canaanite" ',[2] it might be that a person in the community recognizes a literary term for the stereotype it invokes.

2. *Matthew's Designated Outsiders*

Matthew uses sparsely terms that designate persons as a particular geo-graphically-based group in the Gospel story. The term ἔθνος for the most part is the term that embodies the general group of persons outside of the Jewish faith, and was discussed in Chapter 1.

While names of cities, villages and other geographical locations are commonplace in Matthew, and any given person may be identified as from a certain locale,[3] there are only eight instances, including the story of the Canaanite Woman, in which designated geographical titles or place-names are used.[4] In some cases it is obvious why the stereotypes are essential to the story; in others, it is not so apparent.

> And he went and dwelt in a city called Nazareth, that what was spoken by the prophets might be fulfilled, 'He [Jesus] shall be called a *Nazarene*'.[5] (2.23)

> And when he came to the other side, to the country of the *Gadarenes*, two demoniacs met him, coming out of the tombs, so fierce that no one could pass that way.[6] (8.28)

---

2.   Bacon, *Matthew*, II, p. 18.

3.   See, for example, 'at Bethany in the house of Simon the leper' (26.6); 'a man of Cyrene, Simon' (27.32); 'many women who had followed Jesus from Galilee, minis-tering to him; among whom were Mary Magdalene, and Mary the mother of James and Joseph, and the mother of the sons of Zebedee' (27.55-56); 'a rich man from Arima-thea, named Joseph' (27.57). Malina and Neyrey (*Calling Jesus Names*, p. 15) write that the 'persons are known according to stereotyping in terms of locale, trade or class, but especially according to the family clan or faction in which they are imbedded'.

4.   A complete listing of all Gospel references to persons with designated geo-graphical titles is supplied in Appendix 4. Malina and Neyrey (*Calling Jesus Names*, pp. 152-54) do not include any of these passages in 'Table 2: List of Negative Labels in Matthew'. They do include Simon the Canaanaean in 'Table 3: List of Positive Labels in Matthew' (p. 156). I would include all but Mary of Magdala in a 'List of Negative Labels in Matthew', that is, each place name invokes a negative stereotype.

5.   Luke does not call Jesus a 'Nazarene', but does say that they (Joseph, Mary and Jesus) go back to their own city of Nazareth. The maid accuses Peter of being with the Nazarene, Jesus, in Mk 14.67.

6.   Mk 5.1//Lk. 8.26 = Gerasenes; Mark's and Luke's variant readings = Gergesenes.

The names of the twelve apostles are these...Simon the *Cananaean*...[7]
(10.2, 4)

...and Judas *Iscariot*, who betrayed him. (10.4b; 26.14)

These twelve Jesus sent out, charging them, 'Go nowhere among the
Gentiles, and enter no town of the *Samaritans*, but go rather to the lost
sheep of the house of Israel'.[8] (10.5-6)

And behold a *Canaanite* woman from that region came out and cried, 'Have
mercy on me, Lord, Son of David; my daughter is badly demonized'.[9]
(15.22)

Now Peter was sitting outside in the courtyard. And a maid came up to him,
and said, 'You also were with Jesus the *Galilean*'.[10] (Mt. 26.69)

There were also many women there, looking on from afar, who had
followed Jesus from Galilee, ministering to him; among whom were Mary
Magdalene, and Mary the mother of James and Joseph, and the mother of
the sons of Zebedee...Mary *Magdalene* and the other Mary were there,
sitting opposite the sepulchre... Now after the sabbath, toward the dawn of
the first day of the week, Mary *Magdalene* and the other Mary went to see
the sepulchre.[11] (Mt. 27.56, 61; 28.1)

Except for the mention of 'Magdalene' three times and 'Iscariot' twice,
each place-name is mentioned only once by Matthew. Six of these designated geographical titles are difficult to explain. The Canaanite Woman is
one of the six and will be discussed at length; the others will be discussed
briefly.

a. *Nazarene*

The designation 'Nazarene' is perplexing because there is no Old Testament or Jewish tradition that claims messianic connections with Nazareth.
While many scholars classify the phrase 'by the prophets' as a formula
citation characteristic of Matthew, the source of the statement has not been
found. This broad appeal to authority on Matthew's part 'indicates that he
has not taken over the words from the scripture, but the sense of them'.[12]

---

7.   For the same term see Mk 3.18; Lk. 6.15; Acts 1.13.
8.   There are no Gospel parallels.
9.   She is called 'a Greek, a Syrophoenician' in Mk 7.26.
10. Mk 14.67 calls Jesus a Nazarene; the parallels in Lk. 22.54-71; Jn 18.25-27
contain no place-names.
11. Cf. Mk 15.40, 47; 16.1, 9; Jn 19.25.
12. Jerome as cited in Beare, *Matthew*, p. 84. Bultmann (*History*, p. 294) ascribes
the 'awkward combination of the historical tradition of Nazareth as Jesus' home town

While suggestions for the origin of the term Ναζωραῖος range from the reference in Judg. 13.5, 7, where Samson's birth is described as 'holy to God from his mother's womb' and he is designated as a Nazir, that is, an ascetic who is set apart or made holy to lead a consecrated life and to save Israel,[13] to the play-on words 'Nazarite' (Num. 6.2) and 'branch',[14] to a

with the messianic dogma of his birth at Bethlehem' to Matthew himself. Bundy (*Jesus*, p. 35) attributes 'the practice of citing a non-existent passage and ascribing it to the prophets collectively' to a rabbinic convention. See further, Str-B, I, pp. 92-96. James A. Sanders ('Ναζωραῖος in Matthew 2.23', in Craig A. Evans and W. Richard Stegner [eds.], *The Gospels and the Scriptures of Israel* [JSNTSup 104; Sheffield: JSOT Press, 1994], pp. 116-28 [127]) agrees with those who render the word 'inhabitant of Nazareth', but also argues that Matthew's wordplay is reminiscent of tactics used by several prophets, for example, Micah, Isaiah and Jeremiah 'to signal the double truth of Jesus' background: the historic home of his youth and the theological grounding of his mission'. Rudolf Pesch (' "He shall be called a Nazorean": Messianic Exegesis in Matthew 1–2', in Evans and Stegner [eds.], *Gospels and the Scriptures of Israel*, pp. 129-78) concludes that as an exegete, Matthew 'has become a "disciple for the kingdom of heaven"... The community of the disciples as the place where the Torah—the community rule of God's people—is brought to fulfillment by Jesus...' (178).

13. John P. Meier, *Matthew* (NTM, 3; Wilmington, DE: Michael Glazier, 1980), p. 16 and David E. Garland *Reading Matthew: A Literary and Theological Commentary on the First Gospel* (New York: Crossroad, 1993), p. 31. According to G. Wigoder (ed.), *The New Standard Jewish Encyclopedia* (p. 697), a *nazir(ite)* is a 'religious devotee who vowed not to drink any intoxicating liquor, nor to have his hair cut, and to avoid ritual uncleanness through proximity to corpses'. See Mt. 11.19 for the accusation that Jesus was a glutton and friend of sinners. According to T.L. Thompson (*Mythic Past*, p. 345), the Nazirite motif in Mt. 2.23 is used as a 'minor joke'.

14. Davies and Allison, *Matthew*, I, pp. 274-83; Lachs, *Commentary*, pp. 13-14; Beare, *Matthew*, p. 85; R. Pritz, ' "He Shall Be Called a Nazorene" ', *Jerusalem Perspective* 4 (1991), pp. 3-4. See also BAGD, *s.v.* 'Ναζαρά', p. 532; McNeile, *Matthew*, p. 21. T. Stramare ('Sara chiamato Nazareno: Era stato detto dai Profeti', *BibOr* 36 [1994], pp. 231-49) does not find the identification of Mt. 2.23 with Isa. 11.1 and Judg. 13.5 so convincing. Pesch (' "He Shall Be Called a Nazorean" ') combines geography and Old Testament exegesis to get New Testament 'Messianic Exegesis'. See J. Sanders ('Ναζωραῖος') for a review and bibliography of the major studies. Håkan Ulfgard ('The Branch in the Last Days: Observations on the New Covenant Before and After the Messiah' [unpublished paper presented at 'The Dead Sea Scrolls in their Historical Context' conference 5-6 May 1998, Edinburgh]) places Mt. 2.23 in the context of what he terms the 'scriptural plant metaphor' also to be found in Qumran texts and suggests the possibility of a close relationship between the earliest Jewish-Christian movement and the Judaism of the Dead Sea scrolls.

Christian invention,[15] a better description of the term is found in Acts 24.5: 'We have, in fact, found this man [Paul] a pestilent fellow, an agitator among all the Jews throughout the world, and a ringleader of the sect of the Nazarenes (Ναζωραίων)'. One suggestion, therefore, is that the Matthean evangelist imposes a post-resurrection meaning on the term as a literary device to foreshadow trouble.[16] Another suggestion is that if Augustine is correct, namely, that the *christianos Nazarenos* are 'born heretics' because they circumcise themselves and otherwise follow Jewish lifestyles and the old Law,[17] then the term is another piece of evidence that Matthew is a law-abiding Jew.

The only other Gospel use of the term is in Mk 14.67,[18] where the spelling is Ναζαρηνοῦ.[19] The connotation is disparaging: 'and seeing Peter warming himself, she looked at him, and said, "You also were with the Nazarene, Jesus".'

15. Luz (*Theology*, pp. 18, 28) claims that the Syrian Christians called themselves Nazarenes. Since Syria is the supposed place of origin for Matthew's Gospel, Luz argues that '"Nazarenes" was the name given to Christians. Jesus, the Nazarene, will therefore bear the same name as his followers, the Matthean community.'

16. Against, for example, J. Enoch Powell (*The Evolution of the Gospel: A New Translation of the First Gospel with Commentary and Introductory Essay* [New Haven: Yale University Press, 1994], p. 61) who suggests that 'N. is not material to the narrative'. According to Luz (*Matthew 1–7*, p. 150), the anticipation of the geographical statements in 2.19-23 is the way of the Messiah of Israel to the Gentiles. Luz also promotes a thesis based on the later tradition that the term 'Nazarean' became a designation for a Christian: 'Thus in Ναζωραῖος an ecclesiological note is sounded: since Jesus comes to Nazareth in the Galilee of the Gentiles, he becomes a Ναζωραῖος, i.e., a "Christian", the teacher and Lord of the community which calls on him and which preaches to the Gentiles'. Raymond E. Brown (*The Birth of the Messiah* [ABRL; New York: Doubleday, 1993] pp. 209-10) is dubious about this theory.

17. A.F.J. Klijn, *Jewish-Christian Gospel Tradition* (Leiden: E.J. Brill, 1992), p. 20.

18. Edwin K. Broadhead ('Jesus the Nazarene: Narrative Strategy and Christological Imagery in the Gospel of Mark', *JSNT* 52 [1993], pp. 3-18) includes four other Markan references (1.9, 24; 10.47; 16.6) as evidence that 'the Nazarene title is transformed into a complex christological image' (p. 17).

19. Martinus C. de Boer ('The Nazoreans: Living at the Boundary of Judaism and Christianity', in G. Stanton and Guy G. Stroumsa [eds.], *Tolerance and Intolerance in Early Judaism and Christianity* [Cambridge: Cambridge University Press, 1998], pp. 239-62) rehearses the history of the Nazoreans in the context of the formation of boundaries between Jews and Christians in the ancient world.

b. *Gadarene*

Textual problems entered early in the understanding of the story of the Gadarene Demoniac (8.28-34).[20] The cited locations for this story are three different countrysides, namely, Gadara (Matthew), Gerasa (Mark and Luke) and Gergesa (other variant readings). The textual problem has traditionally been associated with identifying only the geographical setting of the pericope.

The Gergesites are included in the same enemies list as the Canaanites in the LXX version of Exod. 23.23-25 and 34.11-16, as well as Deut. 7.1-6 and 20.16-18, but are not included in the MT.[21] Josephus mentions both Gergesus and Gadara. He includes the city of Gergesus with Canaan, Sidon and Samareus in the same discussion:

> The sons of Canaan were these: Sidonius, who built a city of the same name; it is called by the Greeks, Sidon...but for the seven others, (Eueus), Chetteus, Jebuseus, Amorreus, Gergesus, Eudeus, Sineus, Samareus, we have nothing in the sacred book but the names, for the Hebrews overthrew their cities.[22]

The association of names with one another in Josephus, as well as their identification in the LXX, supports Origen's opinion that the city of Gergesa is the correct one.[23] Gergesa also fits the geographical context of the pericope best, in that it is nearest a steep bank that leads into a sea (Mt. 9.32).[24] The name used by Matthew, namely, Gadara, is inexplicable; I would argue for the use of Gergesa. In addition to the above-mentioned reasons, the inclusion of its inhabitants on the enemies list of Israel intensifies the concept of outsiders in Matthew's Gospel.[25]

20. Davies and Allison (*Matthew*, II, pp. 78-79) discuss the variants and traditions. See also Swanson, *Mark*, p. 245.

21. These passages will be discussed in the next section, 'Canaanites in the Old Testament'.

22. Josephus, *Ant.* 1.6.2. The city of Gadara is Josephus' setting for a war in which the Gadarenes are made prisoners and killed (*War* 3.7.1); later Vespasian completely overtakes the city of Gadara (*War* 4.7.3).

23. So McNeile, *Matthew*, p. 111.

24. Davies and Allison (*Matthew*, II, p. 79) agree that Γεργεσηνῶν 'could well restore a reading lost in the pre-Markan tradition'.

25. Since the place-name (whichever one is used) indicates that those who are healed are outsiders, the affiliation with Canaan offers further evidence for those who consider the demoniacs to be Gentiles. See, e.g., Beare, *Matthew*, pp. 218-19; Lachs, *Commentary*, p. 164; Wainwright, *Matthew*, p. 105. Those who wish to leave the issue open include Davies and Allison, *Matthew*, II, p. 83; Filson, *Matthew*, p. 116; McNeile, *Matthew*, p. 113; Plummer, *Matthew*, p. 133.

c. *Cananaean and Iscariot*

The third and fourth cases of place-naming include two of the disciples, Simon the Cananaean and Judas Iscariot. Mark and Matthew call Simon a Cananaean; Luke calls him a Zealot in both the Gospel and Acts; the KJV mistook it for Canaanite; Jerome thought it meant 'from Cana'. Most scholars render Σίμων ὁ Καναναῖος 'Simon the Zealot',[26] a term that distinguishes Simon from the other disciples. One tradition maintains that Simon was a member of the party of the Zealots. Davies and Allison report the modern consensus that it is 'doubtful whether "zealot" came to refer distinctively to revolutionaries before the Jewish war in the sixties'.[27] According to John J. Rousseau and Rami Arav, 'Simon the Zealot (or Cananaean) could indeed have been a political-religious militant; a Zealot current apparently existed well before 66 B.C.E'.[28] I suggest that, as in the case of the term 'Nazarene', 'Zealot' may be a post-War term imposed on the text by Matthew as a literary device—in this instance, to foreshadow violence. (In any case, unless Σίμων ὁ Καναναῖος can be connected to Canaan or Cana, the term does not exactly fit the category of a place-name.)

Possibilities of the term Ἰούδας ὁ Ἰσκαριώτης (Ἰσκαριώθ in Mark and Luke) range from 'a man of Qeriyyot' to 'liar, hypocrite', to 'deliverer', to 'a man of ruddy complexion, red-headed'.[29] While the question of Matthew's (and Mark's) intended meaning remains unanswered, the evidence most intriguing in light of Matthew's designated outsiders is that of the Hebrew place–name Kerioth.

Kerioth is mentioned twice in the Hebrew Bible as a city in the enemy land of Moab (Jer. 48.20-25; Amos 2.1-3).[30] It appears then that the

---

26. That is, not as 'Canaan' or 'Cana' but from the Aramaic word *qan'an*, 'zealot'. See Beare, *Matthew*, p. 239; Davies and Allison, *Matthew*, II, p. 156; Filson, *Matthew*, pp. 126-27; Horsley, *New Documents*, I, p. 94; Lachs, *Commentary*, p. 179; McNeile, *Matthew*, p. 132; Plummer, *Matthew*, p. 147.

27. Davies and Allison, *Matthew*, II, p. 156. According to Meier (*Matthew*, p. 105), the term 'Cananaean' does suggest that Simon was 'a member of the fiercely nationalistic Jewish group ready to resist Rome by force'.

28. John J. Rousseau and Rami Arav, *Jesus and His World: An Archaeological and Cultural Dictionary* (Minneapolis: Fortress Press, 1995), pp. 51-52.

29. Davies and Allison, *Matthew*, II, p. 157; Gundry, *Matthew*, p. 183; William Klassen, *Judas: Betrayer or Friend of Jesus?* (Minneapolis: Fortress Press, 1996); Lachs, *Commentary*, p. 179; Maccoby, *Judas Iscariot and the Myth of Jewish Evil* (Glencoe: Free Press, 1992), p. 128; McNeile, *Matthew*, p. 133.

30. Klassen (*Judas*) does not include these references in his study. As mentioned, Ps. 86 (LXX) states that the citizens of Tyre are claimed by God; a similar

disciple Judas cannot necessarily be assumed to be Jewish; if he is a Moabite, he is a designated enemy of Israel and the story needs to be examined in that light rather than that he is symbolic of the fate of the Jewish people.[31] Matthew apparently has a bigger interest in Judas Iscariot than do the other Gospel writers because it is the only Gospel that includes a narrative about Judas' death (27.3-10;[32] see Zech. 11.12-13 [30 shekels of silver] and Jer. 18.1-3; 32.6-15 [potter's field]).[33] While the Matthean text does not say that Judas was buried in the potter's field designated for foreigners, the story appears to be reminiscent of Jeremiah.

d. *Samaritans*

The charge to the disciples to 'go nowhere among the Gentiles, and enter no town of the Samaritans' (10.5-6) has already been considered in Chapter 1 with the emphasis on Gentiles. In the present discussion, it is worth repeating that this is Matthew's only mention of Samaritans.[34] According to Ingrid Hjelm, 'an increasing anti-Samaritan attitude developed in the course of rabbinic discussions in the early centuries of this era... Samaritans underwent the fate of being not only formally excluded from this self-defined post-biblical Judaism, but were also likened to heathens.'[35] Like the Canaanites and other designated enemies of Israel, Samaritans were not allowed to become proselytes. Thus, the Gentiles and Samaritans are alike: they are not Jews, they are outsiders.[36]

---

understanding of the traditional enemy Moab, as one to whom the God of Israel also lays claim, can be found in Ps. 60 ('Moab is my washbasin').

31. Maccoby, *Judas Iscariot*, pp. 47, 101-26. Hooker (*Mark*, p. 113) reiterates the uncertainty of the term Iscariot, but mentions that both Judaea and Moab had villages of that name. She questions whether Mark understood the term since he fails to explain it. If the disciple is non-Jewish, however, then the question of his first name must be reckoned; perhaps he is Judean, but the only non-Galilean in Jesus' group.

32. See also Acts 1.16-20.

33. A.G. Moeser ('The Death of Judas', *BibTod* 30 [1992], pp. 145-51) views Judas' suicide as a matter of honor and shame.

34. Mark does not refer to the Samaritans; Luke uses the term three times and John mentions them four times.

35. Ingrid Hjelm, *The Samaritans and Early Judaism: A Literary Analysis* (CIS, 7; JSOTSup, 303; Sheffield: Sheffield Academic Press; 1999), p. 76. She argues that Mt. 10.5-6 is a neutral text in that the focus is on 'the lost sheep of the house of Israel', that is, Gentiles, Samaritans and the Canaanite Woman simply do not belong.

36. Davies and Allison (*Matthew*, II, p. 166) include a brief history of the Samaritans as well as a comparison of Matthew's order of 'Gentiles, Samaritans and Jews' to Luke's 'Jews, Samaritans and Gentiles'. The term Σαμαρίτης can refer to

e. *Galilean*

Matthew changes Mark's (14.67) 'the Nazarene, Jesus' to 'Jesus the Galilean' (26.69). He later uses the term Nazareth (26.71), but in the same pericope Mark (14.70) and Luke (22.59) attach 'Galilean' directly to Peter rather than to Jesus. The servant girl uses the title 'Jesus the Galilean' in a derogatory sense,[37] that is, to emphasize the fact that Jesus is regarded as an outsider in the situation at hand.[38] Jouette M. Bassler argues that the 'Galilean' epithets, at least in the Gospel of John, 'no longer function on the literal level, but convey primarily symbolic information about a person's reaction to Jesus quite apart from the geographical location or identity of the person'.[39] I argue that the place names function on a symbolic level, signifying negative stereotypes in Matthew as well.[40]

Solomon Zeitlin looks to Josephus for a distinction between geography and name calling, saying that 'undoubtedly the term "Galileans" in this passage [*War* 4.9.10. 558] does not have a geographical connotation but it has the sense of a contingent, on a par with the Zealots'.[41]

It is of note that Luke speaks of Galileans causing trouble:

> At that very time there were some present who told him about the Galileans whose blood Pilate had mingled with their sacrifices. He asked them, 'Do

religious persuasion *or* simply to Greek settlers from Samaria. So Horsley and Llewelyn (eds.), *New Documents*, II, p. 110. According to Bickerman (*Jews in the Greek Age*, p. 186), the Samaritans pretended to be the true Canaanites, at least in territorial contests with the Jews. From her analysis, Hjelm (*Samaritans*, p. 237) concludes that Samaritans and Jews never did form a single state.

37. Filson, *Matthew*, p. 284.

38. Likewise, Peter is an outsider in Mark's and Luke's Gospels as the 'Galilean'.

39. Jouette M. Bassler, 'The Galileans: A Neglected Factor in Johannine Community Research', *CBQ* 43 (1981), pp. 243-57 (252-53). Freyne (*Galilee*, p. 124) also argues that 'the underlying assumption [in John]…is that the Galileans do not know the law and are not, therefore, law-abiding'. See Jn 4.45 and 7.15 for evidence.

40. Schweizer (*Good News*, p. 500) agrees that the term Galilean is derogatory in Matthew. According to Freyne (*Galilee*, p. 89), there is a mixed attitude about Galilee in Matthew: on the one hand, Galilee has a stake in Jesus' career, but 'recedes from view, and the reader's attention is directed instead to the lost sheep of the house of Israel', contrary to Mark.

41. Solomon Zeitlin, 'Who Were the Galileans?' *JQR* 64 (1974), pp. 189-203 [196]. Ruth Vale ('Literary Sources in Archaeological Description: The Case of Galilee, Galilees and Galileans', *JSJ* 18 [1987], pp. 209-26 [226]) cautions that 'Galileans' discovered in the literary sources must be compared with archaeological evidence.

you think that because these Galileans suffered in this way they were worse sinners than all other Galileans?' (Lk. 13.1-2)

Judas the Galilean [who] arose in the days of the census and drew away some of the people after him; he also perished, and all who followed him were scattered. (Acts 5.37)[42]

Mark also implies trouble: 'The chief priests and the scribes were looking for a way to arrest Jesus by stealth and kill him; they said, "Not during the festival, or there may be a riot among the people"' (14.1b-2).[43]

f. *Magdalene*

It is ironic that Mary Magdalene (Μαρία ἡ Μαγδαλανή), a woman to whom ill repute is traditionally ascribed, may offer the least of the problems, although even here a mixed message prevails. There is a question as to whether the original reference to the city is to Magdala, Magadan, Dalmanutha (Mt. 15.39//Mk 8.10) or Tarichea.[44] Since neither Magadan nor Dalmanutha has been identified geographically, McNeile, for example, thinks that the better-known 'Magdala' was substituted.[45] Susan Haskins, in her comprehensive study on Mary Magdalen, is more definite about the geographical location and 'the putative disadvantage of her birthplace:

Mary Magdalen's second name, *Magdalini* in Greek, signified her belonging to el Mejdel, a prosperous fishing village on the north-west bank of the lake of Galilee, four miles north of Tiberias. Its apparent notoriety in

42. One cannot be certain that the label Galilean in this context necessarily equates with 'rebel' or 'revolutionary'; it could merely be a geographical designation for Luke. However, Rousseau and Arav (*Jesus and His World*, pp. 51, 100) do agree that Judas the Galilean was a revolutionary leader (from Gamla).

43. See Gerd Theissen ('Die Tempelweissagung Jesu: Prophetie in Spannungsfeld von Stadt und Land', *TZ* 32 [1976], pp. 144-58 [149]) for the plausibility of an apprehension about Galileans in Jerusalem. For a comprehensive study of the term Galilee in Mark's Gospel, see Malbon, *Narrative Space*. According to her ('Galilee and Jerusalem', pp. 242-55 [253]), 'the Marcan meaning remains: The traditional order (associated with Judea) is challenged by a new order (associated with Jesus of Nazareth in Galilee)'.

44. See Swanson, *Mark*, p. 121.

45. McNeile, *Matthew*, p. 234. A problem does exist, not in ch. 27, but in 15.39: 'And sending away the crowds [those who followed Jesus after the Canaanite woman's daughter was healed], he got into the boat and went to the region of Magadan'. The reading 'Magdala' can be found in the lesser uncials of Matthew, as well as in Mark's parallel (8.10) which has the preferred reading of 'Dalmanutha'.

the early centuries of Christianity—it was destroyed in AD 75 because of its infamy and the licentious behaviour of its inhabitants—may have helped later to colour the name and reputation of Mary Magdalen herself.[46]

Jerome and others state that 'Magdala' means 'towers'[47]—nothing inherently wrong there. According to Carla Ricci, 'the bad reputation the town enjoyed in rabbinic literature after the first century appears to stem from corruption brought about by excessive wealth. Perhaps this element had some hand in perpetuating the confusion over attributing the character of "sinner" to Mary Magdalene.'[48]

Thus, it appears that the purpose of the name-calling is to heighten stereotyped attitudes. Out of the eight stories, four are held in common with Mark. Of those four stories, Matthew changes the geographical title in three of them: the Gadarene Demoniac, the Canaanite Woman, and the Courtyard Scene. While even the Markan accounts connote an outsider's status, Matthew's emendations intensify the marginality.

3. Canaanites in the Old Testament

Matthew's community undoubtedly understood the antecedent for the description of the woman, namely, that a distinction was to be made between biblical heroes (Israelites) and villains (Canaanites). To date, however, no one has put forth a satisfactory explanation for her designation as a 'Canaanite'.[49] Scholars, like Davies and Allison, categorize the proposals set forth to explain Matthew's redaction of her description and agree that

46. Susan Haskins, *Mary Magdalen: Myth and Metaphor* (New York: Harcourt Brace & Company, 1993) p. 15. Although Haskins and others often refer to Mary's 'conversion', it is in the context of converting from her alleged sexual sin to a proper life rather than from one religion to another. See also Jorunn Jacobsen Buckley, ' "The Holy Spirit is a Double Name": Holy Spirit, Mary, and Sophia in the *Gospel of Philip*', in Karen L. King (ed.), *Images of the Feminine in Gnosticism* (Studies in Antiquity and Christianity; Philadelphia: Fortress Press, 1988), pp. 211-27 (214-17); Elaine Pagels, 'Pursuing the Spiritual Eve: Imagery and Hermeneutics in the *Hypostasis of the Archons* and the *Gospel of Philip*', in King (ed.), *Images of the Feminine*, pp. 187-206 (203); Antoinette Clark Wire, 'The Social Functions of Women's Asceticism in the Roman East', in King (ed.), *Images of the Feminine*, pp. 308-23 (321).

47. Jerome, 'Letter cxxvii'.

48. Carla Ricci, *Mary Magdalene and Many Others: Women Who Followed Jesus* (Minneapolis: Fortress Press, 1994), p. 130. It should be noted that it is only later in Luke (8.2) and the later ending of Mark that Mary is described as the one 'from whom [Jesus] had cast out seven demons' (16.9).

49. The term 'Canaanite' is misused in today's archaeology and ancient Near

most modern exegetes have supposed the change to 'Canaanite' was made because of its Old Testament associations: one automatically thinks of Israel's enemies. Thereby is evoked 'Israel's deeply-engrained fear of and revulsion towards Gentile ways'—which in turn allows one to see in Jesus the overcoming of such fear and revulsion.[50]

The Markan term 'Syrophoenician' is a geographical denotation, referring to a 'district which was so called because Phoenicia belonged to the province of Syria...and could thus be differentiated from Libophoenicia around Carthage'.[51] Both terms, that is, Syrophoenician and Canaanite, are elusive, and so the two Gospel descriptions of the woman need to be examined.

The original meaning of 'Phoenician' is probably 'people who trade in purple'.[52] As traders, these Phoenicians were not considered to be honest, but 'the reason may only have been that the Phoenician merchants were foreigners'.[53]

However, scholars are at odds on the definitions of 'Phoenician' and 'Canaanite'. Alessandra Nibbi's claim that these terms 'represent no more than socio-cultural or socio-geographical groups of mixed content which we shall probably never fully understand',[54] helps to illustrate the problem that confronts us with Matthew's substitution of the word 'Canaanite' for 'Syrophoenician'. Her emphasis that 'ethnic identity, culture and language are three quite separate problems'[55] must be taken seriously. She cautions against the deduction that the terms 'Canaanite' and 'Syrophoenician' can be substituted for one another because the terms 'Canaan' and 'Canaanite' may be Semitic in language and/or culture and/or ethnic descent, or not![56]

Eastern studies if it is used as a historical construct. For a proper context, see such scholars as T.L. Thompson (*History*, p. 311). Lemche (*Prelude*, p. 104) reiterates that the inhabitants of the geographic locale known as 'Canaan' did not refer to themselves as 'Canaanites'—that is, the word is a narrative construct composed by the opposition. In fact, 'the first known population to be called "Canaanite" was a fourth-century C.E. North African peasant population during the days of Augustine of Hippo'.

50. Davies and Allison, *Matthew*, II, p. 547.

51. BAGD, *s.v.* 'Συροφοινίκισσα', p. 794. See further V. Taylor, *Mark*, p. 349; Burkill, *New Light*, p. 72 n. 2; Albright and Mann, *Matthew*, p. 187.

52. Lemche, *Canaanites*, p. 157.

53. Lemche, *Canaanites*, p. 157.

54. Alessandra Nibbi, *Canaan and Canaanite in Ancient Egypt* (Hawksworth: Bocardo, 1989), p. 7. See further Eleanor B. Amico, 'The Status of Women at Ugarit' (unpublished Doctural dissertation, University of Wisconsin, 1989).

55. Nibbi, *Canaan*, p. 7.

56. Nibbi, *Canaan*, p. 11.

Another suggestion, based on the earliest reference to the term 'Canaanite' in a Mari letter of the eighteenth century BCE, is that the term 'Canaanite' refers to a class or category of people who were Phoenician traders or, perhaps, thieves. In an Egyptian text, Canaanites are referenced also as a category of people, but not as an ethnic group.[57]

There are problems with the Mari letter. According to Lemche, those people called 'Canaanites' may have been ethnically of a different stock from the ordinary population of Mari, because they came from the geographical area known as Canaan, or because 'Canaanite' was a designation resulting from connotations with the sociological term *habiru*. If the last choice is the case, 'the Canaanites of Mari may well have been refugees or outlaws rather than ordinary foreigners from a certain country (from Canaan)'.[58]

Dubious and ambiguous evidence has made a history and geography of the Canaanites almost impossible thus far. A discussion of that very ambiguity in the context of current debate is necessary for an understanding of the various images portrayed by the Old Testament writers, whose ideas in turn, I suggest, are reflected in the Gospel of Matthew.[59]

57. Nibbi, *Canaan*, p. 17. See further, G. Dossin, 'Une mention de Cananéens dans une lettre de Mari', *Syria* 50 (1973), pp. 277-83.

58. Lemche, *Canaanites*, p. 28. See further, Manfred Weippert (*The Settlement of the Israelite Tribes in Palestine* [SBT, 21; Naperville, IL: Allenson, 1967], p. 97) who takes a literal translation of '"Canaanite brigands", which may well mean "highwaymen of foreign origin", whether or not they were actually Canaanites coming from Phoenicia'.

59. The vast quantity of material available on the identity of the Canaanites in the Old Testament needs to be acknowledged. Works not already cited include: G.W. Ahlström, *Who Were the Israelites?* (Winona Lake, IN: Eisenbrauns, 1986); Diana Edelman (ed.), *The Fabric of History* (JSOTSup 127; Sheffield: JSOT Press, 1991); K. Engelken, 'Kanaan als nicht-territorialer Terminus', *BN* 52 (1990), pp. 47-63; Israel Finkelstein, *The Archaeology of the Israelite Settlement* (Jerusalem: Israel Exploration Society, 1988); *idem*, 'Searching for Israelite Origins', *BARev* 14.5 (1988), pp. 34-45, 58; David Jobling, *The Sense of Biblical Narrative: Structural Analyses in the Hebrew Bible* (JSOTSup, 39; Sheffield: JSOT Press, 1978), especially pp. 88-134; Niels Peter Lemche, *Ancient Israel: A New History of Israelite Society* (The Biblical Seminar, 5; Sheffield: JSOT Press, 1988); *idem*, *Early Israel*; Doran Mendels, *The Land of Israel as a Political Concept in Hasmonean Literature: Recourse to History Second Century B.C. Claims to the Holy Land* (Texte und Studien zum Antiken Judentum, 15; Tübingen: J.C.B. Mohr, 1987); Carol Meyers, *Discovering Eve* (New York: Oxford University Press, 1988); T.L. Thompson, *The Historicity of the Patriarchal Narratives: The Quest for the Historical Abraham* (BZAW, 133; Berlin: W. de Gruyter, 1974), and

As a prelude to the discussion of the Canaanites, the concept of 'Israel' and 'Israelites' must be taken into consideration. All of history is a reconstruction and, therefore, not necessarily and probably not the 'real thing'. To that end, a distinction between biblical or literary Israel and Israel as a historical community in ancient Palestine must be recognized.[60]

Philip R. Davies, after T.L. Thompson,[61] for example, detects three different Israels: the Israel of History (the inhabitants of the northern Palestinian highlands during part of the Iron Age), the Israel of the Bible (literary) and Ancient Israel (a scholarly construct).[62] Thompson and Davies, along with Lemche, Ahlström, Van Seters, Finkelstein and others, changed the paradigm for researching scriptural texts (specifically Old Testament and/or the Dead Sea Scrolls in each case) with the integrative philosophy and methodology of historical science that calls into serious question the historicity of any sacred writing.[63]

his review of the quest for historicity since that publication ('Historiography in the Pentateuch: Twenty-Five Years after Historicity', *SJOT* 13 [1999], pp. 258-83); *idem*, *The Origin Tradition of Ancient Israel*. I. *The Literary Formation of Genesis and Exodus 1–23* (JSOTSup, 55; Sheffield JSOT Press, 1987); John Van Seters, *Abraham in History and Tradition* (New Haven: Yale University Press, 1975); *idem*, *In Search of History: Historiography in the Ancient World and the Origins of Biblical History* (New Haven: Yale University Press, 1983); *idem*, *Prologue to History: The Yahwist as Historian in Genesis* (Louisville, KY: Westminster/John Knox Press, 1992); Keith W. Whitelam, 'Recreating the History of "Israel"', *JSOT* 35 (1986), pp. 45-70.

60. Niels Peter Lemche, 'New Perspectives on the History of Israel', in Florentino Garcia Martinez and Ed Noort (eds.), *Perspectives in the Study of the Old Testament and Early Judaism: A Symposium in Honour of Adam S. Van der Woude on the Occasion of his 70th Birthday* (VTSup, 73; Leiden: E.J. Brill, 1998), pp. 42-60. Lemche argues six theses regarding Israel in ch. 2, 'Understanding of Community', pp. 186-93. For a wide spectrum on the issues with 33 reprinted articles, see V. Philips Long, *Israel's Past in Present Research: Essays on Ancient Israelite Historiography* (SBTS; Winona Lake, IN: Eisenbrauns, 1999).

61. T.L. Thompson, *The Early History of the Israelite People* (SHANE, 4; Leiden: E.J. Brill, 1992).

62. Philip R. Davies, *In Search of 'Ancient Israel'* (JSOTSup, 148; Sheffield: Sheffield Academic Press, 1992). Davies responds to the questions of possibility for writing a history of ancient Israel and whether or not the Old Testament/Hebrew bible can be used in such a history in 'Whose History? Whose Israel? Whose Bible? Biblical Histories, Ancient and Modern', in Lester L. Grabbe (ed.), *Can a 'History of Israel' Be Written?* (JSOTSup, 245; ESHM, 1; Sheffield: Sheffield Academic Press, 1997), pp. 104-22.

63. The ramifications can be enormous, regardless of which side one takes on the issues. See, for example, Iain W. Provan, 'Ideologies, Literary and Critical: Reflections

Included in the biblical stories about Israel that belong in the realm of
constructed history is the narrative about the Israelite conquest of
Canaan.[64] Lemche summarizes the history of research regarding the Old

on Recent Writing on the History of Israel', *JBL* 114 (1995), pp. 585-606; T.L.
Thompson, *The Mythic Past: Biblical Archaeology and the Myth of Israel* (Basic
Books, 1999); *idem*, 'A Neo-Albrightean School in History and Biblical Scholarship?',
JBL 114 (1995), pp. 683-98; Philip R. Davies, 'Method and Madness: Some Remarks
on Doing History with the Bible', *JBL* 114 (1995), pp. 699-705; *idem*, 'Introduction:
Minimum or Maximum?', in Volkmar Fritz and Philip R. Davies (eds.), *The Origins of
the Ancient Israelite States* (JSOTSup 228; Sheffield: Sheffield Academic Press, 1996),
pp. 11-21. For a critique of early Old Testament deconstructionists, see, for example,
George Mendenhall, 'The Hebrew Conquest of Palestine', *BA* 25 (1962), pp. 66-87;
Norman Gottwald, 'Domain Assumptions and Societal Models in the Study of Pre-
Monarchic Israel', in G.W. Anderson, P.A.H. DeBoer, Henry Cazelles, J.A. Emerton,
W.L. Holladay, R.E. Murphy, E. Nielsen, R. Smend and J.A. Soggin (eds.), VTSup 28
(Leiden: E.J. Brill, 1975), pp. 89-100; *idem*, *The Hebrew Bible: A Socio-Literary
Introduction* (Philadelphia: Fortress Press, 1985), Niels Peter Lemche, 'Is it Still
Possible to Write a History of Ancient Israel?', *SJOT* 8 (1994), pp. 165-90. See also
Keith W. Whitelam (*The Invention of Ancient Israel: The Silencing of Palestinian
History* [London: Routledge, 1996]) for a critique of European and North American
reconstructions of ancient Israel and argument for creating a history of the Palestinians.
    64. Lemche, 'New Perspectives', p. 42. According to Nadav Na'aman ('The
Canaanites and Their Land: A Rejoinder', *UF* 26 [1995], pp. 397-418), Lemche
(*Canaanites and Their Land*) disrupted scholarly consensus, namely, that Canaan (and
the Promised Land) included the Egyptian province in Asia and/or the Phoenician
coast and/or was a synonym for 'trader'. Na'aman agrees with Lemche insofar as a
heavy theological overlay divorces the Old Testament from historical reality (p. 415),
but wants it both ways by arguing that the Canaanites as former inhabitants of Palestine is from a memory 'rooted in the people's consciousness, and their image was
invoked by Israelite scribes to convey a message according to their own historiographi-
cal objectives and didactic-theological aims' (p. 415). In Lemche's reply ('Where
Should We Look for Canaan? A Reply to Nadav Na'aman', *UF* 28 [1996], pp. 767-
72), he includes Na'aman among biblical discoursers rather than ancient Near East
scholars. Anson F. Rainey ('Who is a Canaanite? A Review of the Textual Evidence',
BASOR 304 [1996], pp. 1-15) also disagrees with Lemche's thesis and argues that
'Canaan as a geographic and social entity was a reality to the various authors' (p. 12).
Lemche's rebuttal can be read in 'Greater Canaan: the Implications of a Correct Reading of EA 151.49-67', *BASOR* 310 (1998), pp. 19-24. In a slightly different vein, he
argues in another piece ('The Origin of the Israelite State—A Copenhagen Perspective
on the Emerence of Critical Historical studies of Ancient Israel in Recent Times',
SJOT 12 [1998], pp. 44-63 [46-47]) that oral tradition is not to be discredited—its
special qualities must be made more precise; oral tradition and history together help to
establish a common destiny, 'i.e. communality, among a certain group of people'.

Testament view of Canaan.[65] In his survey and analysis of the Canaanites in the Old Testament, Lemche's goals are:

> to evaluate the character of this information in the Old Testament…to delineate a history of tradition of the Old Testament understanding of Canaan and its inhabitants…[and] to put forward hypotheses concerning the intention lying behind the Old Testament writers' description of the Canaanites and their society.[66]

His hypotheses have a direct bearing on this study and so are summarized here, not to historicize the tradition, but to shed light on Matthew's understanding of Old Testament writings and consequent use of them.

Lemche divides references to the Canaanites and their land in the Old Testament into two main groups.[67] The first group, found primarily in the Pentateuch and the Deuteronomistic History, simply identifies the Canaanites as being the principal enemy:

> The understanding of Canaan and the Canaanites in these biblical books is…stereotypical and inflexible and makes it clear that the Canaanites and their land had no independent history of their own; they were only included in the historical narratives in order to further the intentions of the narrators. The biblical Canaanites thus had no historical role to play, and the Old Testament historical literature cannot be used as information about the *historical* Canaanites, simply because the Canaanites of the Old Testament are not historical persons but actors in a 'play' in which the Israelites have got the better, or the hero's part.[68]

Matthew also uses actors or characters in the gospel writing; the dilemma is whether or not the function of the Canaanite woman's character in the story has been properly identified through traditional interpretation.

Writings from the prophets and a limited number of other Old Testament passages illustrate the second group of references to the Canaanites. It is the second group, according to Lemche, that demonstrates 'the unreal

---

Lemche's argument (that is, the Copenhagen perspective) is not that there was no historical Israel, but that the following historical questions must be asked: 'What was this Israel?…Why is the formation of the state of ancient Israel told in this particular way? What kind of answer have its authors provided to their audience? When and how did it happen?' (p. 63).

65. Lemche, *Canaanites*, pp. 63-71. So T.L. Thompson, *History*, pp. 310-16.

66. Lemche, *Canaanites*, p. 71.

67. Lemche, *Canaanites*, p. 154.

68. Lemche, *Canaanites*, p. 155.

character of the evidence of the first group'.[69] He claims that 'no comparably coherent picture emerges in the prophetic books', and even when conformity does occur, 'it is easy to show that the author has been influenced by the ideas of the Pentateuch and the Deuteronomistic History'.[70] He thus arrives at the following conclusions:

1. The oldest reference to the Canaanites in the Old Testament is probably the one found in Hos 12.8: 'A trader, in whose hands are false balances, he loves to oppress. Ephraim has said, "Ah, but I am rich, I have gained wealth for myself"; but all his riches can never offset the guilt he has incurred' (Hos. 12.7-8). Lemche identifies the Ephraimite as a Canaanite, saying that Hosea has changed a foreign ethnic designation into a sociological connotation because 'the Canaanite Ephraim also becomes a trader'.[71] Thus neither term is ethnic; Ephraimite is a geographically-determined word and Canaanite is an economic one.

2. Only the ethnic sense of the word, that is, not the socio-economic sense as in the prophets following Hosea, survived in the Psalms.[72]

3. In the Wisdom Literature, for example, Job and Proverbs, 'Canaan finally lost the last traces of having been an ethnic term',[73] although the LXX still allows for such interpretation.

4. The historical literature portrays the concept of Canaan differently from the prophetic tradition.[74] Justification for this statement includes the fact that the 'connotation of merchant never appears in this part of the Old Testament'.[75] In addition, 'the concept of Canaan in the historical books is interwoven with the Old Testament historians' description of the fate of Israel and plays no independent role of its own'.[76] Lemche claims that 'the superior

69. Lemche, *Canaanites*, p. 155.
70. Lemche, *Canaanites*, p. 155.
71. Lemche, *Canaanites*, p. 156. Earlier, Lemche argues that 'this sociological understanding of the Canaanites may go back to Hosea himself and may have survived in the Old Testament tradition following Hosea, or it may predate Hosea' (p. 146). In any case, he contends that the sociological designation as a 'trader', 'tradesman', 'merchant', and so on, does not constitute the *original* sense of the word.
72. Lemche, *Canaanites*, p. 157.
73. Lemche, *Canaanites*, p. 157.
74. Lemche, *Canaanites*, p. 158.
75. Lemche, *Canaanites*, p. 158.
76. Lemche, *Canaanites*, p. 158.

aim of the history writers…[was] clearly…to explain the trouble-some character of Israel's relations with its land, before the settle-ment, after the settlement, and, finally, after the possession of the land was lost during the Exile'.[77] The Old Testament writers were not writing history, rather a novel, 'the theme of which was the origin of Israel and its ancient history'.[78]

5. The Old Testament cannot be used to delineate geographical boundaries for 'Canaan'—the evidence is conflicting.[79]

6. In Old Testament literature the Canaanites are an 'ideological prototype'. The Old Testament writers portray the Canaanites in such a stereotypical way that they 'are allowed only to act inside the framework of the historical reconstruction and cannot depart from the role allotted to them…the Canaanites represented a phenomenon which was considered to be extraneous and hostile to the Israelites'.[80]

Important to this study is that the Canaanites of the Old Testament were considered opponents of the Israelites. Accordingly, the term 'Canaanite' was a synonym for the opponent and thus 'the Canaanites were allowed no entry to the Jewish community nor permitted to intermarry with them'.[81]

77. Lemche, *Canaanites*, p. 158.

78. Lemche, *Canaanites*, p. 158. Lemche defines 'novel' and suggests that authors can choose two approaches to the treatment of history: 'In both cases authors of a historical novel will have as their aim to entertain their public. In order to do so the historians may choose to write a novel describing the past history of intended readers in such a way as to explain to them their present situation, and, perhaps, their own individuality and identity. The history writer may, however, also choose to tell the audience what is going to happen, and adopt a method of describing the past in such a way that the description of the historical development will at the same time promote a programme for the future direction of the society' (pp. 158-59). It is precisely the Old Testament program of stereotyping Canaanites that enables Matthew to use the term 'Canaanite' so effectively in the story of the woman from Tyre and Sidon.

79. Lemche, *Canaanites*, p. 160.

80. Lemche, *Canaanites*, p. 165. Lemche further claims that 'the grudge against the Canaanites in the historical books was not a part of the heritage of the exiles but originated in conditions which perhaps only arose after the official return of the Jews to Jerusalem after 538 BCE, and, furthermore, that the answer to the question, "Who were the Canaanites?" should be looked for in the post-exilic period and not in either pre-exilic or exilic times.'

81. Lemche, *Canaanites*, pp. 165-66. As he pursues this line of thought, Lemche postulates that the Canaanites 'were likely to have constituted that part of the

Lemche's conclusions can be analyzed by looking at Old Testament references to the Canaanites.[82] The more conspicuous uses of the term are highlighted.

The eponymous ancestor of the Canaanites is introduced in Gen. 9–10:

> The sons of Noah who went out of the ark were Shem, Ham, Japheth. Ham was the father of Canaan. These three were the sons of Noah; and from these the whole earth was peopled. (Gen. 9.18-19)

The story is then told of Noah's drunkenness and the curse he puts on his grandson, Canaan:

> And Noah recovered from the wine and knew all that his younger son had done to him. And he said 'Cursed be the servant Canaan, a slave shall he be to his brothers'. And he said, 'Blessed be the Lord God of Shem, and Canaan shall be his bond-servant. May God make room for Japheth, and let him dwell in the habitations of Shem, and let Canaan be his servant'. (Gen. 9.24-27)[83]

The story in Gen. 9.24-27 is followed by a genealogy in ch. 10, which includes the birth of Canaan's first-born son, Sidon:

> And Canaan begot Sidon his first-born...and after this the tribes of the Canaanites were dispersed. And the boundaries of the Canaanites were from Sidon till one comes to Gerara and Gaza, till one comes to Sodom and Gomorrah... (Gen. 10.15a, 18b-19)[84]

Many scholars have suggested that these are historical passages and are, therefore, a prelude to the portrayal of the Canaanites as notorious throughout the Old Testament for their deviant sexual behavior: that is, Noah's curse on Canaan represents God's sentence on the Canaanites for

---

Palestinian population which was thought to be the enemies of the Jews of Jerusalem... These opponents...could have been the predecessors of the Samaritans, that is, the population living north of Jerusalem' (p. 168). The stories of the Canaanite Woman (Mt. 15.21-28) and the Samaritan Woman (Jn 4.7-42) should perhaps be examined together, not only from a source-critical perspective, but a sociological one as well.

82. A complete count from Hatch and Redpath are listed in Appendix 6.

83. It is from this biblical text that Julian Sheffield ('The Canaanite Woman, Mat. 15.21-28: A Slave Proselyte?' [unpublished paper delived at the SBL Annual Meeting, Boston, 1999]) sees another possibility from my study of the woman as a proselyte, that is, she may also be a slave.

84. The introduction of 'Canaan' and 'Sidon' in the same text was discussed in Chapter 1, p. 44.

their sins.[85] Lemche, however, cites inconsistencies and intrusions into the narrative context that prohibit a 'precise "ethnographic" knowledge' from Genesis 10. He concludes that the author who relays the Noah–Ham–Canaan anecdote possesses no real historical knowledge about the ancient Canaanites. Rather, it reflects an attitude that can be found in the rest of the Pentateuch and in the deuteronomistic literature: 'It is thus possible to consider Gen. 9.18-27 as expressing a fundamental rejection of the Canaanite culture and nation'.[86] Lemche maintains that the story of the crime of Ham is an 'inclusion result[ing] from a firmly established anti-Canaanite attitude among the Israelite population already in the days of J'.[87] It is this attitude that suits the purpose of Matthew.

The second reference to Canaan comes in the Abraham and Sarah narrative. As the land promised to Abraham and Sarah, Canaan plays an important role in Israel's tradition. Lemche discusses the Abraham narrative in terms of 'place' (Canaan) and 'anti-place' (Israel), terms that he has borrowed from Geert Hallbäck.[88] 'From the first moment, when Yahweh promises Abraham that his descendants shall inherit a certain country and until Joshua realizes that this promise has become true, the anti-place, Israel, struggles in order to become rooted in one place, that is, in the land of Canaan.'[89]

Abraham is not only considered to be the first proselyte, but according to Sandmel, 'the Rabbinic Literature conceives of Abraham, and of Sarah,

85. Claus Westermann (*Genesis* [BKAT, I/1; 2 vols.; Neukirchen–Vluyn: Neukirchener Verlag, 1974], II, pp. 644-73, 694-99), disagrees with the idea that Ham's offense and the sins of the Canaanites can be linked; it is simply a 'family-quarrel-type' story. T.L. Thompson (*History*, p. 360) perceives the use of the Shem, Ham and Japheth genealogy as a 'Functional Variant' to the origin tradition for the purpose of, in this case, narrating 'the aetiology of human society's spread over the earth'. Albert I. Baumgarten ('Myth and Midrash: Genesis 9.20-29', in Jacob Neusner [ed.], *Christianity, Judaism and Other Greco-Roman Cults* [SJLA, 12; 4 vols.; Leiden: E.J. Brill, 1975], III, pp. 55-71) discusses the origins of the story in Gen. 9.20-29 and provides a midrashic interpretation. See further T.L. Thompson, *Tradition*, pp. 77-80.

86. Lemche, *Canaanites*, pp. 115-16.

87. Lemche, *Canaanites*, p. 77. He also says of Gen. 10 that 'we can say that the author in this case made use of a number of traditional ethnic names without connecting them with concrete political and geographical entities' (p. 78).

88. Geert Hallbäck, 'Sted og Anti-sted: Om forholdet mellem person og lokalitet i Markus-evangeliet', *Religionsvidenskabeligt Tidsskrift* 11 (1987), pp. 55-73.

89. Lemche, *Canaanites*, pp. 103-104. The relationship between a historical analysis and a narrative study of a text can be found in Lemche, *Early Israel*; T.L. Thompson, *Narratives*; *idem*, *Tradition*, pp. 105-106 n. 46a).

as master missionaries, dedicated to converting Gentiles, and it attributes to the Haran episode (based on the wording of Gen. 12.5) a great moment of mass proselyting'.[90] Abraham's role as the first proselyte will be discussed later in this chapter.

Canaan is not only the land promised to Abraham and his descendants (Gen. 17.7-8): it is also featured in other Old Testament passages: it is the place where Hagar conceives one of Abraham's children (16.1-6); it is the burial place of Abraham and Sarah, Isaac and Rebekah, Jacob and Leah (49.29-33); it is the final resting place of Joseph's body (Josh. 24.32). While the land of Canaan is good, the Old Testament portrays the people of Canaan as bad. Men are restricted from taking wives from the Canaanites[91] (Gen. 24.2-3, 36; 28.6, 8; Deut. 7.1-4//Exod. 34.11-17), and, of course, Esau disobeys by doing just that (Gen. 36.2).

Relevant to this investigation is the account of another such intermarriage:

> And it came to pass at that time that Judah went down from his brothers, and came as far as to a certain man of Adullah, whose name was Hirah. And Judah saw there the daughter of a Canaanite man, whose name was Shua; and he took her, and went in to her. And she conceived and bore a son, and called his name, Er...and Judah took a wife for Er his first-born, whose name was Tamar... (Gen. 38.2-3, 6)

In summary, Tamar's husband dies. By refusing to honor the Levirate marriage law, Tamar's father-in-law is in essence cheating her out of bearing a child, so she poses as the prostitute whom Judah turns to after his wife dies. Tamar gets pregnant; Judah denies that he is the father; Tamar proves that Judah is the father; she gives birth to twin boys, Zerah and Perez. Matthew alludes to this story of Tamar, a Canaanite woman, in the genealogy at the very beginning of the Gospel and it will be discussed in more detail later.

While it has been shown that the Old Testament unquestionably offers a dual portrait of the term 'Canaan(ite)' for Matthew to exploit, a limited number of other Old Testament references must be cited. The most damaging discourses against the Canaanites are found in Exodus and Deuteronomy:

90. Sandmel, *Judaism and Christianity*, pp. 22, 50 nn. 44, 49. See further David Daube, *Ancient Jewish Law: Three Inaugural Lectures* (Leiden: E.J. Brill, 1981), p. 9 nn. 38-40.

91. For an analysis of this prohibition, see Shaye J.D Cohen, *The Beginnings of Jewishness: Boundaries, Varieties, Uncertainties* (Berkeley: University of California Press, 1999), pp. 241-62.

> For my angel shall go as your leader, and shall bring you to the Amorites, and Hittites, and Perizzites, and Canaanites, and Gergesites, and Hivites, and Jebusites, and I will destroy them. You will not worship their gods, nor serve them: you will not do according to their works, but shall utterly destroy them, and break to pieces their pillars. And you shall serve the Lord your God, and I will bless your bread and your wine and your water, and I will turn away sickness from you. (Exod. 23.23-25; cf. 34.11-16)[92]

A 'fully developed anti-Canaanite programme'[93] emerges:

> From the book of Exodus onwards the story aims directly at one goal: the land of promise which was given by Yahweh to Israel and its fathers as their inheritance. This is now the focus of attention... The promise...is, however, not unconditional: a negative condition is attached to it, the prohibition against any contact with the inhabitants of Canaan. The Canaanites have to be exterminated if Israel is to remain in its land.[94]

There are two passages in Deuteronomy that, according to Lemche, are evidence that the ancient Israelite 'historians' ' "knew" that any number of nations had lived in the land of Israel before Israel conquered Canaan, namely the Hittites, and the Girgashites'.[95] The shorter one is cited here:

> Of these you shall not take anything alive; but you shall surely curse them, the Hittites and the Amorites, and the Canaanites, and the Perizzites, and the Hivites, and the Jebusites, and the Gergesites; as the Lord your God commanded you; that they may not teach you to do all their abominations, which they did to their gods, and so you should sin before the Lord your God. (Deut. 20.16-18; cf. 7.1-6)

After a discussion of these varied lists of enemies who are to be destroyed, Lemche concludes that 'these lists of the pre-Israelite nations of Palestine cannot be considered historical documents from which we may draw information as to the ethnic composition of the Palestinian population before the arrival of the Israelites'.[96] He thus reinforces his thesis that, in spite of the presupposition on the part of traditional biblical scholarship

---

92. Kaufman Kohler ('Amorites—In Rabbinical and Apocryphal Literature', in Singer [ed.], *Jewish Encyclopedia*, I, pp. 528-30 [529]) equates the Canaanites with the Amorites: 'To the apocryphal writers of the first and second pre-Christian century [e.g. *Jubilees* and the *Apocalypse of Baruch*] they are the main representatives of heathen superstition, loathed as idolaters, in whose ordinances Israelites may not walk (Lev. 18.3)'.

93. Lemche, *Canaanites*, p. 113.

94. Lemche, *Canaanites*, p. 113.

95. Lemche, *Canaanites*, p. 83.

96. Lemche, *Canaanites*, p. 84.

that the Canaanites formed a distinctive people or nation in the ancient world,[97] the anti-Canaanite sentiment in the Hebrew Bible is an ideological theme and is not based on any set of 'historical facts'.

Part of the anti-Canaanite sentiment that is embodied in the biblical tradition prohibits Canaanites from converting to Judaism. According to Bamberger:

> As a matter of theory, the Canaanites were ineligible, since the Bible decreed their extermination from the land (Deut. 20.16). The Rabbis differed as to whether converts might be received from Canaanites dwelling outside the borders of Palestine. Nevertheless, Rahab and (with limitations) the Gibeonites were accepted—a fact which causes the later scholars some difficulty.[98]

The reality of the prohibition, however, is that 'this law is always understood by the Rabbis to refer, not to conversion, but to intermarriage with legitimate Jews. There was never any objection to accepting converts from these peoples; and we have several specific instances of such conversions on record.'[99] The key to the seemingly contradictory texts may lie in Deut. 23.3:

> The Ammonite or Moabite shall not enter the assembly of the Lord; even *until the tenth generation* he shall not enter into the assembly of the Lord even for ever: because they met you not with bread and with water by the way, when you went out of Egypt.[100]

In Matthew's genealogy, Salmon and Rahab comprise the tenth generation; the rabbis regard Rahab as an exemplary proselyte. Since Rahab is a Canaanite, that is, an enemy of Israel rather than a *ger*, her unlikely role as a proselyte is significant.

---

97. Lemche, *Canaanites*, p. 23.

98. Bamberger, *Proselytism*, p. 33. Van Houten (*Alien*) distinguishes between Israelites, Canaanites or any other large group of people, and aliens, as well as the spectrum that biblical Israelite Law takes in regard to the *ger*.

99. Bamberger, *Proselytism*, p. 33. Sandmel (*Judaism*, p. 229) argues that in order to rationalize intermarriage, the rabbinic explanation was quite simple: 'their brides had antecedently become converts to Judaism'. Cohen ('From the Bible to the Talmud: The Prohibition of Intermarriage', *HAR* 7 [1983], pp. 23-39 [36]) discusses the same Old Testament prohibitions and emphasizes the fact that 'not all of the ancient discussions on this topic mirror social reality'.

100. The emphasized phrase 'ten generations' is interpreted as 'forever' in the Mishnah (*m. Yeb.* 8.3).

4. *Canaanites in Matthew*

In Mt. 15.21-28, the woman is immediately identified as 'a *Canaanite* woman from those regions'.[101] The term Χανανα(α is a *hapax legomenon* in the New Testament.[102] Alice Dermience calls it 'a foreign and archaic appellation',[103] and correctly argues against those commentators who equate the term with Mark's 'Syrophoenician'.[104] 'Canaanite' is instead an

---

101. G. Schwarz ('ΣΥΡΟΦΟΙΝΙΚΙΣΣΑ—ΧΑΝΑΝΑΙΑ [MARKUS 7.26/MAT-THAUS 15.22]', *NTS* 30 [1984], pp. 626-28 [627]) makes the observation that Matthew's Canaanite Woman is without variants handed down; not so Mark's Greek, Syrophoenician Woman.

102. While the term 'Canaanite' is used only once in the New Testament, there are two references to 'Canaan': in Stephen's speech (Acts 7.2, 8-11), 'Canaan' is a general geographical description; in Paul's address (Acts 13.16-19), he is tracing Israelite history, borrowing from both Deut. 7.1 and Josh. 14.1. There is also a variant reading in Jn 14.22 in which Judas is a Κανανιτης. For a discussion of the *hapax legomenon*, see Lemche, *Canaanites*, p. 58; E.A. Russell, 'Canaanite Woman', pp. 268-70; Wainwright, *Matthew*, p. 225 n. 17. There is at least one other example of an archaic people in the New Testament, namely, Acts 2.9, the 'Elamites': 'And how is it that we hear, each of us in his own native language? Parthians and Medes and Elamites and residents of Mesopotamia, Judea and Cappadocia, Pontus and Asia, Phrygia and Pamphylia, Egypt and the parts of Libya belonging to Cyrene, and visitors from Rome, both Jews and proselytes' (Acts 2.8-10). Ernest Haenchen (*The Acts of the Apostles: A Commentary* [Philadelphia: Westminster Press, 1971], p. 170) writes that the Medes and Elamites 'had long been past history…[but] those names convey to the reader the impression that the Christian mission is already reaching out "to the ends of the earth"!' So Conzelmann, *The Acts of the Apostles* (Hermeneia; Philadelphia: Fortress Press, 1984, 1987), p. 14. The same applies to the Canaanites in Matthew's story, but in an exaggerated manner, because the mission is extended even to the enemies of Israel. This is, of course, consistent with Matthew's earlier instruction to 'Love your enemies' (Mt. 5.43//Lk. 6.27).

103. Dermience, 'La péricope', p. 29. See further, S. Legasse, 'L'épisode de la Cananéenne d'après Mt 15, 21-28', *BLE* 73 (1972), pp. 21-40 (26).

104. Plummer (*Matthew*, p. 215), for instance, takes Mark's description in the literal sense and says simply that 'this woman was a Greek-speaking descendant of the old inhabitants of Syrian Phoenicia'. Plummer cites Josephus (*Con. Apion* 1. 13): 'These Phoenicians "bore the greatest ill-will" towards the Jews; and this hostility helps to explain our Lord's attitude towards one of these hereditary foes of Israel'. See Kilpatrick, *Matthew*, pp. 132-33, and Theissen, *Miracle Stories*, p. 126, regarding the Markan description of the woman. Lightfoot (*Commentary*, II, p. 261) discusses 'a Canaanite woman-servant'. Likewise, according to Lachs (*Commentary*, p. 248), the expression may be from early rabbinic sources which distinguish between the Hebrew slave and the Canaanite slave (*Mek.* Exod. 21.26; *m. Qid.* 1.3.).

all-encompassing designation or metaphor for any foreigner to Judaism, whether by race, religion or trade. For that matter, anything historically reminiscent as contemptible to the Jews could be called 'Canaanite'.[105] It is within this context that the Matthean evangelist continues to use some of the same literary ploys as the Old Testament story tellers when they talk about the 'Canaanites', but emends their theology to be inclusive within Judaism rather than exclusive.[106]

According to Harrisville, Matthew is changing Mark's political description of the woman to religious in nature: 'the Evangelist's use of the word is for the purpose of heightening the religious opposition between Israel and the Gentiles'.[107] It is suggested by Selvidge that 'by using the word *Canaan*, Matthew stirs up...ancient fear and perhaps hatred of the foreigner, the unknown one—the one that became the enemy of Abraham'.[108]

The Old Testament tradition of the role of foreign women in Israel's

---

105. Dermience, 'La péricope', p. 30. So Meier, *Marginal Jew*, II, p. 675. David Novak (*The Image of the Non-Jew in Judaism: An Historical and Constructive Study of the Noahide Laws* [Toronto Studies in Theology, 14; New York: Edwin Mellen Press, 1983], p. 60) affirms the same archaism of the term 'Canaanite' in the Talmud: 'Just as the Canaanites of Biblical times were seen as being the very epitome of lawlessness and, therefore, were denied the protection of Jewish law, so lawlessness leads to similar results in later times with any Gentiles with whom Jews happen to come into contact. In other words, the later use of the term "Canaanite" is by analogy. There were no "Canaanites" in the Talmudic period.' While the scope of this study does not permit a discussion of so-called Canaanite religions, it is important to note that much of what we 'know' is derived from the biblical perspective, that is, it is a caricature defined by the biblical writers' perspectives and motives. See Delbert R. Hillers, 'Analyzing the Abominable: Our Understanding of Canaanite Religion', *JQR* 75 (1985), pp. 253-69 (258). Perkinson ('Canaanitic Word', p. 64) interprets the term 'Canaanite' as a metaphor: 'For the mind steeped in Israelite history, "Canaanite" glimmers summoning up a troubled image of polytheism, sacred prostitution, and ethnicity beyond the pale. The word opens an old memory, a rent in Matthew's text. It marks the woman herself as metaphor, as more (and less) then mere flesh and blood.' See also Pui-Lan Kwok, *Discovering the Bible in the Non-Biblical World* (Maryknoll: Orbis Books, 1995), pp. 71-73.

106. As will be pointed out, Matthew likes to use mirror images (that is, opposites) and this will be another example: the 'Canaanites' are the enemies and to be avoided at all cost in the Old Testament; Matthew wants to bring them around again as evidenced in a proselytic call in the so-called Great Commission. See Glenna S. Jackson, 'Are the "Nations" Present in Matthew?', *Hervormde Teologiese Studies 56* (2000), pp. 1043-56.

107. Harrisville, 'Woman of Canaan', pp. 280-81.

108. Marla J. Selvidge, *Daughters of Jerusalem* (Kitchener, Ontario: Herald Press, 1987), p. 79.

history must be carefully considered in order to understand their presence in Matthew's story.[109] Not only is there a tradition of them saving Israel,[110] but curiously enough, the women of enemy people may convert to Judaism. The later Sages, according to Zeitlin, 'in order to reconcile the contradictory and opposing view between the book of Ruth and the book of Deuteronomy [23.3], said that the Pentateuchal prohibition regarding the Moabites referred only to the male but not to the female'.[111] Matthew, therefore, includes Canaanite women in the Gospel story at two points, the genealogy and the story of the woman from Tyre and Sidon.[112]

The Moabites and Canaanites have been brought together many times in Hebrew Scriptures, most importantly for this discussion in the book of Ruth. The story of Tamar in Genesis 38 is sometimes understood to be a parallel narrative to the book of Ruth because the plot in both narratives is nearly the same: a childless widow is encouraged to return to her own kin, but each woman wants a son for her deceased husband; the laws regarding the Levirate marriage come into play in both stories; the conflict is resolved because of an 'incorrect' application of the laws; both narratives contain genealogical information.[113] Both women are foreigners: a Canaanite and a

---

109. Tamara C. Eskenazi ('Out From the Shadows: Biblical Women in the Post-exilic Era', *JSOT* 54 [1992], pp. 25-43 [25]) draws on Elephantine documents 'to suggest a context for understanding the opposition to foreign women'. While her conclusions are specifically tied to postexilic times, one of them is worth considering in regard to 'foreign women' in general: 'The fear of mixed marriages with their concomitant loss of property to the community makes most sense when women can, in fact, inherit' (p. 35). It may be that the prescriptive prohibition was socio-religious, but the descriptive prohibition was socio-economic. For the role of 'foreign women' in biblical narrative, see Athalaya Brenner, *The Israelite Woman: Social Role and Literary Type in Biblical Narrative* (JSOTSup, 21; Sheffield: JSOT Press, 1989), pp. 115-22; France, 'Scripture, Tradition and History'.

110. For example, Zipporah (Exod. 4.24-26); Rahab (Josh. 2; 6.22-25); Jael (Judg. 4.17-22). George W. Stroup ('Between Echo and Narcissus: The Role of the Bible in Feminist Theology', *Int* 42 [1988], pp. 19-32 [20]) includes several foreign women (e.g. Tamar and Rahab) in his category of 'sisters and daughters...[who] fill the history of the church and dwell in the shadows of the stories of the Bible'. For a list of other Old Testament women of virtue, including proselytes, see Claude Orrieux (*'Prosélytisme Juif'? Histoire d'une erreur* [Paris: Belles, 1992], pp. 147-48).

111. Zeitlin, *Studies*, II, p. 408.

112. Foreign women are absent in Mark, except for the story of the Syrophoenician Woman.

113. See, e.g., Lemche, *Canaanites*, p. 116; *idem, Early Israelites*, pp. 258-259. While the parallels are there, I am not as convinced as Daube (*Law*, p. 43) that 'it is

Moabite. The direct connection between the two stories is contained in two references in Ruth:

> And all the people who were in the gate said, 'We are witnesses': and the elders said, 'The Lord make your wife who goes into your house, as Rachel and as Leah, who both together *built* the house of Israel, and wrought mightily in Ephrathah, and there shall be a name to you in Bethlehem. And let your house be as the house of Perez, whom *Tamar* bore to Judah, of the seed which the Lord shall give you of this handmaid'. (Ruth 4.11-12; cf. the birth of Perez in Gen. 38.27-29)

According to Sharon Pace Jeansonne, the phrase 'build up' (v. 11) refers to 'establishing a people', literally 'having a child', for example Sarai intends to be 'built up' through Hagar (Gen. 16.2). Another example is 2 Sam. 7.27 where God will 'build up' David, or establish a dynasty.[114]

The author of Matthew indicates in the Gospel's genealogy that the Davidic dynasty was built through four foreign women, that is, two Canaanites, a Moabite, and a Hittite, noted enemies of Israel.

5. *Matthew's Genealogy*

Several elements from Matthew's genealogy are repeated in the story of the Canaanite Woman. In her first plea for help (15.22),[115] the Canaanite

---

certain that there is in Ruth a persistent harking back to the Tamar incident' or Andre LaCocque (*The Feminine Unconventional: Four Subversive Figures in Israel's Tradition* [Overtures to Biblical Theology; Minneapolis: Fortress Press, 1990], p. 93 n. 28) who suggests that it is 'by artistic transpositions [that] Tamar the Canaanite becomes Ruth the Moabite' (p. 95).

114. Sharon Jeansonne, *The Women of Genesis: From Sarah to Potiphar's Wife* (Minneapolis: Fortress Press, 1990), p. 19. 'Establishing' a dynasty and 'continuing it' seem to have the same meaning here. See further Gillian Feeley-Harnik, 'Naomi and Ruth: Building Up the House of David', in Susan Niditch (ed.), *Text and Tradition: The Hebrew Bible and Folklore* (SBLSS; Atlanta: Scholars Press, 1990), pp. 163-84; Adele Berlin, 'Ruth and the Continuity of Israel', in Judith A. Kates and Gail Twersky Reimer (eds.), *Reading Ruth: Contemporary Women Reclaim a Sacred Story* (New York: Ballantine Books, 1994), pp. 255-60.

115. Bruce Malina (*The New Testament World: Insights from Cultural Anthropology* [Louisville, KY: John Knox Press, 1981], p. 81) calls the result of this request a 'patron-client relationship' in his discussion of dyadic relationships. In this case, however, Jesus has given mixed messages about being a 'patron' of non-Jews: in 8.28-34 he heals the Gadarene demoniac, but in 10.5-6, he instructs the disciples to go nowhere among the Gentiles, but only to the 'lost sheep of the house of Israel'.

woman identifies Jesus as the Son of David.[116] This is in contrast to the Syrophoenician woman's request, which is set in the third person in Mk 7.26b and does not include the reference to David: 'And she begged him to cast the demon out of her daughter'.[117]

The Old Testament texts concerning Hiram, King of Tyre, and his relationship with King David and King Solomon not only illustrate that something good can come from that city, but also indicate that a link between the people of Tyre and their knowledge of traditions and stories about King David can be made by Matthew's community.

The inclusion of the title 'son of David' in v. 22 is significant in the context of the story of the Canaanite Woman for many reasons, not the least of which is its direct association with the book of Ruth. Matthew's first use of the term 'son of David' begins the Gospel:

The book of the genealogy of Jesus Christ, the son of David... (1.1)

Most scholars agree that the author of Matthew emphasizes Jesus' descent from David in order to establish him as the Messiah and king of Israel in

---

116. Davies and Allison (*Matthew*, II, p. 548) note that the woman consistently addresses Jesus as 'Lord'. The term, they say, 'lies somewhere between "sir" and the informed Christian confession. This helps keep her boldness in check. She may debate with Jesus, but that does not diminish her recognition of his superiority.' See further France, *Matthew*, pp. 284-86; Held, 'Matthew', p. 235; Hubert Frankemölle, *Jahwebund und Kirche Christi: Studien zur Form-und Traditionsgeschichte des 'Evangeliums' nach Matthäus* (Münster: Aschendorff, 1974), pp. 167-68. For Jack Dean Kingsbury (*Matthew: Structure, Christology, Kingdom* [Minneapolis: Fortress Press, 1975], pp. 99-113), *kyrios* is 'relational' and 'confessional', that is, the term expresses a relationship between Jesus and those who call him that, and illustrates his capacity as the 'messiah', 'Son of David', 'Son of God' and 'Son of Man'. According to A.-J. Levine (*Social and Ethnic Dimensions*, pp. 138-39), the reference to 'Canaanite' legitimizes the subordination of the Gentiles. For a history of the term 'Son of David', see W.D. Davies, *Christian Engagements with Judaism* (Harrisburg, PA: Trinity Press International, 1999), pp. 175-78.

117. Gundry (*Matthew*, pp. 310-12) correctly states in his comparison of Matthew's emendations of Mark's account in this verse that 'the addressing of Jesus as the Son of David anticipates the limitation of his ministry to Israel (vv. 24, 26) and the woman's agreement with that limitation (v. 27)' (p. 311). Bauer (*Structure*, p. 147) is also correct in stating that the addressing of Jesus as 'Lord' by the Canaanite Woman is in line with others who approach him in faith, but his statement that thus 'Matthew achieves...continuity by assimilating in various ways throughout the Gospel the earthly Jesus to the living Lord of the church', assumes a Christian perspective on the part of the Matthean author.

continuity with Israel's history.[118] There is also evidence from the Talmud, Midrash and both the Palestinian and Babylonian recensions of the *Shemoneh Esreh* in which the Messianic designation is 'Son of David'. The prevailing view of both Christian and Jewish traditions is that the Messiah would be Davidic.[119]

In addition to the three times that David is mentioned in the genealogy, he is referred to another 12 times in Matthew's Gospel, all but twice (Mt. 12.3; 22.43-45) within the phrase 'son of David'. Five of the 'son of David' references are in conjunction with healing stories involving people who would not be expected to 'see' or know Jesus as the Messiah (9.27; 12.22-23; 15.22; 20.30-31; 21.14-15).[120]

While David is the first ancestor mentioned, Matthew also reminds the community of the Abrahamic tradition at the beginning of the Gospel:

118. See, e.g., Luz, *Matthew*, pp. 108-109; Bauer, 'The Kingship of Jesus in the Matthean Infancy Narrative: A Literary Analysis', *CBQ* 57 (1995), pp. 306-23; John Mark Jones, 'Subverting the Textuality of Davidic Messianism: Matthew's Presentation of the Genealogy and the Davidic Title', *CBQ* 56 (1994), pp. 256-72. It is commonly known that Matthew's Jesus as the 'son of David' is a peculiarity when it is through the earthly father, Joseph, who is not his biological father, that Jesus inherits his Davidic ancestry.

119. Johnson, *Purpose*, p. 120. He divides the discussion of the Messiah into three parts: 'the Messiah ben David' (pp. 116-20), 'the Messiah ben Aaron' (pp. 120-31), and 'the Levitical Messiah' (pp. 131-38). Noting the work of Geza Vermes (*Jesus the Jew: A Historian's Reading of the Gospels* [Philadelphia: Fortress Press, rev. edn, 1981]), David M. Bossman ('Authority and Tradition in First Century Judaism and Christianity', *BTB* 17 [1987], pp. 3-9 [6]) argues that 'Jesus is filling a political role and the messianic theme here follows a royal identification which more readily relates to the divinely constituted state than to the family'.

120. These healing stories reflect the usage of the term 'Son of David' as used in the LXX. Solomon, as υἱὸς Δαυίδ (1 Kgs 2.1; 2 Chron. 1.1; 35.3), becomes a healer and exorcist. For further discussion see Klaus Berger, 'Die königlichen Messiastraditionen des Neuen Testaments', *NTS* 20 (1973), pp. 1-44; *idem*, 'Zur Problem der Messianität Jesu', *ZTK* 71 (1974), pp. 1-30; Davies and Allison *Matthew*, I, p. 136; Dennis Duling, 'Solomon, Exorcism, and the Son of David', *HTR* 68 (1975), pp. 235-52; *idem*, 'The Therapeutic Son of David: An Element in Matthew's Christological Apologetic', *NTS* 24 (1978), pp. 392-410; Johnson, *Genealogies*, p. 226. Bruce D. Chilton ('Jesus ben David: Reflections on the *Davidssohnfrage*', *JSNT* 14 [1982], pp. 88-112) argues against Duling, claiming that Matthew does not use the title 'Son of David' in a therapeutic context. Theissen (*Social Reality*, p. 137) reiterates that while Jesus is a son of David, 'what marks him out are his miraculous healings, not his political ambitions (Mt. 12.23; 9.27; 15.22)'.

The book of the genealogy of Jesus Christ, the son of David, the son of Abraham. (1.1)[121]

Abraham is traditionally the first proselyte in biblical narrative.[122] Not only is it made clear in Genesis 12 and 15 what he is to do to gain God's special favor, but the pseudepigraphical *Apocalypse of Abraham* relates Abraham's conversion from idolatry in great detail.[123] Abraham is the prototype of the perfect proselyte throughout rabbinic literature.[124] It was

121. A.-J. Levine ('Matthew', p. 253) writes that 'beginning with a genealogy, Matthew emphasizes Jesus' Hebrew ('son of Abraham') and royal ('son of David') lineage'. Lachs (*Commentary*, p. 2) emphasizes the same two elements and adds a third: 'to refute slanderous accusations, apparently widespread, to the effect that Jesus was of illegitimate birth due to his mother's improper behavior. This slander is presumably very old, perhaps first century, for it is already refuted in the Gospel of John, "We are not born of fornication" (8.41)'. Scholars disagree about this interpretation: for example, R. Alan Culpepper (*Anatomy of the Fourth Gospel: A Study in Literary Design* [New Testament Foundations and Facets; 2 vols.; Philadelphia: Fortress Press, 1983], I, p. 171) interprets the text as Lachs does; Haenchen (*A Commentary on the Gospel of John* [Hermeneia; 2 vols.; Philadelphia: Fortress Press, 1984], II, p. 29) and Rudolf Bultmann (*The Gospel of John: A Commentary* [Philadelphia: Westminster Press, 1971], p. 316) interpret the issue to be not one of Jesus' ancestry but of the Jews' parentage. For a history of the term 'Son of Abraham', see W.D. Davies, *Christian Engagements*, pp. 178-81.

122. According to Lachs (*Commentary*, p. 42), Abraham is the 'father of proselytes' and a proselyte then 'becomes a "son of our father Abraham"' (see Mt. 3.9). See also Luz, *Theology*, p. 26. Thomas M. Bolin ('A Stranger and an Alien Among You' [Genesis 23.4]: The Old Testament in Early Jewish and Christian Self-Identity', in Hills [ed.], *Common Life*, pp. 57-76) examines the repeated theme of Abraham as a 'foreigner/alien residing in the land of Canaan'.

123. For further discussion of the *Apocalypse of Abraham* and a comparison with biblical and other pseudepigraphical works, see George W.E. Nickelsburg (*Jewish Literature Between the Bible and the Mishnah* [Philadelphia: Fortress Press, 1981], pp. 294-99).

124. Albert A. Goldstein, 'Conversion to Judaism in Bible Times', in Eichorn (ed.), *Conversion*, pp. 13-15. Sandmel (*First Christian Century*, p. 22) cites Abraham and Sarah as master missionaries in rabbinic literature; Sandmel, *Judaism and Christian Beginnings*, p. 228. Geza Vermes (*Scripture and Tradition in Judaism: Haggadic Studies* [SPB, 40; Leiden: E.J. Brill, 1961], pp. 67-75, 83-85) discusses the Haggadic development of the life of Abraham, specifically the tradition of rejection of his father Terah's other gods. For a defense of the exegetical interpretation of Abraham, see Hayim Goren Perelmuter (*Siblings: Rabbinic Judaism and Early Christianity at their Beginnings* [New York: Paulist Press, 1989] p. 117).

Abraham's children who would continue in the covenant with the Lord.[125]

The Davidic aspect of the stories of Tamar and the wife of Uriah does exist, but, according to John Paul Heil, the subsequent use of the Canaanite Rahab and the Moabite Ruth in the genealogy reinforces the 'inclusive, universalist dimension of the Abrahamic promises'.[126] Heil adds: 'And Mary's giving birth to the Davidic Christ will continue Rahab's and Ruth's fulfillment of the universalist promise of Abraham'.[127] He then refers to the 'Davidic Christ's fulfillment of the Abrahamic promise when he heals the daughter of a Gentile woman (15, 21-28)'.[128]

Andries G. Van Aarde observes that the Matthean narrative point of view is not about biological descent, but vocation. For example, 'in Matthew 3.7-9 the true children of Abraham are described as people doing certain things: "they bear fruit that befits repentance" (3.8), or, more generally, they bear good fruit (7.17)'.[129] As will be shown, the vocation of the Canaanite woman from Tyre and Sidon is that of a proselyte into the Jewish community of Jesus and his disciples.

The 'taintedness' of the genealogy is pointed out in V. Aptowitzer's discussion of the debate between the Hasmoneans and the anti-Hasmoneans regarding the ancestry of David. Johnson summarizes that dispute: 'The Sadducees (representing the later Hasmonean point of view) held that, because of the illegal aspects of the marriage of Judah and Tamar, both David and his descendants were of tainted descent. Moreover, they

---

125. Zeitlin, *Studies*, II, p. 407. Rodney T. Hood ('The Genealogies of Jesus', in Allen Wikgren [ed.], *Early Christian Origins* [Chicago: Quadrangle, 1961], pp. 1-15 [8]) discusses the resulting smugness on the part of the Jews that aroused the prophetic wrath of John the Baptist who warned that God can produce children of Abraham out of stones if God so chooses (Mt. 3.9). For a rehearsal of Philo's and Josephus' discussion of Abraham's conversion and his relationship with the Gentiles, see Vermes (*Scripture*, pp. 79-81) and Sandmel (*Judaism and Christian Beginnings*, p. 231).

126. John Paul Heil, 'The Narrative Roles of the Women in Matthew's Genealogy', *Bib* 72 (1991), pp. 538-45 (540).

127. Heil, 'Narrative Roles', p. 543.

128. Heil, 'Narrative Roles', p. 543. G.E. Ford ('The Children's Bread and the Gods [Mt. xv. 21-28; Mk. vii. 24-30]', *ExpTim* 23 [1911–12], pp. 329-30 [329]) connects Gal 3.7 ('Know therefore that they which be of faith, the same are children of Abraham') with Jesus' answer to the Canaanite woman in 15.28 ('O woman, great is thy faith').

129. Andries Van Aarde, 'The *Evangelium Infantium*, the Abandonment of Children, and the Infancy Narrative in Matthew 1 and 2 from a Social Scientific Perspective', in Eugene H. Lovering (ed.), *SBLSP* 31 (Atlanta: Scholars Press, 1992), pp. 435-49 (445).

pointed to the Gentile ancestry of David in the Moabitess Ruth'.[130] Indeed, according to rabbinic sources:

> R. Abba b. Kahana opened, 'Tremble, and sin not' (Ps. iv, 5). David said to the Holy One, blessed be He, 'How long will they rage against me and say, 'Is he not of tainted descent? Is he not a descendant of Ruth the Moabitess?'... Ye also, are you not descended from two sisters [Rachel and Leah]? Look upon your own genealogy and be still. And Tamar who married your ancestor Judah—is it not a tainted descent? She was but a descendant of Shem the son of Noah. Have you then an honourable descent?' (*Ruth R.* 8.1)

Shem is the brother of Ham, who was the father of Canaan (Gen. 9.18-19). The other allusion to Tamar in the book of Ruth is included in the mention of her son Perez:

> Now these are the generations of Perez: Perez begot Hezron: Hezron begot Ram; and Ram of Amminadab. And Amminadab begot Nahshon; and Nahshon begot Salmon. And Salmon begot Boaz; and Boaz begot Obed. And Obed begot Jesse; and Jesse begot David. (4.18-22)[131]

The author of Matthew combines both references from Ruth in the genealogical opening of the Gospel:

> Abraham was the father of Isaac, and Isaac the father of Jacob, and Jacob the father of Judah and his brothers, and Judah the father of Perez and Zerah by *Tamar*, and Perez the father of Hezron, and Hezron the father of Ram, and Ram the father of Amminadab, and Amminadab the father of Nahshon, and Nahshon the father of Salmon, and Salmon the father of Boaz

---

130. V. Aptowitzer, *Parteipolitik der Hasmonäerzeit im Rabbinischen und Pseudo-epigraphischen Schrifttum* (Vienna: Verlag der Kohut-Foundation, 1927), p. 92, as quoted in Johnson, *Genealogies*, pp. 132-33.

131. Robert L. Hubbard (*The Book of Ruth* [Grand Rapids: Eerdmans, 1988], pp. 280-85) discusses each of the descendants in 'The Genealogy of Perez', noting Canaanite birth places. Jack M. Sasson ('A Genealogical "Convention" in Biblical Chronography?', *ZAW* 90 [1978], pp. 171-85 [171-72]) proposes that 'minimal alterations were made in inherited lists of ancestors in order to place individuals deemed worthy of attention in the seventh...position of a genealogical tree'. As part of his evidence, he notes that 'Boaz, hero of the story [of the book of Ruth], occupied the seventh slot. In order to preserve Boaz in this position, moreover, the genealogist of Ruth was forced to begin his line, not with the name of the eponymous ancestor Judah, but with that of the lesser liminary Perez' (p. 184). I argue that while the author of Ruth may have had reasons to exclude Judah from the genealogy, Matthew recaptured Judah's (that is, Judah's and Tamar's) name in order to emphasize the extreme marginality of the Canaanite origins of Jesus.

by *Rahab*, and Boaz the father of Obed by *Ruth*, and Obed the father of
Jesse, and Jesse the father of David the king. And David was the father of
Solomon by the wife of Uriah [*Bathsheba*]...(1.2-6)

A genealogy is a traditional way to begin a story or a prophecy,[132] and is
usually dominated by males;[133] for example, Luke's genealogy (3.23-38)
follows the mainstream of an all-male lineage.[134] However, genealogists
are not always motivated by antiquarian interest or historical curiosity, but
are more often concerned with statements about relationships in contemporary times.[135] The task, therefore, is to establish the relationship of the
'most distinctive feature'[136] of the Matthean genealogy—namely, the

132. See, e.g., Zeph. 1.1. There are also genealogies in Gen. 3, 10 (which highlights
Canaan and Sidon), 11; 1 Chron. 3; Ezra 7, Jud. 8. See further, Gerard Mussies,
'Matthew's Pedigree of Jesus', *NovT* 38 (1986) pp. 32-47; Joachim Gnilka, *Das
Matthäusevangelium* (2 vols.; Freiburg: Herder, 1986), II, pp. 1-14. See David R.
Bauer ('The Literary and Theological Function of the Genealogy in Matthew's
Gospel', in Bauer and Powell [eds.], *Treasures*, pp. 129-59) for a narrative critical
examination of the genealogy.

133. According to Mussies ('Pedigree', p. 38), 'O.T. genealogies are mainly tables
of male descendants', but he cites 1 Chron. 2 as having 'no less than fourteen
women...mentioned by name'. Greek pedigrees are predominantly male, but women
are mentioned in some. Laffey (*Introduction*, p. 116) likewise notes that 'genealogies
are one expression of patriarchal culture'. Laffey also identifies major exceptions in the
Deuteronomistic History: Joab, Abishai, and Asahel—their mother is Zeruiah (2 Sam.
2.18) (p. 117). Bruce J. Malina and Richard L. Rohrbaugh (*Social-Science Commentary on the Synoptic Gospels* [Minneapolis: Fortress Press, 1992], p. 25) agree that
the New Testament genealogies are patrilineal and, therefore, are 'important testimony
to the male's status as bearer of rights in the community'. Malina and Rohrbaugh avoid
mentioning the foreign women and erroneously claim that 'the Matthean form gives
special stress to fatherhood'.

134. Mussies ('Pedigree', pp. 39-43) discusses the Matthean and Lukan 'harmoni-
zation' solutions that Tertullian and Julius Africanus (via Eusebius) propose (p. 40), as
well as the deliberate changes made in N, θ, W, and B: 'Their authors apparently all
four started from the assumption that it was Luke and not Matthew who had to be
corrected' (p. 42). See further J.C. Anderson, 'Mary's Difference', pp. 190-99. Daube
(*New Testament*, pp. 27-36) suggests that 'Mary is made to resemble Ruth' in Luke's
story of the annunciation.

135. Harrington, *Matthew*, p. 31.

136. Krister Stendahl, 'Quis et Unde? An Analysis of Mt 1-2', in G. Stantan
Interpretation, pp. 56-66 (56); Hood, 'Genealogies', p. 2; Herman C. Waetjen, 'The
Genealogy as the Key to the Gospel According to Matthew', *JBL* 95 (1976), pp. 205-
30 (218). See also Bernard Brandon Scott, 'The Birth of the Reader', *Semeia* 52
(1990), pp. 83-102.

mentioning of the four women Tamar, Rahab, Ruth and Bathsheba ('the wife of Uriah') to Matthew's purpose in writing the gospel. According to Harrington, the relationship is in the right timing of important themes as part of God's plan for salvation, that is, 'the roots of Jesus in the history of Israel, the surprising instruments that God uses, the peculiar assortment of people that make up the ancestors of Jesus, [and] the tension between tradition and newness'.[137]

The significance of the four named women included in Matthew's genealogy (Tamar in v. 3, Rahab and Ruth in v. 5, and the wife of Uriah [Bathsheba] in v. 6) needs to be explored not only because of their sex, but because of their non-Israelite origins as well.

There are three traditional proposals for the inclusion of the women in the genealogy.[138] The first, as espoused by Jerome, is that 'the four Old Testament women were regarded as sinners; and their inclusion fore-shadowed for Matthew's readers the role of Jesus as the Savior of sinful men [sic]'.[139] The second proposal, first made popular by Martin Luther, is that:

> The women were regarded as foreigners and were included by Matthew to show that Jesus, the Jewish Messiah, was related by ancestry to the Gentiles. According to the Bible, Rahab and (probably) Tamar were Canaanites, while Ruth was a Moabite. Bathsheba is not identified in the Old Testament as a foreigner; but it is as the wife of Uriah (*the Hittite*) that Matthew identifies her, and indeed this peculiar designation constitutes the strongest argument for the proposal that the four women were to be thought of as foreigners in the genealogy of the Messiah.[140]

The third proposal is the claim that the four Old Testament women share two common elements with Mary, the mother of Jesus, in that there is

> something extraordinary or irregular in their union with their partners—a union which, though it may have been scandalous to outsiders, continued

---

137. Harrington, *Matthew*, p. 33.

138. R.E. Brown, *Birth*, pp. 71-74. See further his 'Gospel Infancy Narrative Research from 1976 to 1986: Part I (Matthew)', *CBQ* 48 (1986), pp. 468-83; Hendrikus Boers, *Who Was Jesus? The Historical Jesus and the Synoptic Gospels* (San Francisco: Harper & Row, 1989, especially 'The Matthean Birth Stories', in ch. B2, pp. 11-16; A.-J. Levine, *Social and Ethnic Dimensions*, pp. 59-88; Freed, 'Genealogy', pp. 3-19; Roger Le Deaut, 'Targumic Literature and New Testament Interpretation', *BTB* 4 (1974), pp. 243-89 (285).

139. R.E. Brown, *Birth*, p. 71.

140. R.E. Brown, *Birth*, p. 72.

the blessed lineage of the Messiah; the women showed initiative or played an important role in God's plan and so came to be considered the instrument of God's providence or of His Holy Spirit... These women were held up as examples of how God uses the unexpected to triumph over human obstacles and intervenes on behalf of His planned Messiah.[141]

The presence of the women in the genealogy is related to Matthew's theology and purpose, that is, 'it did foreshadow the role of the Messiah who was to bring Gentiles into God's plan of salvation—people who, though not Jews, were like Jesus in their descent from Abraham'.[142]

While I would like to agree with Wainwright that the presence of the four women serves as a critique of patriarchy,[143] and I partially agree with Wim J.C. Weren that the purpose of the genealogy is to show that 'Jesus [is] the purpose of Israel's history, but this history has achieved its aim not by the effort of men but by the extraordinary concerted action of female forces',[144] a better understanding is that of Craig L. Blomberg and Richard

---

141. R.E. Brown, *Birth*, pp. 73-74. Gail Paterson Corrington (*Her Image of Salvation* [Louisville, KY: Westminster/John Knox Press, 1992], p. 152), however, disagrees; that is, at least on the part of Uriah's wife, the irregular behavior is on the part of King David, not Bathsheba. Ann Belford Ulanov (*The Female Ancestors of Christ* [Boston: Shambhala, 1993], p. 84) supports the thesis that the four women's 'scandalous behavior both forecasts and supports Mary's scandalous pregnancy'. For insights on incest, especially in the cases of Tamar and Ruth, see Susan Reimer Torn, 'Ruth Reconsidered', in Kates and Reimer (eds.), *Reading Ruth*, pp. 336-46. See also Athalya Brenner (ed.), *A Feminist Companion to Ruth* (The Feminist Companion to the Bible, 3; Sheffield: Sheffield Academic Press, 1993). T.L. Thompson (*Mythic Past*, p. 46) explains the wordplay on *kanaf* in the story of Ruth.

142. R.E. Brown, *Birth*, p. 74. John Nolland ('The Four [Five] Women and Other Annotations in Matthew's Genealogy', *NTS* 43 [1997], pp. 527-39) finds only modified interest on the part of Matthew in these traditional proposals; the women's function is to prepare the reader for Mary's role in salvation history. Schaberg's controversial thesis (*The Illegitimacy of Jesus* [San Francisco: Harper & Row, 1987]) is that all five women (including Mary) gave birth to illegitimate children. See also Schaberg's review of several feminist interpretations of the infancy narrative ('Feminist Interpretations of the Infancy Narrative of Matthew', *JFSR* 13 [1997], pp. 35-62). As she states, they 'touch a nerve in Christian and scholarly psyches' in that 'the theories of the "incarnation" and "divinity" of Jesus, of the activity of the Spirit, of the role of women in the process of "redemption", of women's sexuality, and of a "Virgin Mother" are all challenged' (35).

143. Elaine Mary Wainwright, 'The Gospel of Matthew', in Schüssler Fiorenza (ed.), *Searching the Scriptures*, II, pp. 642-43.

144. Wim J.C. Weren, 'The Five Women in Matthew's Genealogy', *CBQ* 59 (1997), pp. 288-305 [290].

Bauckham. According to Blomberg, it is not the women's pedigrees that were stressed, but the 'Jewish tradition [that] emphasized their roles as proselytes',[145] and according to Bauckham,

> the reason for Tamar's appearance in the genealogy cannot be that she was regarded as a Gentile…[but that] she could be a proselyte, though the fact that this goes unnoticed would be consistent with Pseudo-Philo's [for instance] lack of interest in those righteous Gentiles of the Old Testament whom Jewish tradition regarded as proselytes.[146]

Philo viewed Tamar as a proselyte by describing her as 'a woman from "Palestinian Syria"…which is simply a contemporary way of saying that she was a Canaanite. From a polytheistic and idolatrous background, she converted to the worship and service of the one true God (*Virt.* 220-222).'[147] That option will be discussed further in the case of each of the foreign women in the genealogy.

Tamar (Mt. 1.3) becomes an ancestor of King David by posing as a prostitute for Judah's pleasure (Gen. 38).[148] Although her ancestry is ambiguous,[149] Jeansonne concludes that Tamar is a Canaanite for at least two reasons: her name means 'palm tree', which signifies that her off-spring will comprise the Israelite tribe that will provide the Davidic line of kings and that the narrator purposely leaves her origins ambiguous, thus letting the reader assume that Judah married a woman from the land of

---

145. Craig L. Blomberg, 'The Liberation of Illegitimacy: Women and Rulers in Matthew 1–2', *BTB* 21 (1991), pp. 144-50 (145). So Sim, 'Gospel of Matthew and the Gentiles', p. 22. However, Sim argues that it is not likely that the Gentiles in Matthew's church would have identified with these women based on their proselytism.

146. Richard Bauckham, 'Tamar's Ancestry and Rahab's Marriage: Two Problems in the Matthean Genealogy', *NovT* 37 (1995), pp. 313-29 [318-19].

147. Bauckham, 'Tamar's Ancestry', p. 320.

148. A clear discussion of history's edification of Tamar, including the fact that she is a proselyte and is also counted among the ancestors of David, can be found in Orrieux, *'Proselytisme Juif?'*, p. 147. For a recent literary analysis of Gen. 38, where the text is seen as an 'ideal narrative', see Anthony J. Lambe, 'Genesis 38: Structure and Literary Design', in Philip R. Davies and David J.A. Clines (eds.), *The World of Genesis: Persons, Places, Perspectives* (JSOTSup 257; Sheffield: Sheffield Academic Press, 1998), pp. 102-20.

149. A.-J. Levine reviews Jewish writings on the subject (*Social and Ethnic Dimensions*, pp. 74-77). Luz (*Theology*, p. 26) states, but does not argue, that Tamar was Aramaic. Weren ('Five Women', p. 289) points out the conflicting evidence for her ancestry.

Canaan rather than going back to his own family or land for a wife.[150]
Through Tamar's insistence that the levirate marriage law be honored, she
becomes the mother of the twins Perez and Zerah.

Rahab, the mother of Boaz (Mt. 1.5), is also a Canaanite. She becomes a
hero for the Israelites through her profession as a prostitute[151] (Josh. 2–6).
The woman named Rahab in Matthew's genealogy is the same Rahab as
the one in the book of Joshua.[152] Her reward for heroic acts on behalf of
the Israelites is announced in Josh. 6.25:

> And Joshua saved alive Rahab the harlot, and all the house of her father,
> and caused her to dwell in Israel until this day, because she hid the spies
> which Joshua sent to spy out Jericho.

Scholars cite the aetiological function of the reference, that is, its justification of the presence of foreigners in Israel, 'foreign women even, who,
rather than being a threat to the Israelites (cf. Josh. 23.12), had functioned
as a real asset'.[153]

Rahab's earlier speech to the Israelite men in Josh 2.9-13 is a confession
of faith in Yahweh:

---

150. Jeansonne, *Women*, p. 101. Malachi 2.11 and Isa. 57.3 include allusions to
Tamar's 'foreign' status. Philo writes (Virt. XL. 221): 'Tamar was a woman from
Palestinian Syria, bred in a house and city which acknowledged a multitude of gods
and was full of images and wooden busts and idols in general'.

151. For commentaries on Rahab's vocation, see Betsy Halpern Amaru, 'Portraits of
Biblical Women in Josephus' Antiquities', *JJS* 39 (1988), pp. 143-70 (160); Phyllis A.
Bird, 'The Harlot as Heroine: Narrative Art and Social Presupposition in Three Old
Testament Texts', *Semeia* 46 (1989), pp. 119-39; Laffey, *Introduction*, p. 86; Susan
Niditch, 'Notes and Observations: The Wronged Woman Righted: An Analysis of
Genesis 38', *HTR* 72 (1979), pp. 143-49; J. Alberto Soggin, *Joshua* (OTL; Phila-
delphia: Westminster Press, 1972), p. 41.

152. Although it can be argued either way as to whether the woman named Rahab in
Matthew's genealogy is the same Rahab as the one in the book of Joshua, I agree with
those who claim she is. I think, for example, that Bauckham ('Tamar's Ancestry', pp.
320-29) has argued persuasively that, based on Matthew's exegetical basis for his
genealogical information, she is. Others who agree include Soggin, *Joshua*, p. 41; R.E.
Brown, '*Rachab* in Mt 1,5 Probably is Rahab of Jericho', *Bib.* 63 (1982), pp. 79-80;
Weren, 'Five Women', pp. 298-99; Yair Zakowitch, 'Rahab als Mutter des Boas in der
Jesus-Genealogie (Matth. I 5)', *NovT* 17 (1975), pp. 1-5. Jerome D. Quinn ('Is
"PAXAB" in Mt 1,5 Rahab of Jericho?', *Bib.* 62 [1981], pp. 225-28), for example,
disagrees.

153. Laffey, *Introduction*, pp. 88-89.

> And she said to them, I know that the Lord has given you the land; for the fear of you has fallen upon us... The Lord your God is God in heaven above, and on the earth beneath. (Josh. 2.9, 11b)

Thus, through her profession of faith in Yahweh, Rahab becomes a member of the Israelite community.[154]

Rahab's inclusion in the two New Testament works centers upon her faithfulness to God:

> By faith the walls of Jericho fell down after they had been encircled for seven days. By faith Rahab the harlot did not perish with those who were disobedient, because she had given friendly welcome to the spies. (Heb. 11.30-31)

Rahab, the Canaanite harlot, is exemplified along with Abraham in James:

> 'Abraham believed God, and it was reckoned to him as righteousness'; and he was called the friend of God. You see that a man is justified by works and not by faith alone. And in the same way was not also Rahab the harlot justified by works when she received the messengers and sent them out another way? For as the body apart from the spirit is dead, so faith apart from works is dead. (Jas 2.23b-26)

According to Orrieux, the example of Rahab the prostitute illustrates equally essential aspects in the approach of future proselytes: repentance and confidence in divine pardon.[155] That influence on the picture of Matthew's Canaanite Woman will be shown in Chapter 3.

Ruth (1.4) is a Moabite and the relationship between Moab and Israel is not unlike the relationship between Canaan and Israel:

> While Israel was staying at Shittim, the people began to have sexual relations with the women of Moab. These invited the people to the sacrifices of their gods, and the people ate and bowed down to their gods. (Num. 25.1-2)

The fact that 'the adjective "Moabitess" appears at least twice in connection with Ruth where the plot does not demand the title (2.2, 21)'[156] em-

---

154. Soggin (*Joshua*, p. 37) historicizes the statement of Rahab in 2.9-13: '[it is] inspired by themes drawn from the ancient confessions of faith of Israel (Deut. 26.5b-9; Josh. 24.2b-13) and sounds very improbable coming from this woman, even allowing for her sudden conversion'. Robert G. Boling and Ernest G. Wright (*Joshua* [AB, 6; Garden City, NY: Doubleday, 1982], p. 146) agree with John McKenzie (*The World of the Judges* [Englewood Cliffs, NJ: Prentice–Hall, 1966], p. 480) that Rahab is quoted as 'rather well read in the Deuteronomic tradition of the exodus and the wilderness'. Josephus' account of Rahab and the spies can be found in *Ant.* 5.1.2.7.

155. Orrieux, *'Proselytisme Juif?'*, p. 149.

156. Dorothea Harvey, 'Book of Ruth', *IDB*, IV, pp. 131-34 (133).

phasizes Ruth's foreignness, and in particular her ancestry, whereby the
Moabite women 'played the harlot' to the Israelites going from Egypt to
Canaan (e.g. Num. 25.1-2). Danna Nolan Fewell and David Miller Gunn
discuss Ruth's religious convictions in light of the argument that Naomi
has lost her husband and sons because of their association with Ruth, an
enemy Moabite:

> YHWH is punishing Naomi—that Naomi claims loudly enough—but for
> what? Is Moab the unspoken reason? Does Ruth therefore attempt to tame
> that fear by removing its theological roots? Understand the speech thus and
> we may hear her saying to Naomi: If you are worried that to continue
> association with a foreign woman with foreign gods is to invite further
> disaster, then don't worry, for I can fix that; I'll change people—your
> people will be my people!—and I'll change gods as well—your god will be
> my god! [1.16][157]

Ruth, the model for future proselytes,[158] and Boaz, the son of the Canaanite-
turned-proselyte Rahab, give birth to Obed, and are thus the ancestral
grandparents of King David.

Bathsheba (wife of Uriah in Mt. 1.6) is a Hittite.[159] She becomes King
David's wife through the murder of her husband (2 Sam. 11).[160] It is
striking that the three female ancestors of King David along with his wife

---

157. Danna Nolan Fewell and David Miller Gunn, *Compromising Redemption:
Relating Characters in the Book of Ruth* (Literary Currents in Biblical Interpretation;
Louisville: Westminster/John Knox Press, 1990), p. 96.

158. Jack M. Sasson, *Ruth: A New Translation with a Philological Commentary and
a Formalist-Folklorist Interpretation* (The Biblical Seminar, 10; Sheffield: JSOT Press,
1989), p. 13. E. van Wolde (*Ruth en Noomi, twee vreemdgangers* [Baarn: Ten Have,
1993], pp. 140-41) points out several similarities between the story of Ruth and the
story of Tamar.

159. Luz (*Theology*, p. 26) understands 'the paraphrase of Bathsheba as the "wife of
Uriah" as an unmistakable signal'; that is, that she was an Israelite before marrying the
Hittite Uriah. Since the biblical evidence does not give us any information about her
before her marriages, we can only speculate as to why Matthew did not call her by
name—perhaps he forgot it.

160. Many scholars claim that Bathsheba was raped. According to J. Cheryl Exum
(*Fragmented Women* [Valley Forge, PA: Trinity Press International, 1993], pp. 172-
76), Bathsheba is also raped symbolically by the narrator of the story. Moshe Garsiel
('The Story of David and Bathsheba: A Different Approach', *CBQ* 55 [1993], pp. 244-
62) concurs that Bathsheba is a 'tragic figure, involved without deliberate will in
adultery and murder, and forced to marry in haste to escape the consequences' (p. 254).
For her role in Israelite's history, see T. Dennis, *Sarah Laughed: Women's Voices in
the Old Testament* (London: SPCK, 1994), pp. 140-75.

are mentioned specifically in Matthew's 'genealogy of Jesus Christ' (1.1) and they are either Canaanite, Moabite or Hittite.[161]

Luz chooses the fact that the women are non-Jews as the reason for their inclusion in the genealogy, and provides an insight with which I both agree and disagree:

> Thus the genealogy contains a universalistic overtone; it is indicated in a hidden way that the son of David, the Messiah of Israel, brings salvation for the Gentiles. This provides a clue for the interpretation of 'son of Abraham' in 1.1, which is seemingly so taken for granted and yet so striking: it reminds us of the broad Jewish tradition which sees Abraham as the father of the proselytes. The shifting of the salvation of Israel to the Gentiles, a predominant theme in the Gospel of Matthew, is addressed in its opening text.[162]

The agreement lies in all but the last sentence. There is no shift from Israel to the Gentiles but rather an avenue for the Gentiles through Israel.[163]

6. *Summary*

Canaanites in the Old Testament are identified as stereotypically bad; their land is good and selected individuals from amongst them are chosen by

---

161. It is also striking that, as A.-J. Levine ('Matthew', p. 262) points out, 'Just as women mediate both a man's entry into this world by giving birth and, in many traditions, his exit by participating in funerary rites, women frame the life of Jesus; they are present in his genealogy and the story of his birth, and they are the primary witnesses to his death and resurrection'.

162. Luz, *Matthew*, p. 110. Montague (*Companion God*, p. 18) assumes that Matthew's purpose is to tell the readers that 'Gentiles are in your future because they are in your past. And our history shows that even in the biological transmission of the promise we can expect surprises.' Patte (*Matthew*, p. 18) observes that the evangelist's convictions are stated in 1.1-25: 'In thematic passages the convictions are expressed in terms of the "readers' old knowledge", as envisioned by the author; the presence of the author's convictions, what is new for the readers, is signaled by the tensions they create by being introduced in the old knowledge of the readers'.

163. It should be noted that Philo also refers to Hagar (*Abr.* 251), Tamar (*Virt.* 221-22), and especially Abraham (*Cher.* 31; *Mut.* 76; *Som.* 1.161) as proselytes. Josephus includes Ruth (*Ant.* 5.9): 'I was therefore obliged to relate this history of Ruth, because I had a mind to demonstrate the power of God, who, without difficulty, can raise those that are of ordinary parentage to dignity and splendor, to which he advanced David, though he were born of such mean parents'. T.L. Thompson (*Mythic Past*, p. 348) makes a poignant statement about Mt. 1–2: 'The role of Jesus in this gospel will be that of an Immanuel who is not only God with us, but will represent God, in the manner of Moses and Joshua before him, as saving people: not from Egypt nor from the Canaanites, but this time from their sins'.

God to serve Israel, especially for the purpose of continuing the Israelite lineage. Matthew's emendation of Mark's 'Syrophoenician' to 'Canaanite' contains the same double-stranded tradition. On the one hand, it speaks of the notorious enemies of Israel who are prohibited from converting to Judaism and are obviously not part of the *ger*; on the other, it directs attention back to Jesus' Canaanite heritage through the proselytic women in the genealogy. The evangelist chooses Mark's story of the Syro-phoenician Woman because of its female specificity—the wives of Israel's enemies are not excluded from conversion into Judaism. Why Jesus then appears to reject the Canaanite Woman in 15.21-28 needs to be explored.

Chapter 3

IN SEARCH OF A NEW PARADIGM

1. *Introduction*

The text of Mt. 15.21-28 can be divided up and translated as follows:

First Request/Rejection

ἐλέησόν με, κύριε υἱὸς
Δαυίδ ἡ θυγάτηρ μου κακῶς
δαιμονίζεται

'Have mercy on me, Lord, Son
of David; my daughter is
badly demonized'.

ὁ δὲ οὐκ ἀπεκρίθη αὐτῇ λόγον.

But he did not answer her a word.

Second Request/Rejection

Καὶ προσελθόντες οἱ μαθηταὶ
Αὐτοῦ ἠρώτουν αὐτὸν λέγοντες
ἀπόλυσον αὐτήν, ὅτι κράζει
ὄπισθεν ἡμῶν.

And his disciples came and
asked him, saying,
'Send her away, for she is
still crying along behind us'.

ὁ δὲ ἀποκριθεὶς εἶπεν
οὐκ ἀπεστάλην εἰ μὰ εἰς
τὰ πρόβατα τὰ ἀπολωλότα
οἴκου Ἰσραήλ.

But he answered, saying,
'I was sent only to
the lost sheep of the
house of Israel'.

Third Request/Rejection

ἡ δὲ ἐλθοῦσα προσεκύνει αὐτῷ
λέγουσα κύριε, βοήθει μοι.

But she came in reverence of him,
saying, 'Lord, help me'.

ὁ δὲ ἀποκριθεὶς εἶπεν
οὐκ ἔστιν καλὸν
λαβεῖν τὸν ἄρτον τῶν
τέκνων καὶ βαλεῖν τοῖς
κυναρίοις.

But he answered, saying,
'It is not pleasing to God
to take the bread of
the children and throw it to
the dogs'.

Fourth Request/Acceptance

ἡ δὲ εἶπεν ναὶ κύριε,	But she said, 'yes Lord,
καὶ γὰρ τὰ κυνάρια	yet even the dogs
ἐσθίει ἀπὸ τῶν χίων	eat the crumbs
τῶν πιπτόντων ἀπὸ	that fall from
τῆς τραπέζης τῶν	the table of
κυρίων αὐτῶν.	their masters'.
τότε ἀποκριθεὶς ὁ Ἰησοῦς	Then Jesus answered,
εἶπεν αὐτῇ	saying to her,
ὦ γύναι, μεγάλη σου ἡ πίστις	'O woman, great is your faith.
γενηθήτω σοι ὡς θέλεις.	Be it done for you as you will'.

While others have recognized the repetitive petitionary form of the story of the Canaanite Woman,[1] there has been no adequate explanation as to the origin of or reason for the three-time request/rejection and fourth-time request/acceptance form in comparison to Mark's shorter form of the same story. Mark's version contains terms that denote proselytism, and so an analysis of these terms will be included in this discussion. However, the primary purpose of this chapter is to demonstrate the verisimilitude of Matthew's theme of proselytism with the form for the story of the Canaanite Woman as influenced by the intertextuality with several Old Testament writings, the most important of which are the Psalms and the book of Ruth.

2. *The Gospel of Mark*

The expansion of Mark's request pattern is both the most important and most obvious change that Matthew makes. There are, however, other emendations that Matthew makes in Mark's vocabulary or details that serve the express purpose of indicating proselytic activity—namely, the woman's initiative, the attitude of worship, the woman's nationality, the presence of the disciples and the exorcism.

---

1.   See, for example, Davies and Allison, *Matthew*, II, p. 541; Theissen, *Miracle Stories*, pp. 181-82; Wainwright, *Matthew*, pp. 219-22; Antoinette Clark Wire, 'The Structure of the Gospel Miracle Stories and Their Tellers', *Semeia* 11 (1978), pp. 83-113. Mack (*Myth*, p. 381) includes the 'Challenge/Response of the Core of the Chreia' in Mark. According to Plummer (*Matthew*, p. 215), 'of these four appeals and answers, Mk. gives only the last two, and we are in ignorance as to the source of the other two'.

a. *Initiative (Mark 7.25a, 26b)*

ἀλλ᾽ εὐθὺς ἀκούσασα γυνὴ	But immediately a woman
περὶ αὐτοῦ, ἧς εἶχεν τὸ	whose little daughter
θυγάτριον αὐτῆς πνεῦμα	was possessed by an
ἀκάθαρτον...	unclean spirit.
καὶ ἠρώτα αὐτὸν ἵνα τὸ	And she begged him
δαιμόνιον ἐκβάλη ἐκ τῆς	to cast the demon out
θυγατρὸς αὐτῆς.	of her daughter.

In both Mark and Matthew, the woman takes the initiative in asking for help. Paget summarizes conventional understanding of Gentiles taking the initiative: 'In the conversionary process the forces were nearly always centripetal (the motivation for conversion nearly always came from Gentiles), rarely centrifugal (the motivation did not come from Jews themselves)'.[2] Cohen agrees—in rabbinic conversion ceremonies, certain texts 'presume that the potential convert will take the initiative by "approaching" or "coming" to be converted... "To approach"...is technical language for presenting oneself for membership or for approval... Cf. the Greek term προσέρχεσθαι, whence "proselyte"'.[3]

2.   Paget, 'Jewish Proselytism', p. 68.
3.   Shaye J.D. Cohen, 'The Rabbinic Conversion Ceremony', *JJS* 41 (1990), pp. 177-203 (181 n. 4). See also BAGD, *s.v.* προσέρχομαι, p. 713. Some will question the strength of an argument that is dependent in any way on early rabbinic materials because of the problems in dating them (e.g. Jacob Neusner, 'Was Rabbinic Judaism Really "Ethnic"?', *CBQ* 57 [1995], pp. 281-305 [281 n. 1]); Feldman (*Jew and Gentile*, p. 492 n. 55) comments on the methodological question involved as to whether to speak collectively of the rabbis or to examine the rabbinic treatises separately . For example, most scholars agree that until the mid-second century CE, no formal rites for conversion existed. Nevertheless, even within those limitations, it is reasonable to assume that what did emerge as formal rites had to come from practices of some sort and for some time. The fact that some rabbinic materials can be dated beginning in the second century means that they were at least in the air during the first-century writing of the Gospels, and there is reason to believe that many of the early Christian writings and rabbinic Jewish writings came out of the same milieu. For other studies paralleling Matthew and rabbinic literature, see Terence L. Donaldson, 'The Law That Hangs (Matthew 22.40): Rabbinic Formulation and Matthean Social World', *CBQ* 57 (1995), pp. 689-709; Wendell E. Langley, 'The Parable of the Two Sons (Matthew 21.28-32) Against its Semitic and Rabbinic Backdrop', *CBQ* 58 (1996), pp. 228-43. Langley argues that it is not a question of dependence, but of comparison and plausibility. Jacob Neusner (*From Scripture to 70: The Pre-Rabbinic Beginnings of the Halakhah* [SFSHJ; Atlanta: Scholars Press, 1998], p. 3) explains the many difficulties of defining

b. *Attitude of Worship (Mark 7.25b)*

...ἐλθοῦσα προσέπεσεν   ...came and fell down at his feet.
πρὸς τοὺς πόδας αὐτοῦ

Mark immediately paints the woman as a humble worshipper. While Matthew does not indicate an attitude of worship immediately, it does appear in the woman's third request in 15.25:

But she came in reverence (προσεκύνει) of him, saying, 'Lord, help me'.[4]

Mark Allan Powell compares three distinct types of worship in Matthew and includes the Canaanite woman in the category of 'supplicatory worship', defined as 'a demonstration of dependence upon and confidence in the one who is worshipped'[5] and notes that this kind of worship depends

and dating Rabbinic Judaism, that is, it is difficult to set temporal limits to the history of ideas. However, 'what is at issue therefore is not where and when episodic facts originate, but how and why facts are taken over and put together into that remarkably cogent structure and system of thought that is embodied by the halakhah of Rabbinic Judaism.' As Neusner says any number of times, 'Origin means nothing, context means everything' (p. xviii). See also Overman (*Matthew's Gospel*, pp. 2-3) who, although he cautions against thinking of formative Judaism and rabbinic Judaism as synonymous, argues that early proponents of rabbinic Judaism may have been at least a part of Matthew's opposition.

4. Gundry (*Matthew*, p. 314) and A.-J. Levine (*Social and Ethnic Dimensions*, p. 145) emphasize the aspect of worship in this verse. However, the verb κλαίω ('to cry'), with an emphasis on inadequacy and submission, is not used in this pericope. Instead, κράζω is used by Matthew in both vv. 22 and 23. (See Johannes Schneider, 'κλαίω' in *TDNT*, III, pp. 722-25. Cf. Ruth 1.9, 14.) Matthew does use κλαίω in reference to Peter in 26.75 (cf. Mk 14.72). It is also interesting that Matthew does not use σέβω in the story of the Canaanite Woman even though it was used in 15.7-9 (cf. Mk 7.6-7): 'You hypocrites! Well did Isaiah prophesy of you, when he said: "This people honors me with their lips, but their heart is far from me; in vain do they worship me [σέβονταί με, cf. Isa. 29.13, LXX], teaching as doctrines the precepts of men".' Gentiles who felt drawn to Judaism but did not formally become proselytes, were called, according to Arthur Darby Nock (*Early Gentile Christianity and Its Hellenistic Background* [New York: Harper & Row, 1964], p. 2; cf. BAGD, *s.v.* σέβω, p. 746), '*Sebomenoi*, "worshippers", and the "worshippers of the Highest God"'. According to Mark and Matthew, those who σέβονταί με are not sincere; thus it would not be an appropriate term to use with the woman from Tyre.

5. According to M.A. Powell ('A Typology of Worship in the Gospel of Matthew', *JSNT* 57 [1995], pp. 3-17 [6]), there are 13 instances of worship in Matthew; nine use the term προσκυνέω (the magi [2.11], a leper [8.2], a ruler [9.18], the disciples [14.33], the Canaanite woman [15.25], a slave [18.26], the mother of James and John

on the initiative of the supplicant. An attitude of worship that connotes proselytism is thus included in both Matthew's and Mark's stories, but Matthew includes another proselyte term to initially introduce the woman:

> …a Canaanite woman from that region came out (ἐξελθοῦσα)… (Mt. 15.22)

The term ἐξέρχομαι has been translated 'came out', but it can also mean to 'leave a congregation' as in 1 Jn 2.19.[6] Matthew demonstrates that the woman has come out of her region, meaning that she is in the process of leaving her own people behind as she converts to the religion of Jesus.[7] There are other instances in Matthew where ἐξέρχομαι means the equivalent of 'to leave behind' with a sense of finality:

> Truly, I say to you, you will never get out (ἐξέλθῃς) till you have paid the last penny. (5.26)

> And he said to them [demons], 'Go'. So they came out (ἐξελθόντες) and went into the swine, and behold, the whole herd rushed down the steep bank into the sea, and perished in the water. (8.32)

> And whatever town or village you enter, find out who is worthy in it, and stay with him until you depart (ἐξέλθητε)… And if any one will not receive you or listen to your words, as you leave (ἐξερχόμενοι) that house or town, shake off the dust from your feet. (10.11, 14)

> When the unclean spirit has gone out (ἐξέλθῃ) of a man, he passes through waterless places seeking rest, but he finds none. (12.43)

Moore correctly concludes that:

> προσήλυτος and its synonyms designate a man who has not merely embraced the monotheistic theology of Judaism, but has addicted himself to the Jewish ordinances and customs, and in so doing severed himself from his people, friends, and kinsmen; for which reason he is to be treated with peculiar benevolence.[8]

[20.20], two women [28.9], and the disciples [28.17]). Luz (*Theology*, p. 72) also notes that the woman's approach is similar to the magi and the disciples.

6. BAGD, *s.v.* ἐξέρχομαι, p. 275.

7. This is not to be confused with the argument as to whether she left her geographical region and went to Jesus or he went to her region (see p. 42, n. 48). Matthew is again using a double entendre with the term ἐξελθοῦσα.

8. G.F. Moore, *Judaism*, II, pp. 327-28. Abraham J. Malherbe (*Social Aspects of Early Christianity* [2nd edn; Philadelphia: Fortress Press, 1983], p. 51) quotes Philo and emphasizes that it was not easy for proselytes: 'Conversion to Judaism created tension between proselytes and their pagan associates and relatives… The proselytes had left their country, their relatives, and their friends for the sake of virtue and

The 'peculiar benevolence' the woman finally receives from Jesus in the story certainly qualifies her as a προσήλυτος.

c. *Nationality (Mark 7.26)*

ἡ δὲ γυνὴ ἦν Ἑλληνίς,	Now the woman was a Greek,
Συροφοινίκισσα τῷ γένει.	a Syrophoenician by birth.

The identification of the woman illustrates another instance of Matthew's change in Mark's terminology for furthering the purpose of proselytism: Mark identifies the woman as 'a Greek, a Syrophoenician by birth [nationality]' (7.26). That description, incidentally, is two verses into the pericope. Her predicament precedes her description, indicating that the impending miracle is more important to Mark than her Gentile status:

> But immediately a woman, whose little daughter was possessed by an unclean spirit, heard of him, and came and fell down at his feet. Now the woman was a Greek, a Syrophoenician by nationality. (7.25-26a)[9]

However, Mark has introduced a concept into the story that has not been carefully examined by biblical scholars: the term Ἑλληνίς can refer to a kind of proselyte, that is, God-fearing Gentiles, as in Acts 17.4 and Jn 12.20.[10]

> And some of them were persuaded, and joined Paul and Silas; as did a great many of the devout Greeks and not a few of the leading woman. (Acts 17.4)

> Now among those who went up to worship at the feast were some Greeks. (Jn 12.20)

According to D.S. Margoliouth, 'the word *Hellenis* is likely to mean "proselyte", and that the woman belonged to this class may have been inferred from her addressing Jesus as "Son of David", though this feature

religion. Recognizing the social disruption caused by their conversion, Philo urges that proselytes be made to feel at home in the divine society to which they had been called.' Neusner ('Was Rabbinic Judaism "Ethnic"?', p. 287) also emphasizes the fact that a proselyte was a true Israelite: 'We find the idea that God should be your God, not only ours; when God becomes your God, you become part of us, and the way of life that we follow is not "ours" but the one that God demands of everyone'.

    9.   Matthew 15.22 inverts the order of predicament and description.

    10.   BAGD, *s.v.* Ἑλλην, pp. 251-52. The basic meaning of Ἑλλην is a person of 'Greek language and culture' and 'in the broader sense, all persons who came under the influence of Greek, i.e. pagan, culture'.

is omitted by Mark'.[11] Margoliouth combines the Matthean and Markan stories; it rather appears that Matthew, influenced by the word Ἐλλενίς in Mark, added 'Son of David' to intensify the concept of proselytism.

The Greeks mentioned in the Gospel of John are proselytes, according to Bultmann, even though the term προσήλυτοι or σεβόμενοι is not used:

> Doubtless they are so-called proselytes; if they are not described as such (as προσήλυτοι or σεβόμενοι) but are called Ἐλλανίς, obviously this is because they should be viewed as representatives of the Greek world. The way they have to take is complicated; they turn to Philip; he informs Andrew about it, and they both then present the request to Jesus. In the words that follow, however, Jesus appears to ignore the request.[12]

This Johannine passage is similar to Matthew's text in 15.23b, where the Canaanite Woman also attempts to go through the disciples to get to Jesus, that is, the Greeks in John 12 go to Philip first, then Philip to Andrew, Philip and Andrew to Jesus, and then finally Jesus ignores them![13] According to Bultmann:

> the Greek world is asking after Jesus! Accordingly the fact that the Greeks must turn to the disciples in order to reach Jesus could also have a symbolic meaning: the access of the Greek world to Jesus is mediated through the apostles… The later Christian usage has served as a pattern for the conception of this scene, according to which a Gentile, who wanted to join the community, had to be recommended by two members of the Church.[14]

Each of the early communities of Jesus followers had its own set of rites for proselytes.

Matthew did not leave the term Ἐλληνίς as it stands in Mark's story of

---

11. D.S. Margoliouth, 'The Syro-Phoenician Woman', *The Expositor* 22 (1921), pp. 1-10 (6). He presumes historicity of the text.

12. Bultmann, *John*, p. 423. Barnabas Lindars (*The Gospel of John* [NCB; Grand Rapids: Eerdmans, 1972], p. 427) also associates Greeks with proselytes 'and to devout Gentiles like Cornelius (Ac. 10.1f)'. A distinction can be made between προσήλυτοι and σεβόμενοι (cf. BAGD, *s.v.* σέβω, p. 746), but Bultmann includes both terms for categories of proselytes among the Greeks. As for the women, the advantage of not having to be circumcised led many more of them than men to conversion (Goldstein, 'Conversion', p. 15).

13. Bultmann, *John*, p. 423 nn. 3-4. The continuity of Jn 12.20-22 and 23-30 is questioned by Bultmann; he suggests that the request of the Ἐλληνές 'remains without an answer' (p. 420). Is it possible that there is a proselytic formula here also? Jn 12.20-26 contains four steps in the request:
'Greeks—Philip—Andrew—Philip/Andrew—Jesus'.

14. Bultmann, *John*, p. 423 n. 5.

the Syrophoenician Woman even though the term indicates proselyte activity. A stronger term that denotes a specific member of Israel's enemies is needed to show the radical nature of proselytism.

d. *The Disciples (Mark 7.24)*

There is no mention of the disciples in Mark's story of the Syrophoenician Woman; in fact, Mark (7.24) makes it clear that Jesus was alone:

> And from there he arose and went away to the region of Tyre. And he entered a house, and would not have any one know it; yet he could not be hid.

The disciples' interaction with the Canaanite Woman in Matthew's story is for the purpose of providing witnesses for her conversion. According to Cohen, by the early or mid-second century, a convert 'must be able to provide witnesses, because the conversion process involves formal interaction with native Jews'.[15] Matthew's story may suggest that the formality of conversion had begun to take place earlier than Cohen suggests.

The necessity of witnesses is also evidenced in the *Pseudo-Clementine Homily* on this story as the disciples intimate that they too asked the Lord to heal the woman's daughter:

> There is amongst us one Justa, a Syro-Phoenician, by race a Canaanite, whose daughter was oppressed with a grievous disease. And she came to our Lord, crying out, and entreating that He would heal her daughter. But He, being asked also by us, said, 'It is not lawful to heal the Gentiles, who are like to dogs on account of their using various [that is, without distinction][16] meats and practices, while the table in the kingdom has been given to the sons of Israel'. (*Ps.-Clem.* 2.19)

e. *Exorcism (Mark 7.30)*

καὶ ἀπελθοῦσα εἰς τὸν οἶκον	And she went home,
αὐτῆς εὗρεν τὸ παιδίον	and found the child
βεβλημένον ἐπὶ τὴν κλίνην	lying in bed,
καὶ τὸ δαιμόνιον ἐξεληλυθός.	and the demon gone.

Mark's story makes it clear that the daughter was not with her mother. A 'healing at a distance' is thus a part of Mark's account.[17] It is not obvious

---

15. Cohen, 'Rabbinic Conversion Ceremony', pp. 195-96.

16. 'Justa, A Proselyte', in *The Clementine Homilies* (*ANF* VIII; Grand Rapids, MI: Eerdmans, 1951), p. 232.

17. Elizabeth Struthers Malbon ['Fallible Followers: Women and Men in the

in Matthew's version that the two females have been separated: 'And her daughter was healed at that hour (15.28b)'.[18]

The LXX takes for granted that δαιμόνιον is a contemptuous term for heathen gods;[19] Matthew uses the term similarly in the story of the blind and mute demoniac:

> Then they brought to him a demoniac who was blind and mute; and he cured him, so that the one who had been mute could speak and see. All the crowds were amazed and said, 'Can this be the Son of David?' But when the Pharisees heard it, they said, 'It is only by Beelzebul, the ruler of the demons, that this fellow casts out the demons'. (12.22-24)

According to 2 Kgs 1.2-4, Baalzebub, the god of Ekron, is a pagan deity and the rival of the God of Israel. The emphasis on an exorcism from Mark's account is not needed by Matthew: therefore, the demon that possesses the woman's daughter in Matthew's version is one of the pagan gods. Rabbinic literature strongly emphasizes the possibility of fulfilling the Law, and if one does so, the seductive activity of demons is greatly reduced.[20] Since the children of adult proselytes who have 'fulfilled the Law' automatically become Jews,[21] the demon loses possession and the

Gospel of Mark', *Semeia* 28 [1983], pp. 29-48 [37]) notes the male//female pairings in Markan miracle stories, for example, the Gerasene demoniac with Jairus's daughter and the hemorrhaging woman; and the Syrophoenician woman's daughter with the deaf mute in the Decapolis. Matthew has extra material in each case between the Markan pairings. For other first-century 'healings at a distance' as a category in hellenistic religions, see Horsley and Llewelyn (eds.), *Documents*, IV, p. 248. Derrett ('Law', p. 174) labels this an 'absent healing' and notes the cultural environment whereby the woman could expect such.

18. Davies and Allison (*Matthew*, II, p. 556), viewing the healing as a medical cure, point out that this is not technically an exorcism, since 'there is no trace of an exorcism ritual'. Wire ('Stories', p. 89) argues the same for the Syrophoenician Woman's daughter because the woman's 'struggle to achieve Jesus' intervention supplants any struggle of Jesus with the unclean spirit and becomes the one organizing interaction of that story'. Duling ('Solomon', pp. 250-51) writes that 'a comparison of Mark's seams with Matthew's healing summaries will show that whereas Mark has a hard focus on exorcisms and a soft focus on healings, for Matthew the emphasis is on healing, not exorcisms'. As will be shown, Matthew's definition of a healing in this story is not one of a medical cure.

19. W. Foerster, 'δαίμων', *TDNT*, II, pp. 1-19 (12).

20. W. Foerster, 'δαίμων', p. 16.

21. Bamberger (*Proselytism*, p. 52) states that 'such children [those of proselytes] "will be agreeable to what their father has done" (Ket. 11a). If, however, the minor has no father, there is somewhat greater doubt.' For a related discussion on how the Law

daughter is healed.[22] Hence, for Matthew, the Markan 'healing at a distance' is not important because the healing is one of conversion.[23]

As a summary of the above discussion, the following chart shows how Matthew takes five elements from Mark that hint of proselytism and strengthens them:

Mark	Matthew
1. ἠρώτα (7.26)	ἐλέησόν (15.22b)
In both Mark and Matthew, the woman takes the initiative, but in Matthew she doggedly pursues him.	
2. ἐλθοῦσα	ἐλθοῦσα
προσέπεσεν (v. 25)	προσεκύνει (v. 25)
Matthew emphasizes the proselytic activity with two verbs.	
3. ἡ δὲ γυνὴ ἦν Ἑλληνίς, Συροφοινίκισσα τῷ γένει. (v. 26)	γυνὴ Χαναναία (v. 22a)
Matthew emphasizes the extreme marginality of the female proselyte by labeling her as a specific enemy of Israel.	
4.	μαθηταὶ (v. 23)
Matthew adds witnesses to the woman's proselytic request.	

affects the female children of Gentiles as well as female proselytes, see Judith Romney Wegner, *Chattel or Person? The Status of Women in the Mishnah* (Oxford: Oxford University Press, 1988), pp. 22-23. Daube (*Ancient Jewish Law*, pp. 22-32) also discusses the issue of children born of a Jewess and a Gentile.

22. According to Derrett ('Law', p. 172), 'the Syro-Phoenician woman requotes scripture, with a common-sense midrash. If her daughter may "eat", the demon must be expelled; for a table cannot be laid for demons (Is lxv II)'! What he says, however, about the woman in Mark's story is not true of Matthew's story, that is, that the Syrophoenician Woman's daughter was cured as a free gift, that Jesus did not act by way of reciprocity, and that the faith of the person involved was irrelevant (p. 183). The discussion of the expansion on Matthew's part will show that, for Matthew, the cure was reciprocity for the mother becoming a Jew.

23. The same may be true of the demons in the country of the Gadarenes (8.28-34). An intriguing connection between child sacrifice in Tyre and the story of the Canaanite Woman and her daughter from Tyre cannot help but be noticed (but not argued in this monograph). See J.A. Dearman, 'The Tophet [A tophet, according to Dearman, is 'a cult-place without a temple where child sacrifice and the incineration of corpses were practiced' (59)] in Jerusalem: Archaeology and Cultural Profile', *JNSL* 22.1 (1996), pp. 59-71.

5. καὶ ἀπελθοῦσα εἰς τὸν οἶκον αὐτῆς εὗρεν τὸ παιδίον βεβλημένον ἐπὶ τὴν κλίνην	ὦ γύναι, μεγάλη σου ἡ πίστις γενηθήτω σοι ὡς θέλεις.
καὶ τὸ δαιμόνιον ἐξεληλυθός. (v. 30)	καὶ ἰάθη ἡ θυγάτηρ αὐτῆς ἀπὸ τῆς ὥρας ἐκείνης. (v.28)
Matthew stresses that the woman will have done for her what she wills; the physical healing is incidental.	

3. *The Psalms and Other Texts*

The Canaanite Woman fits well into a literary category of people 'who would stand in "loyal opposition" to God and to God's ways of executing justice'.[24] There is Old Testament precedent for arguing with God, especially when prayer is expected to bring about a resolution of an impending crisis.[25] 'Where else in the Old Testament', according to Balentine, 'does one find such bold presentations of individuals [Moses, Elijah and Joshua] standing *tête à tête* with God, challenging, interrogating, petitioning and being taken seriously? Not only do they assault God; at times they even prevail.'[26] If the precedent is that God's mind could be changed, as the story goes, then perhaps Jesus would change his mind also.[27] Thus Matthew

24. George W. Coats, 'The King's Loyal Opposition: Obedience and Authority in Exodus 32–34', in G.W. Coats and Burke O. Long (eds.), *Canon and Authority* (Philadelphia: Fortress Press, 1977), pp. 91-109; Samuel E. Balentine, 'Prayers for Justice in the Old Testament: Theodicy and Theology', *CBQ* 51 (1989), pp. 597-616 (603). The phrase 'loyal opposition' sounds like an oxymoron, and means to argue even with God for what is thought to be right. See also Patrick D. Miller, *They Cried to the Lord: The Form and theology of Biblical Prayer* (Minneapolis: Fortress Press, 1994).

25. Balentine, 'Prayers for Justice'. O'Day ('Surprised by Faith', p. 299) affirms the Canaanite Woman's standing 'in the tradition of Abraham and Moses who were not afraid to bargain with God; she is profoundly linked with all the broken and needy petitioners who sang Israel's songs of lament, with all those who cling to the faithfulness to the promise. She is not a Jew; she is, nevertheless, fully Jewish.' The Canaanite Woman is not born a Jew, but becomes one.

26. Balentine, 'Prayers for Justice', p. 613. See also Gen. 32.22-28 where Jacob wrestles with an angel and wins; thus his name is changed to 'Israel', that is, one who struggles with God and wins.

27. It has been theorized that the fourth request in the Matthean version of the woman's argument is in the form of a legal debate. Derrett ('Law', p. 162), capitalizing on Burkill's notion of Apartheid, suggests that the story may be a product of the church's legal problems.

continues the Davidic motif that was begun in the genealogy by incorporat-
ing not only the literary form of some Davidic Psalms,[28] but the theology of
refuge as well.

The relationship between God and God's people is clearly expressed
through the lament. Michael Neary cites Deut. 26.5-11, in which a 'cry for
help and deliverance, reminiscent of the lament psalms [is] central to the
cultic credo'.[29] The passage states: 'we cried (ἀνεβοήσαμεν)...the Lord
heard...and gave us...a land flowing with milk and honey' (Deut. 26.7, 9).
According to Neary, the theme of the Lament is evident throughout biblical history and is noteworthy in Israel's liturgical celebration, 'indicating
that it reflects the traditional form in which the faith is presented. That cry
of the people/hearkening of God becomes for Israel a way of self-
understanding which is central to [its] theology and history.'[30]

Neary reiterates that the theme of cry/rescue becomes a prototype, a
biblical metaphor for deliverance, a paradigm for the structure of God's
saving activity, which continued into the narrative of the Judges.[31] It also

28. Six of the specific Psalms discussed below contain various attributions to
David: as a shiggaion (Ps. 6, LXX), as a psalm (Pss. 30, LXX and 21, LXX), as a maskil
(Ps. 54, LXX), as a prayer (Ps. 85, LXX), or as a miktam (Ps. 56, LXX). David C.
Mitchell (*The Message of the Psalter: An Eschatological Programme in the Book of
Psalms* [JSOTSup, 252; Sheffield: Sheffield Academic Press, 1997], pp. 26-28) argues
that the Psalms' eschatological or messianic hermeneutic of the New Testament is no
different from contemporary first-century Israel, for example, Qumran, the Pharisees
and the rabbis.

29. Michael Neary, 'The Importance of Lament in the God/Man Relationship in
Ancient Israel', *ITQ* 52 (1986), pp. 180-92 (182).

30. Neary, 'Importance of Lament', p. 182. This is not unique for Judaism,
however. Gods and petitions are an obvious part of Assyrian, Babylonian and Egyptian
religious literature as well.

31. Neary, 'Importance of Lament', p. 183. See Exod. 2.23b-25 (ἀνεβόησαν); 3.7-
8; Judg. 2.18; 3.9 (ἐκέκραξαν), 15; 4.3; 6.6. See Hermann Gunkel and Joachim
Begrich (*Introduction to Psalms: The Genres of the Religious Lyric of Israel* [trans.
James D. Nogalski; Mercer Library of Biblical Studies; Macon, GA: Mercer University
Press, 1998]) for a classic study of the Psalms. See further, Samuel E. Balentine,
'Prayers in the Wilderness Traditions: In Pursuit of Divine Justice', *HAR* 9 (1985), pp.
53-74. Jerome F.D. Creach (*Yahweh as Refuge and the Editing of the Hebrew Psalter*
[JSOTSup, 217; Sheffield; Sheffield Academic Press, 1996]) proposes, in a more re-
cent literary study, that editorial interest and, therefore, a directive for reading the
present Psalter can be discerned through a related field of words associated with the
idea of 'refuge'. See especially his discussion of the term as metaphor (pp. 50-73).
Norman Whybray (*Reading the Psalms as a Book* [JSOTSup, 222; Sheffield: Sheffield

continues into the narrative of Matthew's Gospel. As will be shown, the story of the Canaanite Woman is a vehicle through which Matthew perpetuates the motif of God's saving activity as evidenced in the Old Testament Psalms, this time for a female proselyte.

The presence of one group of proselytes, the 'God-fearers',[32] is frequent in the Psalms. Therefore, two categories of psalms will be included in this discussion: those psalms that specifically include or are voiced by proselytes, and those psalms that contain special language and imagery analogous to Matthew's story of the Canaanite Woman. In many cases, these categories overlap. Language and imagery in the Psalms also overlap, but an attempt will be made to discuss specific psalms and other appropriate writings in the same order as particular verbs signify a new request on the part of Matthew's story of the Canaanite Woman, that is, ἐλεέω,[33] κράζω, βοηθέω and εἶπον. A fifth category of proselytic activity in the form of the phrase, 'In the shadow of your wings, I take refuge', is then briefly discussed.

a. *ἐλέησόν με/οὐκ ἀπεκρίθη αὐτῇ λόγον (Matthew 15.22-23)*
Out of the 16 times that ἐλέησόν με is found in the Psalms,[34] five include an address to the 'Lord', that is, ἐλέησόν με, κύριε.[35] Psalms 6, 9, 30 and

Academic Press, 1996) discusses the difficulty of categorizing psalms and of stereotyping redactional purposes or theologies; David C. Mitchell (*Message of the Psalter*, pp. 78-82) rehearses the past and present theories on the redactional agenda behind the Psalter.

32. From an Old Testament perspective, Goldstein ('Conversion', p. 24) states that '"God-fearers" represent to the psalmist worshipers of God who are not of Jacob's seed'. He lists the 'God-fearers' as a fourth category of religious communicant in Israel, the others being priest, Levite and native Israelite.

33. Malina and Rohrbaugh (*Social-Science Commentary*, p. 110) indicate that the term 'mercy...means the willingness to pay back...one's debts of interpersonal obligation to God and fellow humans...the reason Jesus owes mercy is that he is "Son of David". Yet as Son of David, his obligations are "only to the lost sheep of the house of Israel".' They then erroneously conclude that 'because of the Canaanite woman's loyalty and commitment to him, he accedes'. I argue that she commits herself to the laws of Judaism, not necessarily to Jesus.

34. See Pss. 6.2; 9.13; 25.16; 26.11; 27.7; 31.9; 41.4, 10; 51.1; 56.1; 57.1; 86.3, 16; 119.29, 58, 132.

35. It is significant that the phrase ἐλέησόν με/ἡμᾶς, κύριε is connected to the title υἱὸς Δαυίδ in the stories of the Canaanite Woman and the Two Blind Men. J.C. Anderson ('Matthew: Gender and Reading', *Semeia* 28 [1983], pp. 3-28 [14-16]) includes the two stories in a chiastic pattern. According to Anderson, 'the faith of the

54 will be discussed, as well as the verb ἀποκρίνομαι in 1 Kings and
1 Maccabees.

1. *Psalm 6 (LXX)*. Psalm 6 is a 'so-called Penitential Psalm' or Lament of
the Individual.[36] Links between such cries for help from Hebrew
Scriptures and the Matthean communities suggest strong possibilities for a
liturgical formula.[37]

> ἐλέησόν με, κύριε, ὅτι ἀσθενής εἰμι (Ps. 6.3, LXX)
> Have mercy on me, Lord, for I am weak.

There are actually four petitions in Psalm 6, followed by an acceptance on
God's part.[38]

outcast supplicants—the blind men and the Gentile woman—contrasts with the sign
seeking of the Jewish leaders who would reject them and with the wavering faith and
understanding of the disciples in the feeding stories'. See also A.-J. Levine (*Social and
Ethnic Dimensions*, pp. 139-40) for the differences in the meaning of 'discipleship'
between the two pericopes. For a discussion of κύριος, see Jack Dean Kingsbury, 'The
Title "Kyrios" in Matthew's Gospel', *JBL* 94 (1975), pp. 246-55, (251-53). On a
related issue concerning Canaanite culture and the Psalms, see Antti Laato, 'Psalm 132
and the Development of the Jerusalemite/Israelite Royal Ideology', *CBQ* 54 (1992),
pp. 49-66; Richard J. Clifford, *The Cosmic Mountain in Canaan and the Old Testament* (Cambridge, MA: Harvard University Press, 1972), pp. 35-79, 149; Hermann
Spieckermann, '"Die ganze Erde ist seiner Herrlichkeit voll" Pantheismus im Alten
Testament?' *ZTK* 87 (1990), pp. 415-36.

36. See Sigmund Mowinckel, *The Psalms in Israel's Worship* (2 vols.; New York:
Abingdon Press, 1962) especially I, ch. 7, pp. 225-46, 'National Psalms of Lamentation in the I-Form', and II, ch. 8, pp. 1-25, 'Personal (Private) Psalms of Lamentation';
A.A. Anderson, *Psalms*, I, pp. 86-87; and Claus Westermann, *Praise and Lament in
the Psalms* (Atlanta: John Knox Press, 1981), pp. 68-69.

37. Wainwright, *Matthew*, pp. 226-27 n. 24. Pierre Auffret ('Note complementaire
sur la structure litteraire du Psaume 6', *BN* 42 [1988], pp. 7-13 [13]) discusses the
opposition between YHWH and Sheol: YHWH will change the situation of the faithful,
the reverse is true for the enemy. Most scholars continue to agree with Weiser's conclusion (*Psalms*, p. 130) that the style is 'characterized by the use of traditional
phrases'. See, e.g., Craig C. Broyles, *The Conflict of Faith and Experience in the
Psalms: A Form-Critical and Theological Study* (JSOTSup, 52; Sheffield: JSOT Press,
1989), p. 182 n. 5.

38. Westermann (*Psalms*, pp. 68-69) breaks the components of this Psalm into the
following: Address and Introductory cry for help; Lament; Confession of trust;
Petition; Motifs; and Praise of God. He arbitrarily categorizes the first two petitions as
the introductory cry for help; petition three is not recognized; petition four is broken
into two petitions, the first to *hear*, and the second to *save*.

Petition 1:   O Lord, rebuke me not in your wrath, neither chasten me in your anger. (v. 2)

Petition 2:   Have mercy on me, O Lord;…heal me, O Lord; (v. 3)

Petition 3:   But thou, O Lord, how long? (v. 4)

Petition 4:   Return, O Lord, deliver my soul: save me for your mercy's sake. (v. 5)

Acceptance: Depart from me, all you that work iniquity; for the Lord has heard the voice of my weeping. The Lord has hearkened to my petition; the Lord has accepted my prayer. (vv. 9-10)

Lined up with Matthew, the chart looks like this:

	Psalm 6	Matthew
1. Request:	O Lord, rebuke me not. (v. 2)	Have mercy on me, Lord, Son of David. (v. 22)
2. Request:	Have mercy on me, O Lord. (v. 3)	She is still crying along behind us. (v. 23b)
3. Request:	O Lord, how long? (v. 4)	Lord, help me. (v. 25)
4. Request:	Save me. (v. 5)	even the dogs eat the crumbs that fall from their masters' table. (v. 27)
Resolution:	The Lord has heard the voice of my weeping. (v. 9)	Be it done for you as you will. (v. 28)

Thus, form parallels can be seen between Psalm 6 and the story of the Canaanite Woman that suggest a possible literary and liturgical reliance on the part of Matthew.

2. *Psalm 9 (LXX)*. Psalm 9 contains the same petition ἐλέησόν με, κύριε and reflects an individual speaker:

> I will give thanks to you, O Lord, with my whole heart;
> I will recount all your wonderful works. I will be glad and exult in you;
> I will sing to your name, O Most High…
> Have mercy on me, O Lord (ἐλέησόν με, κύριε)!
>   look on my affliction which I suffer of my enemies,
> O you who lifts me up from the gates of death, that I may declare all your
>   praises in the gates of the daughter of Zion:
> I will rejoice in your salvation. (9.2, 14-15, LXX)

This Psalm may be spoken as a cultic act in the Temple where the needy person prays to God.[39] 'That I may declare all your praises' in v. 15, accord-

---

39. A.A. Anderson, *Psalms*, p. 105.

ing to Anderson, is correctly interpreted as 'that I may declare Yahweh's saving deeds before other worshippers (cf. verse 2)'.[40] In other words, v. 2 ('I will give thanks to you, O Lord, with my whole heart; I will recount all your wonderful works') is reflected in v. 15. Again, Matthew divulges familiarity with this form of petitionary prayer when the Canaanite woman makes the same request: she initiates proper proselytic activity by asking for help and, as a result, her daughter is healed. The proper form for proselytism will be discussed at length in the next major section.

3. *Psalms 30 (LXX) and 54 (LXX).* Psalm 30 (LXX) contains two of the pleas that are present in the story of the Canaanite Woman, but more importantly illustrates the assumption on the Psalmist's part that the petition for help will be heard:

> Have mercy on me, Lord (ἐλέησόν με, κύριε)
> for I am afflicted. (30.10)

> But I said in my extreme fear,
> I am cast out from the sight of your eyes:
> therefore you heard (εἰσήκουσασ) my supplication
> when I cried to you (κεκραγέναι με πρὸς μέ). (30.23)

Psalm 54 is also an example of the assumption that one will be heard:

> Give ear to my prayer, O God; Hide not thyself from my supplication! Attend to me, and hear (εἰσακουσόν) me.

According to Samuel Balentine, the Psalm contains

> a plea not only for a response but also for a divine intervention which will offset the suppliant's present sense of God's hiddenness... Thus God's answer, or the lack of it, is for the suppliant inseparably bound up with his experience of God's presence or hiddenness in his own circumstances.[41]

Jesus, however, 'did not answer her a word'.[42] The equivalent of this verse is not found in Mark's story of the Syrophoenician Woman. Albright

---

40. A.A. Anderson, *Psalms*, p. 112.

41. Samuel E. Balentine, *The Hidden God: The Hiding of the Face of God in the Old Testament* (Oxford Theological Monographs; Oxford: Oxford University Press, 1983), p. 153.

42. Again, see Balentine's work on petitions for God to 'hear' and 'answer' (e.g. Pss. 86.1; 102.3), in *Hidden God*, especially pp. 151-55. Old Testament precedent is that if one cries, one will be heard. Gundry (*Matthew*, p. 312) notes 15.12, 'where Matthew inserted a reference to the word Jesus spoke to the Pharisees. Even to the Pharisees! This poor woman's faith has to overcome silence.'

and Mann note the inconsistency of the narrative at this point: 'Both the silence of Jesus and the near-desperate cry of the disciples are interesting in the light of commentators' assertions that this gospel (in contrast with the supposedly earlier Mark) treats Jesus and his disciples with increased reverence'.[43]

From a historicizing point of view, the possibilities for explaining Jesus' ignoring of the woman range from pretending to play into the hands of the disciples to 'draw them out and let them express themselves'[44] to 'mental preoccupation'[45] to ignorance.[46] A particularly intriguing hermeneutical interpretation of Psalm 54 (LXX) by Ulrike Bail offers another possibility for the story of the Canaanite Woman:

> No one has ever considered whether particular experiences of violence towards women can be located in the Psalms... The intention is not to offer a reconstruction of a historically identifiable distress or of a so-called real problem as the background to a specifically female experience of violence; instead, the question is whether the structure of the language used in the Psalms can give space to the specific experience of violence suffered by women.[47]

43. Albright and Mann, *Matthew*, p. 187. The role of the disciples in Matthew continues to be a topic of interest; see, for example, Richard A. Edwards, 'Uncertain Faith: Matthew's Portrait of the Disciples', in Frank Segovia (ed.), *Discipleship in the New Testament* (Philadelphia: Fortress Press, 1985), pp. 47-61; Jack Dean Kingsbury, 'The Verb *Akolouthein* ('to Follow') as an Index of Matthew's View of his Community', *JBL* 97 (1978), pp. 56-73; Ulrich Luz, 'The Disciples in the Gospel According to Matthew', in G. Stanton (ed.), *Interpretation*, pp. 98-128; Michael J. Wilkins, *The Concept of Disciples in Matthew's Gospel* (NovTSup, 59; Leiden: E.J. Brill, 1988), pp. 126-72. Warren Carter ('Kernels and Narrative Blocks: The Structure of Matthew's Gospel', *CBQ* 54 [1992], pp. 463-81 [476]) includes the story of the Canaanite Woman in the category of the 'disciples understand[ing] Jesus' identity and respond[ing] positively'.

44. James D. Smart, 'Jesus, the Syro-Phoenician Woman—and the Disciples', *ExpTim* 50 (1938–39), pp. 469-72 (471).

45. B. Horace Ward, 'Our Lord's Hard Saying to the Syro-Phoenician Woman: Matt. xv. 26; Mark vii. 27', *ExpTim* 13 (1901-1902), p. 48.

46. J. Ireland Hasler, 'The Incident of the Syrophoenician Woman (Matt. xv. 21-28; Mark vii. 24-30)', *ExpTim* 45 (1934), pp. 459-61 (460).

47. Ulrike Bail, '"O God, hear my prayer": Psalm 55 and Violence Against Women', in Athalaya Brenner and Carole Fontaine (eds.), *Wisdom and Psalms: A Feminist Companion to the Bible* (*The Feminist Companion to the Bible* [Second Series] Sheffield: Sheffield Academic Press, 1998), pp. 242-63 (243). For another feminist reading of the Psalms, see Beth LaNeel Tanner, 'Hearing the Cries Unspoken:

Bail further suggests that it is possible 'that the woman who prayed this psalm also composed it. Its title could, therefore, read, "A woman's Lament: Speaking against Silence".'[48] Without running too far in one's imagination, it could be said likewise for the original teller of the story of the Canaanite Woman.

a. ἀποκρίνομαι

A form of the verb ἀποκρίνομαι is found in each of Jesus' four responses to the woman. Of the seven times that a form of the phrase οὐκ ἀπεκρίθη occurs in the New Testament and LXX, all are in some manner related to religious fidelity. The first two instances in the Old Testament, 1 Kgs 18.21 and 2 Kgs 18.35-36, are both within the context of religious self-identity:

> And Elijah came near to all the people, and said, 'How long will you go limping with two different opinions? If the Lord is God, follow him; but if Baal, then follow him'. And the people did not answer him a word (καὶ οὐκ ἀπεκρίθη ὁ λαὸς λόγον). (3 Kgdms 18.21, LXX)[49]

> 'Who among all the gods of the countries have delivered their countries out of my hand, that the Lord should deliver Jerusalem out of my hand?' But the people were silent and answered him not a word (καὶ οὐκ ἀπεκρίθησαν αὐτω λόγον), for the king's command was, 'Do not answer him'. (4 Kgdms 18.35-36, LXX)

The issue again in 1 Maccabees 2 is the refusal on the part of the Jews to obey Antiochus:

> And they said to them, 'Enough of this! Come out and do what the king commands, and you will live'. But they said, 'We will not come out, nor will we do what the king commands and so profane the sabbath day'. Then

An Intertextual-Feminist Reading of Psalm 109', in Brenner and Fontaine (eds.), *Wisdom and Psalms*, pp. 283-301.

48. Bail, '"O God"', p. 244.

49. In the second instance, Jerusalem is being besieged by Sennacherib. Rabshakeh asks, 'Who among all the gods of the countries have delivered their countries out of my hand, that the Lord should deliver Jerusalem out of my hand?' The people refuse to answer: 'But the people were silent and answered him not a word, for the king's command was, "Do not answer him (καὶ ἐκώφευσαν καὶ οὐκ ἀπεκρίθησαν αὐτῷ λόγον, ὅτι ἐντολὴ τοῦ βασιλέως λέγων, οὐκ ἀποκριθήσεσθε αὐτῷ)"' (4 Kgdms. 18.35-36, LXX). In the third instance, Job has difficulty getting answers from anyone in his dilemma of trying to explain God's actions. See especially Elihu's response in Job 32.4-16: οὐκ ἀπεκρίθησαν ἔτι, ἐπαλαίωσαν ἐξ αὐτῶν λόγους...ὅτι ἔστησαν, οὐκ ἀπεκρίθησαν (vv. 15-16).

the enemy hastened to attack them. But they did not answer them (καὶ οὐκ ἀπεκρίθησαν αὐτοῖς) or hurl a stone at them or block up their hiding places, for they said, 'Let us all die in our innocence; heaven and earth testify for us that you are killing us unjustly'. So they attacked them on the sabbath, and they died, with their wives and children and cattle, to the number of a thousand persons. (1 Macc. 2.33-38)[50]

The only other New Testament reference is Mk 14.61, where Jesus answers in silence on a question pertaining to religious fidelity:

And the high priest stood up in the midst, and asked Jesus, 'Have you no answer to make? What is it that these men testify against you'? But he was silent and made no answer (οὐκ ἀπεκρίνατο οὐδέν) (Mk 14.60-61a)

b. κράζω

The verb κράζω, which describes the Canaanite Woman's second request (the disciples say that 'she is still crying along behind us'), can be found in Psalm 21 (LXX). It is exemplary of a psalm that not only refers to those 'that fear the Lord' but also contains many terms that are included in the story of the Canaanite Woman and so will be dealt with at length. Incidentally, it is the same Psalm that both Mark and Matthew include in the death scene.[51]

O God, my God, why have you forsaken me?...
O my God, I will cry (κεκράξομαι) to you by day,
    but you will not hear...
But you, the praise of Israel ('Ισραηλ),
    dwell in a sanctuary...
(Our fathers) cried (ἐκέκραξαν) to you,
    and were saved...
For many dogs (κύνες) have compassed me...
I will declare your name to my brethren:
    in the midst of the congregation I will sing praise to you.
You that fear the Lord,[52] praise him:
    all you seed of Jacob, glorify him:
    let all the seed of Israel ('Ισραηλ) fear him...
    when I cried (κεκραγέναι) to him, he heard me...
The poor shall eat (φάγονται) and be satisfied...
All the ends of the earth shall remember and turn to the Lord:

50. See also 1 Macc. 15.25 where Athenobius does not answer Simon a word: καὶ οὐκ ἀπεκρίθη αὐτῷ λόγον.
51. See Mk 15.34b and Mt. 27.46b and surrounding contexts.
52. See Pss. 115.11 and 135.20.

and all the kindreds of the nations shall worship (προσκυνήσουσιν)
    before him.
For the kingdom is the Lord's;
    and he is the governor of the nations.
All the fat ones of the earth have eaten (ἔφαγον) and worshipped
    (προσεκύνησαν):
all that go down to the earth shall fall (προπεσοῦνται) down before him.
(Ps. 21.2, 3, 4, 6, 17, 23-24, 25, 27-30 [LXX])

The verb κράζω (Ps. 21.2, 5, 24, LXX) can be found frequently in both the
LXX and the New Testament, and ranges in meaning from cries of insane
persons and epileptics to the death-cry of Jesus on the cross to the cry of
the woman in childbirth in the Apocalypse.[53] In the story of the Canaanite
Woman, the disciples complain ὅτι κράζει ὄπισθεν ἡμῶν ('she is crying
after us').[54] The term κράζω is the Greek rendering of the Hebrew term
qara'. According to Walter Grundmann, *qara'* 'occurs predominantly in
the Ps. in the context of crying or calling on God in some individual or
national emergency. God hears such crying in His grace and delivers the
oppressed.'[55] He then adds, 'but God may also refuse to hear... He will
not hear an ungodly people.'[56] In this case, Matthew not only makes use of
common terminology between the Psalm and the story of the Canaanite
woman, but imposes content parallelism as well, that is, Jesus ignores the
woman's first request (Mt. 15.23) as though he has not heard her. Like
God's remoteness in the Psalm, the aloofness of Matthew's Jesus is
troubling, but not impenetrable.[57]

53. BAGD, *s.v.* κράζω, pp. 447-48.
54. According to Gundry (*Matthew*, p. 312) the disciples were not asking Jesus to
get rid of the woman by granting her request, but wanted him to send her away *without*
granting it. See Davies and Allison (*Matthew*, II, pp. 549-50) for a review of
interpretations. See further Frank J. Matera, 'The Plot of Matthew's Gospel', *CBQ* 49
(1987), pp. 233-53 (249); Murphy-O'Connor, 'Structure of Matthew', p. 382.
55. Walter Grundmann, 'κράζω', *TDNT* III, pp. 898-903 (899). He cites Exod.
22.22 among many: 'You shall not afflict any widow or orphan. If you do afflict them,
and they cry out to me, I will surely hear their cry; and my wrath will burn.' Frank J.
Matera (*Passion Narratives and Gospel Theologies: Interpreting the Synoptics through
their Passion Stories* [Theological Inquiries; New York: Paulist Press, 1986], p. 115)
points out that the verb κράζω is used frequently in the LXX to indicate 'deep and
heartfelt prayer'. Wainwright (*Matthew*, p. 227) suggests that the prayer in the story of
the Canaanite Woman may have been a liturgical formula in the Matthean community.
56. Grundmann, 'κράζω', p. 899. See Mic. 3.4; Zech. 7.13; Jer. 11.11. Psalms 25
and 34 also contain the prayers of non-Jewish petitioners.
57. The role that the motif of silence plays in the form of the story of the Canaanite

One other New Testament use of the phrase ἔκραζεν λέγουσα is almost parallel with Mt. 15.21-28. A slave girl, presumably a pagan,[58] bothers Paul until he heals her:

> As we were going to the place of prayer, we were met by a slave girl who had a spirit of divination and brought her owners much gain by soothsaying. She followed Paul and us, crying (αὕτη κατακολουθοῦσα τῷ Παύλῳ καὶ ἡμῖν ἔκραζεν λέγουσα), 'These men are servants of the Most High God, who proclaim to you the way of salvation'. And this she did for many days. But Paul was annoyed, and turned and said to the spirit, 'I charge you in the name of Jesus Christ to come out of her'. And it came out that very hour. (Acts 16.16-18)

c. βοηθέω

A prayer common to both the New Testament and the LXX is found in the Canaanite Woman's third request with the verb βοηθέω. Thirty-two different Psalms contain βοηθέω and/or its derivatives. Many scholars understand the woman's plea to be from the LXX, and Wainwright again claims that it 'may have been used in the liturgy as a liturgical formula'.[59]

Common language, images and synonyms exist between Psalm 85 (LXX) and Matthew's story of the Canaanite Woman.

Psalm 85 (LXX)	*Matthew 15*
Κλῖνον, κύριε, τὸ οὖς σου καὶ ἐπάκουσόν μου,	ὁ δὲ οὐκ ἀπεκρίθη αὐτῇ λόγον.
Incline your ear, O Lord, and answer me, (v. 1a)	but he did not answer her a word. (v. 23a)

Woman will be discussed further. Broyles (*Conflict of Faith and Experience*, p. 192) examines the motif of silence in Psalm 22. Matthew apparently likes many aspects of this particular Psalm (cf. Mt. 27.46b) because another important motif is that of universalism. According to Norbert Lohfink and Erich Zenger (*The God of Israel and the Nations: Studies in Isaiah and the Psalms* [trans. Everett R. Kalin; Collegeville, MN: Liturgical Press, 2000], p. 63), Psalm 22 is a vision of the endtime conversion of the nations to YHWH, that is, one that extends to the universal sphere. As I have argued elsewhere ('Are the "Nations" Present in Matthew?'), the story of the Canaanite woman is the bridge that connects Matthew's genealogy to the so-called Great Commission, that is, a call for the nations to unite under Matthew's notion of Judaism, not Christianity.

58. Theissen (*Miracle Stories*, pp. 258-59) discusses 'non-Jewish petitioners', including the Syrophoenician Woman in Mk 7.27, and agrees with Origen's estimation of miracle cult in early Christianity; that is, Origen repeatedly emphasized the missionary significance of miracles (Cels. I.38; I.46; VIII.47). Ramsey MacMullen agrees (*Paganism in the Roman Empire* [New Haven: Yale University Press, 1981], p. 95).

59. Wainwright, *Matthew*, p. 237.

ἐλέησόν με, κύριε,
οὔτι πρὸς δὲ κεκράξομαι
ὅλην τὴν ἡμέραν.

Have mercy on me, Lord, for to you
do I cry all the day. (v. 3)

ἐν ἡμέρα θλίψεώς μου
ἐκέκραξα πρὸς σέ,
ὅτι εἰσήκουσάς μου.

In the day of my trouble I cry to you,
For you answer me. (v. 7)

Πάντα τὰ ἔθνη,
ὅσα ἐποίησας, ἥξουσιν
καὶ προσκυνήσουσιν
ἐνώπιόν σου, κύριε,
καὶ δοξάσουσιν τὸ ὄνομά σου,

All the nations, you have made,
will come and kneel down before you,
Lord, and will glorify your name.
(v. 9)

ἐπίβλεψον ἐπ' ἐμὲ καὶ
ἐλέησόν με,
δὸς τὸ κράτος σου τῷ παι δί
σου καὶ σῶσον τὸν υἱόν τῆς
παιδίσκης σου.

Turn to me and have mercy on me,
give your strength to your child and
save the son of your handmaid. (v. 16)

ὅτι σύ, κύριε, ἐβοήθησάς μοι
καὶ παρεκάλεσάς με.

because you, Lord, have helped me
and comforted me. (v. 17c)

...ἔκραζεν λέγουσα ἐλέησόν
με, κύριε υἱὸς Δαυίδ...

...cried, Have mercy on me, Lord,
son of David... (v. 22a)

...ἀπόλυσον αὐτήν,
ὅτι κράζει ὄπισθεν ἡμῶν.

...send her away,
for she is still crying along behind
us. (v. 23b)

ἡ δὲ ἐλθοῦσα
προσεκύνει
αὐτῷ λέγουσα κύριε,
βοήθει μοι.

But she came and knelt before him,
saying Lord, help me. (v. 25)

ἐλέησόν με,
κύριε υἱὸς Δαυίδ
ἡ θυγάτηρ μου
κακῶς δαιμονίζεται.

Have mercy on me, Lord, son of
David; my daughter is badly
demonized. (v. 22b)

...κύριε, βοήθει μοι.

...Lord, help me. (v. 25)

According to Whybray, Ps. 85.11 (LXX) ('Teach me your way, O Lord,
that I may walk in your truth; give me an undivided heart to revere your
name') contains the 'recognition that only by attending to Yahweh's
instruction is it possible to achieve true reverence for Yahweh and true
obedience to his will',[60] rather than through one's own self-designated

60. Whybray, *Reading the Psalms*, p. 76.

entitlement. Lohfink and Zenger suggest that the calibrated position of Psalm 85 (LXX) speaks for the universal liberation of the nations by the actualization of YHWH's royal reign and that it 'also looks forward to the decisive eschatological turning when the God of the Sinai covenant is revealed'.[61] Matthew may again be appealing to a Psalmist for help in instilling the notion that Jesus is the one who has the correct view of God's salvation, especially for the enemies of Israel.

d. εἶπον

Psalm 21 was addressed in the discussion of κράζω, but it also supplies the answer to another change that Matthew makes in Mark's story of the Syrophoenician Woman.

Matthew	Mark
ἡ δὲ	ἡ δὲ
εἶπεν ναὶ κύριε,	ἀπεκρίθη καὶ λέγει αὐτῷ κύριε
καὶ γὰρ τὰ κυνάρια	καὶ τὰ κυνάρια
ἐσθίει ἀπὸ τῶν ψιχίων	ὑποκάτω τῆς τραπέζης
τῶν πιπτόντων ἀπὸ τῆς	ἐσθίουσιν ἀπὸ τῶν ψιχίων
τραπέζης τῶν κυρίων αὐτῶν.	τῶν παιδίων.
But she said, 'Yes Lord, yet even the dogs eat the crumbs *that fall from the tables* of their *masters*'. (15.27)	But she answered him, 'Yes, Lord; yet even the dogs *under the table* eat the *children's* crumbs'. (7.28)

The Psalm demonstrates that the poor who eat (φάγονται) and are satisfied will praise the Lord (Ps. 21.26); those who eat (ἔφαγον) also worship (προσεκύνησαν) and 'fall down (προπεσοῦνται) before him' (21.29). Likewise, Matthew shows that after 'worshipping (προσεκύνει) (15.25), even dogs eat (ἐσθίει)' the crumbs that fall (πιπτόντων) from their masters' tables (15.27).

Those who eat	Dogs eat,
also worship	after worship,
and fall down before him.	the crumbs that fall.
(paraphrase of Ps. 21)	(paraphrase of Mt. 15.25, 27)

---

61. Lohfink and Zenger, *God of Israel*, p. 157. Robert L. Cole (*The Shape and Message of Book III [Psalms 73–89]* [JSOTSup, 307; Sheffield Academic Press, 2000], pp. 126, 136-59) includes a lengthy discussion of the unique Davidic superscription of Psalm 85 (LXX).

Psalm 68 (LXX), which Matthew also uses in 27.34, 48, provides a link to make this clearer.[62]

> Because zeal for your house has eaten me (κατέφαγέ με) up, the insults of those who insulted you have fallen (ἐπέπεσον) on me. (Ps. 68.10, LXX)

In this context, the insults have been 'inherited'.[63]

I have been eaten	Dogs [want to] eat
by my zeal for your house	of the house of Israel
and have inherited	in order to inherit
from you.	from the masters.
(Ps. 68.10, LXX)	(Mt. 15.27, 24, 27)

Both the Johannine evangelist and Paul quote this same Psalm:

> His disciples remembered that it was written, 'Zeal for your house will consume me (κατέφαγέ με)'. (Jn 2.17)

Bultmann endorses the idea that κατέφαγέ με refers to 'an expression of [Jesus' emotional] consuming zeal'.[64]

> For Christ did not please himself; but as it is written, 'The insults of those who insult you have fallen [ἐπέπεσον] on me'. (Rom. 15.3)

The verse immediately following explains Paul's notion that Jesus inherited our suffering.[65]

> For whatever was written in former days was written for our instruction, so that by steadfastness and by the encouragement of the scriptures we might have hope. (Rom. 15.4)

What the dogs eat is also of interest in the woman's argument. The term ψιχίον (crumb) is used only three times in the New Testament, and not at all in the LXX.[66] It originates in Mark, and also shows up in variants to Lk. 16.21, where Lazarus 'desired to be fed with the scraps (τῶν ψιχίων) that

---

62. According to Lindars (*John*, p. 140), Ps. 68 (LXX) is 'quarried for quotations by New Testament writers more than any other Old Testament passage'.

63. BAGD, *s.v.* πίπτω, pp. 659-60.

64. Bultmann, *John*, p. 124.

65. So Paul Achtemeier, *Romans* (Interpretation; Atlanta: John Knox Press, 1985), p. 224.

66. However, G.R. Evans ('Crumbs, Gleanings and Fragments: An Exegetical Topos', *Recherches de Théologie ancienne et médiévale* 50 [1983], pp. 242-45) includes, along with Ruth 2.2 as a 'fragments topos', the story of the Canaanite/Syrophoenician Woman.

fell from the rich man's table; moreover the dogs came and licked his sores'. Although there are two different terms for 'crumbs' in the New Testament, ψιχίον and ψωμίον, Mark's and Matthew's use of the first is due to the nuance of each: ψομίον is a broken-off piece of bread, an appropriate word had the woman been regarded as one of the 'lost sheep of the house of Israel'; ψιχίον is the smallest morsel possible, a crumb or scrap, that is, *not* one of the lost sheep of the house of Israel.[67]

e. ἐν τῇ σκιᾷ τῶν πτερύγων σου ἐλπιῶ (*'In the shadow of your wings, I take refuge'*)

Traditional proselyte language is apparent in many Psalms through the phrase 'In the shadow of your wings, I take refuge' (see, e.g., Pss. 16.8; 35.8; 56.2; 60.5, 90.4 [all references are to the LXX]). The metaphor is suggested by the watchful care of a mother bird.[68] A passage from

---

67. The woman's response about eating the crumbs is in accord with other writers of the age, for example, Aristophones says that 'crumbs belong to the heroes' (Diogenes Laertius, *Lives of Eminent Philosophers* [LCL; 2 vols.; Cambridge, MA: Harvard University Press; London: Heinemann, 1925], II, p. 351). The writer of the *Gospel of Philip* was influenced by the Canaanite woman's words as is evidenced in the use of the saying as a sacramental image: 'But let the others yearn just to listen to her voice and to enjoy her ointment, and let them feed from the crumbs that fall from the table, like the dogs. Bridegrooms and brides belong to the bridal chamber. No one shall be able to see the bridegroom with the bride unless [one becomes] one (Wesley W. Isenberg, 'The Gospel of Philip [II. 3]', in James M. Robinson [ed.], *The Nag Hammadi Library in English* [San Francisco: Harper & Row, 4th edn, 1996], pp. 139-60 [158]). Some scholars suggest that 15.27 could refer to 'Matthew's eucharistic editing of Jesus' feeding the five thousand [14.13-21]' (Gundry, *Matthew*, p. 316) or point to the story's chiastic relationship to the feeding stories, 14.13-21 and 15.32-38 (J.C. Anderson, 'Matthew', p. 15). According to Donaldson (*Jesus on the Mountain*, p. 130) the crowds who gather to be fed in v. 30 are 'the lost sheep of the house of Israel' of v. 24. Fiorenza (*In Memory of Her*, pp. 137-38) suggests a similar position for the story of the Syrophoenician Woman. However, based on Burkill's article concerning eucharistic language ('Syrophoenician Woman', pp. 30-32), that is, Jn 13.26, 27, 30, uses the term ψωμίον [morsel] to designate 'a broken-off piece of bread as opposed to a scrap or crumb of bread [ψιχίων]', I would have to disagree with Gundry and Anderson and question Donaldson and Fiorenza. Schweizer (*Matthew*, p. 329) misunderstands the story and claims that the woman has become submissive by speaking of the 'master's table', and that the 'bits of bread' 'are used to wipe food off the hands'.

68. A.A. Anderson, *Psalms*, p. 150. He quotes Gerhard von Rad who links the idea of seeking refuge in Yahweh with 'the function of the sanctuary as asylum for one who was being pursued. But it became divorced from this sacred institution and, given a

Deuteronomy illustrates that refuge may be taken from dangers imposed by either human foes or demonic forces, as in the case of the daughter of the Canaanite Woman:

> As an eagle would watch over his brood, and yearns over his young, receives them having spread his wings, and takes them up on his back: the Lord alone led them, there was no strange god with them. (Deut. 32.11-12)[69]

According to Michael C. Astour's investigation of the Arabic verb *kana'a*, Hebrew and Aramaic cognates are '(a) "to fold wings and to descend to earth" (said of a large bird), and (b) "to bow, to incline toward the horizon"'.[70] The first usage was considered in the above texts. From the second usage, the term *kana'a* points out the irony of the woman's humility in προσεκύνει (v. 25) as it is combined with her refusal to take 'no' for an answer three different times.[71] The metaphor, 'under whose wings you have come to take refuge', and its relationship to proselytism will be considered next in light of the book of Ruth.

4. *The Book of Ruth*

While there is a modern debate as to whether the folktale[72] of Ruth was written to settle the issue of 'universalism versus exclusivism',[73] the rabbis who wrote the Midrashim regarded the book of Ruth as such. The specific message of proselytism in Ruth, according to Neusner, includes:

spiritual sense, passed over into the general language of prayer' (p. 289). G.F. Moore (*Judaism*, I, p. 330) also cites this 'favorite figure in the Psalms for the confident security of the religious man...beneath the wings of God, or beneath the shade of his wings, as the young of birds do under their mother's wings for safety from danger'. In addition to Ps. 56, see Pss. 16.8; 35.7; 60.4; 90.4; Hos. 14.8; Isa. 54.15 (LXX).

69. See Silvia Schroer ('"Under the Shadow of your Wings": The Metaphor of God's Wings in the Psalms, Exodus 19.4, Deuteronomy 32.11 and Malachi 3.20, as Seen Through the Perspectives of Feminism and the History of Religion', in Brenner and Fontaine [eds.] *Wisdom and Psalms*, pp. 264-82 [267-76]) for the argument that the 'eagle' is really a goose-vulture; nonetheless, a portrayal of YHWH as a watchful protector exhibiting 'parent-like' behaviour.

70. Michael C. Astour, 'The Origin of the Terms "Canaan", "Phoenician", and "Purple"', *JNES* 24 (1965), pp. 346-50 (348).

71. Possible wordplay may also exist between Χαναναία and κυνάρια. See A.-J. Levine, *Social and Ethnic Dimensions*, p. 151.

72. Sasson, *Ruth*, p. 214.

73. Sasson, *Ruth*, pp. 246-47. See also Michael S. Moore ('Ruth the Moabite and the Blessing of Foreigners', *CBQ* 60 [1998], pp. 203-17).

1. The admission of the outsider depends upon the rules of the Torah... Those who know the rules are able to apply them accurately and mercifully.
2. The proselyte is accepted because the Torah makes it possible to do so, and the condition of acceptance is complete and total submission to the Torah. Boaz taught Ruth the rules of the Torah, and she obeyed them carefully.
3. Those proselytes who are accepted are respected by God and are completely equal to all other Israelites...
4. What the proselyte therefore accomplishes is to take shelter under the wings of God's presence, and the proselyte who does so stands in the royal line of David, Solomon, and the Messiah... The point is made that Ruth the Moabitess, perceived by the ignorant as an outsider, enjoyed complete equality with all other Israelites.[74]

Boaz employs the metaphor, 'under whose wings you have come to take refuge', as he speaks to Ruth:

'The Lord recompense you [Ruth] for what you have done, and a full reward be given you by the Lord, the God of Israel, under whose wings you have come to take refuge!' Then she said, 'You are most gracious to me, my lord, for you have comforted me and spoken kindly to your maid-servant, though I am not one of your maidservants'. (Ruth 2.12-13)[75]

The origin of the figure of speech as a formal metaphor for proselytes is, according to Bamberger, the book of Ruth:

It [the book of Ruth] shows that a foreign-born woman *can* assume and fulfill properly the religious obligations which entrance into the Jewish group demands. Here also the national and religious elements are combined: 'Thy people shall be my people and thy God my God'. Here also we meet for the first time a phrase which, in slightly modified form, becomes almost a technical term at a later date for conversion: 'to take refuge beneath the wings of the Lord' (Ruth 2.12).[76]

74. Neusner, *The Judaism Behind the Texts: The Generative Premises of Rabbinic Literature* (SFSHJ 4; Atlanta: Scholars Press, 1994), pp. 49-50. Hoenig ('Conversion', p. 35) writes that 'tracing King David, the progenitor of the Messiah, back to the convert Ruth was indeed a strong invitation for the open acceptance of all true proselytes'.

75. Francis Landy ('Ruth and the Romance of Realism, or Deconstructing History', *JAAR* 62 [1994], pp. 285-317 [300-301]) discusses Boaz's role as 'redeemer' in both a metaphorical and literal sense.

76. Bamberger, *Proselytism*, p. 15. So G.F. Moore, Judaism, I, p. 330. See Pss. 17.8; 36.8; 57.2; 61.5; 91.4 (LXX); Hos. 14.7; Num. 8.7; Isa. 54.15.

It is in the book of Ruth that the phrase first appears with the meaning of 'to be converted to Judaism'.[77]

Matthew's form of the Canaanite Woman's request for her daughter's healing and Jesus' refusal to do so can be traced to the book of Ruth, not only through the concept of proselytism, but also through the form. While there is no direct quotation, Matthew's form mirrors the tradition that is rooted in the book of Ruth: Naomi makes the requests and Ruth the proselyte turns her down, whereas the Canaanite-proselyte makes the requests while Jesus turns her down.

Prior to Ruth's profession of fidelity to Naomi in 1.16, Naomi instructs Orpah and Ruth to return to their homeland in Moab, where they have not only kinspeople but also their own gods (1.15). Other Old Testament passages indicate that God is angered by the Israelites' worship of the gods of Moab just as much as their worship of the gods of Sidon (Judg. 10.6; Ps. 83.7).[78] Naomi tells the women three different times to return, only to have her request rejected once by Orpah and all three times by Ruth.[79] When Ruth refuses yet a fourth time, Naomi is silent.[80]

---

77. Hoenig, 'Conversion', p. 35. See also Peter Theodore Nash, 'Ruth: An Exercise in Israelite Political Correctness or a Call to Proper Conversion?', in Holloway and Handy (eds.), *Pitcher is Broken*, pp. 347-54. The story of Joseph and Aseneth, a poetic midrash on a scandalous marriage between a Jew and an Egyptian Gentile, also uses the phrase 'under your wings'. After Aseneth has converted to Judaism, she is the one to whom future proselytes will look: 'In you many nations will take refuge with the Lord God, the Most High, and under your wings many peoples trusting in the Lord God will be sheltered' (*Jos. Asen.* 15.7). See further Richard I. Pervo, 'Aseneth and Her Sisters: Women in Jewish Narrative and in the Greek Novels', in A.-J. Levine (ed.), *'Women Like This': New Perspectives on Jewish Women in the Greco-Roman World* (SBL Early Judaism and Its Literature, 1; Atlanta: Scholars Press, 1991), pp. 145-60.

78. Just like the city of Sidon, the country of Moab had a dual tradition with Israel—on the one hand, a designated enemy (cf. Num. 22.1-4; 25.1-5; Deut. 23.3) and on the other hand, a refuge during a time of famine. See Phyllis Trible ('Ruth: A Text in Therapy', *USQR* 51 [1997], pp. 33-42) for a development of the country of Moab. Trible quotes Tamar Frankiel ('Ruth and the Messiah', in Keakes and Reimer [eds.], *Reading Ruth*, pp. 321-35) for whom the country of Moab symbolizes the drawing of good out of evil, and Torn ('Ruth Reconsidered', pp. 336-46) who imagines that Ruth redeems Moab. Ulanov (*Female Ancestors*, pp. 49-52), however, sees Moab 'as a place where the feminine quite overpowers the masculine', rather than a land where women bring goodness out of evil.

79. See Mona DeKoven Fishbane ('Ruth: Dilemmas of Loyalty and Connection', in Kates and Reimer [eds.] *Reading Ruth*, pp. 298-308) for an insightful analysis of the

1. Request: And Naomi said to her daughters-in-law, 'Go now, return each to the house of her mother'. (1.8a)[81]

   Rejection: And they said to her, 'We will return with you to your people'. (1.10)

2. Request: And Naomi said, 'Return now, my daughters; and why do you go with me?' (1.11a)

   Rejection: 'Have I yet sons in my womb to be your husbands?' (1.11b)

3. Request: 'Turn now, my daughters…' (1.12)

   Rejection: And they lifted up their voice, and wept again; and Orpah kissed her mother-in-law and returned to her people; but Ruth followed her. (1.14)

4. Request: And Naomi said to Ruth, 'Behold your sister-in-law has returned to her people and to her gods; turn now you also after your sister-in-law'. (1.15)

   Response: And Ruth said, 'Entreat me not to leave you, or to return from following you; for wheresoever you go, I will go, and wheresoever you lodge, I will lodge; your people shall be my people, and your God my God…' (1.16)

   Acceptance: And Naomi seeing that she was determined to go with her, ceased to speak to her any more. (1.18)

According to Bamberger and others, this request and rejection pattern became a formula for proselytism into the Hebrew faith in the rabbinic tradition:

relationship between Ruth and Naomi.

80. This is another true mirror image, that is, Naomi is silent after the fourth request while Jesus is silent after the first request; silence on Naomi's part indicates acceptance while silence on Jesus' part indicates rejection.

81. Naomi asks Ruth and Orpah each to return to her 'mother's house' rather than to their father's house. According to D.R.G. Beattie (*Jewish Exegesis of the Book of Ruth* [JSOTSup, 2; Sheffield: JSOT, 1977], p. 54), this is probably related to the stipulations set for a priest's daughter if she marries an outsider or is widowed or divorced in Lev. 22.12-13. However, R. Meir's reason that 'a heathen indeed has no father' better suits the thematic purpose of proselytism in the book of Ruth because, according to L. Rabinowitz (*Midrash Rabbah: Ruth* [New York: Soncino, 1983], p. 35), 'in Jewish law, the child of a non-Jewish marriage has only mother-right'. Matthew's story of the Canaanite Woman reflects 'mother-right'.

Turn back, my daughters, go your way [Ruth 1.12]. R. Samuel b. Nahmani said in the name of R. Judah b. Hanina: Three times is it written here 'turn back', corresponding to the three times that a would-be proselyte is repulsed; but if he persists after that, he is accepted. R. Isaac said: (It is written,) 'The stranger [*ger*] did not lodge in the street [Job 31.32]: A man should rebuff with his left hand, but bring near with the right. (*Ruth R* 2.16)[82]

Prospective converts were to be discouraged in order to determine their sincerity, as well as to let them know that it is not easy to be a Jew. But the discouragement was not to be for too long:

The rule that we must not discourage the candidate by too long and detailed an exposition of the law is based by R. Elazar on Ruth 1.18 [*Yeb.* 47ab]; 'When she saw that she was steadfastly minded to go with her, she left off speaking unto her'.[83]

---

82. Bamberger, *Proselytism*, p. 40; Daube, *Law*, p. 20; Rabinowitz, *Ruth*, p. 36. Also see Daube, *New Testament*, especially ch. V.B, 'The Pattern of Instruction', pp. 113-40. Daube (*New Testament*, p. 125) delineates five divisions in the Talmudic baptismal instruction, of which the 'test' is the first division. It should be noted that Daube acknowledges the fact that although there was a certain degree of standardization in Jewish catechism, 'there are enough variations to show that no rigidly fixed syllabus was followed. Different teachers still emphasized different aspects. There never was a single *Ur*-catechism.' According to Ramsay MacMullen and Eugene N. Lane (*Paganism and Christianity, 100–425 C.E.: A Sourcebook* [Minneapolis: Fortress Press, 1992], pp. 150-51), Philo states that the Gentiles wishing to become a part of the Jewish community should not be spurned, but given special friendship and more than ordinary good will. Cf. Philo, *Virt.* 108 and *Spec. Leg.* 1.52-53.

83. Bamberger, *Proselytism*, p. 40. Rabbi Eliezer is a contemporary of New Testament writers (c. 90 CE); Schrage (*Ethics*, p. 85) defines Jesus in terms of Jewish ethics and cites parallels with Rabbi Eliezer. Feldman (*Jew and Gentile*, p. 339) tells of Rabbi Eliezer being in danger of excommunication because of his contacts with the early Christians at the end of the first century. Neusner discusses the problems inherent in researching the historical rabbis in, for example, *Eliezer ben Hyrcanus* and *Rabbinic Literature and the New Testament: What We Cannot Show, We Do Not Know* (Valley Forge, PA: Trinity Press International, 1994), especially pp. 21-40. Cohen ('Ceremony', p. 197) writes that 'for the midrash [on Ruth], Ruth was the archetypal convert, and her declaration of fidelity to Naomi was understood to be a response to Naomi's instruction in Judaism'. So Martin Goodman, 'Proselytising in Rabbinic Judaism', *JJS* 40 (1989), pp. 175-85 (178); Daube, *Law*, pp. 5-20. As an aside, I will say that I am well aware that 'what we cannot show we do not know' and I do not want to be guilty of a 'promiscuous citation' (Neusner, *Rabbinic Literature*, p. 9). That is, *Ruth R.* probably did not reach closure until the sixth century CE. In combination with other indications that Matthew enlarged Mark's story of the Syro-Phoenician woman to

That means that a prospective convert should be denied three times to test his or her sincerity, but if persistence still reigns, he or she is allowed to enter the faith of the Jews.[84] Ruth proved to be ' "absolutely steadfast" [and] Naomi desists from further dissuasion and takes her with her to Judah. This one becomes the ancestress of the house of David.'[85] According to the Rabbis, Ruth 1.16 means that 'I am fully resolved to become converted under any circumstances, but it is better that it should be at your hands than at those of another' (*Ruth R.* 2.22). Naomi's response in 1.18 is

show how one becomes a member of the community, I add as another piece of evidence the attributed sayings of first-century rabbis and propose a late first-century association between the oral tradition surrounding Matthew's Gospel and the oral tradition of the rabbinic writers. Furthermore, I suggest, since 'documents did not begin on the day they reached closure' (Neusner, *Rabbinic Literature*, p. 9), that the conversion formula stemming from the story of Ruth is one of those instances when the pool of oral tradition was common to the Matthean evangelist who used the tradition and to the rabbis who eventually wrote the tradition down. Since Matthew included Ruth in the genealogy as one of four examples of enemy women-turned-saviors of the Israelites, it is reasonable to think that the Evangelist knew other traditions surrounding her character. I am also suggesting when other stories in Matthew's Gospel are explored with an eye toward proselytism or with the question, 'Does this pericope tell us "how one becomes a member of the community"?' that the problem of dating the attributions of the first-century rabbis will remain interesting, but not critical, for this thesis. I also submit that the problem of dating Matthew's Gospel is similar to the problem of dating first-century rabbinic attestations:

	Matthew	*Eleazar (Ruth R.)*
first century:	'written'	'written'
second century onwards:	'attested to'	'attested to'
fourth century:	canonized	
sixth century:		canonized

Neusner (*From Scripture to 70*, pp. 16-22) again points out the problems of 'attestations'.

84. Cohen ('Ceremony', p. 198) writes that 'a 'tough interview' does not necessarily mean that the interviewer wants the candidate to fail'. Arthur Darby Nock (*Conversion: The Old and the New in Religion from Alexander the Great to Augustine of Hippo* [London: Oxford University Press, 1933], p. 213) also alludes to the rejection method, but as it applies to Christianity: '[The pagan] was then informed of certain beliefs and was told that if he accepted them and promised to live by them he would be admitted to baptism and thereafter to the communal meal. This idea of something from which he was excluded pending the fulfillment of conditions might then act as a further stimulus. We all desire to enter grounds marked *Private*, especially if there goes through them a footpath which is said to lead to the New Jerusalem.'

85. Daube, *Law*, p. 20.

that 'she began to unfold to her [Ruth] the laws of conversion' (*Ruth R.*
2.22).

Even though Ammonite and Moabite men were excluded (Deut. 23.3), it
was lawful for Ruth to convert because she was a female.[86] In fact, it was
on account of the blessings of the foreign women that the line of David
was not wholly exterminated.[87] According to Neusner, conversion is discouraged because it is a difficult undertaking:

> because the Judaism of the dual Torah discourages conversion, lest becom-
> ing part of holy Israel prove cheap and trivial, Naomi's task is to tell Ruth
> what is involved in accepting the yoke of the Torah. The Torah imposes
> heavy responsibilities, separates Israel from Gentiles, and sanctifies life; all
> of this takes work, commitment, and a constant play of conscience. It is
> Naomi's task to tell Ruth that what she imagines to do is difficult.[88]

The Targum to Ruth[89] also contains a strong proselytic message:

> And they said to her, [['We shall not return to our people, nor to our
> God. Rather,]]//we shall return with you to your people, [[to become
> proselytized'.]]
> ...They raised their voices and wept again [another time.]
> ...But Ruth said, 'Do not urge me to leave you, to turn back and not to
> follow you; [[for I demand to be proselytized...']][90]

86. The Talmud states, 'An Ammonite, but not an Ammonitess; A Moabite, but not
a Moabitess' (*b. Yeb.* 76b). (See also *b. Yeb.* 69a; *b. Ket.* 7b; *b. Qid.* 75a.) M.S. Moore
('Ruth', pp. 215-16) rehearses the explanation from *b. Yeb.* 77a: '(1) Since the biblical
text gives a specific reason for the prohibition of Moabites and Ammonites ["because
they did not meet you on the way with food and water"], and (2) since respectable
women would not walk on public highways in ancient times, one must conclude (3)
that no Ammonite or Moabite woman can fairly be held responsible for this crime, and
this means (4) that Ammonite and Moabite women cannot be prohibited from attending Yhwh's assembly. Therefore, (5) Ruth is a legitimate ancestor of David.'

87. Jacob Neusner, *The Midrash Compilations of the Sixth and Seventh Centuries:
An Introduction to the Rhetorical, Logical, and Topical Program: Ruth Rabbah* (BJS,
189; 4 vols.;Atlanta: Scholars Press, 1989), IV, p. 146.

88. Jacob Neusner, *The Mother of the Messiah in Judaism: The Book of Ruth*
(Valley Forge, PA: Trinity Press International, 1993), p. 82.

89. See M.S. Moore ('Ruth', p. 213) for the thesis that the targum to Ruth is a
'xenophobic diatribe against Israel's enemies, real or imagined'.

90. Etan Levine, *The Aramaic Version of Ruth* (AnBib, 58; Rome: Biblical Institute
Press, 1973), pp. 52-56. (Double brackets indicate interpretation added to the Hebrew
Bible.) According to Levine, 'a pre-Mishnaic, and perhaps pre-Christian dating of
basic elements [are] incorporated within the targum to Ruth' (p. vi).

E. Levine comments that 'the added "another time" reflects the law that a perspective proselyte must be rebuffed. It implies their having wept before; Naomi has rejected the daughter-in-laws' first request (v. 10) to be proselytized, and here repeats her rejection, "another time"'. Orpah, of course, 'went on her way', but Ruth persisted, so that, according to E. Levine, 'Naomi was then duty-bound to convey the laws for a would-be proselyte to her'.[91] Therefore, 'the targum consistently presents the dialogue as a formal, juridical transaction, meeting the requirements for religious conversion'.[92]

As will be shown below in the numerical sequence of the requests from the two stories, Matthew expands the two-fold request from the Markan account into a four-fold request and inserts the entire request/rejection sequence into the above formula for conversion, that is, the woman is turned down three times, she comes back a fourth time and her request is granted. Matthew emends Mark's first request in the third person to a first-person plea, proceeds to use the essence of Mark's rejection to that request, but waits to insert it in a third request, includes Mark's second request as a fourth and final request, and then inserts a different form of acceptance to end the pericope. Jesus is, according to this evangelist, following a Jewish custom for testing a prospective proselyte.[93]

The Markan third-person narrative reads:

And she begged him to cast the demon out of her daughter. (Mk 7.26)[94]

Matthew's first-person plea is followed by a rejection, then another request/ rejection, and a third request:

1. Request: 'Have mercy on me, Lord, Son of David; my daughter is badly demonized'. (Mt. 15.22b)
    Rejection: But he did not answer her a word.[95] (15.23a)

---

91. E. Levine, *Aramaic Version of Ruth*, p. 55.

92. E. Levine, *Aramaic Version of Ruth*, p. 56.

93. Against Schweizer (*Matthew*, p. 330), who states that 'no injunction to follow the Law is imposed on her. The cry of faith, which resembles that of Peter (14.30; cf. Ps. 22.20; etc.) suffices: "Lord, help me!"'

94. Theissen (*Stories*, pp. 54-55) discusses 'Pleas and Expressions of Trust' in the story of the Syrophoenician Woman. According to Werner H. Kelber (*The Oral and the Written Gospel: The Hermeneutics of Speaking and Writing in the Synoptic Tradition, Mark, Paul, and Q* [Philadelphia: Fortress Press, 1983], p. 48), the cure in the Syrophoenician Woman is merely incidental: 'the focus of interest falls entirely on the auxiliary motif of request'.

2. Request: And the disciples came and asked him, saying, 'Send her away, for she is still crying along behind us'. (15.23b)[96]

   Rejection: He answered, 'I was sent only to the lost sheep of the house of Israel'. (15.24)

3. Request: But she came worshipping him, saying, 'Lord, help me'. (15.25)

The essence of Mark's first rejection is moved to form Matthew's third rejection:

> And he said to her, 'Let the children first be fed, for it is not right to take the children's bread and throw it to the dogs'. (Mk 7.27)

   Rejection: But he answered, 'It is not right to take the bread of the children and throw it to the dogs'. (Mt. 15.26)

Mark's second request reads:

> But she answered him, 'Yes, Lord; yet even the dogs under the table eat the children's crumbs'. (Mk 7.28)

The essence of Mark's second request is inserted into Matthew's fourth request:

4. Request: She said, 'Yes, Lord, yet even the dogs eat the crumbs that fall from the table of their masters'. (Mt. 15.27)

The answer to Mark's second request reads:

> And he said to her, 'For this saying you may go your way; the demon has left your daughter'. And she went home, and found the child lying in bed, and the demon gone. (Mk 7.29-30)

Matthew's answer to a fourth request is:

---

95. A.-J. Levine (*Social and Ethnic Dimensions*, p. 140) also interprets that to be ignored is to be denied: 'His silence after the woman's first request must be taken as a refusal'.

96. Lachs (*Commentary*, p. 248) suggests that what I have labeled as a second request is really an attempt on the part of the disciples to help her out. He has two possibilities: (1) *auton* (send *it* away) could be substituted for *auten* (send *her* away), meaning 'release the demon which is afflicting her daughter'; (2) even without the emendation, *auten* with the verb *apoluo* could mean 'release her (the daughter) from the grasp of the demon of illness'. Neither Greek grammar nor the second part of the request ('for she is still crying along behind us') support his theory, namely, the demon inside the daughter is not 'still crying along behind us'.

Acceptance: Then Jesus answered her, 'O woman, great is your faith! Be it done for you as you will'. And her daughter was healed at that hour. (Mt. 15.28)[97]

The following synopsis shows the alignment of Mark's account of the Syrophoenician Woman, Matthew's account of the Canaanite Woman, and the form from Ruth that Bamberger attributes to the rabbinic formula for testing a prospective proselyte:

		Ruth	*Mark*	*Matthew*
1. Request:		But Naomi said to her two daughters-in-law, 'Go, return each of you to her mother's house…' (1.8a)	And she begged him to cast the demon out of her daughter. (7.26)	'Have mercy on me, Lord, Son of David; my daughter is badly demonized'. (15.22b)
Rejection:		And they said to her, 'No, we will return with you to your people'. (1.10)		But he did not answer her a word. (15.23a)
2. Request:		But Naomi said, 'Turn back, my daughters, why will you go with me?' (1.11a)		And his disciples came and asked him, saying, 'Send her away, for she is still crying along behind us'. (15.23b)
Rejection:		'Have I yet sons in my womb that they may become your husbands?' (1.11b)		But he answered, saying, 'I was sent only to the lost sheep of the house of Israel'. (15.24)
3. Request:		'Turn back, my daughters, go your way'. (1.12)		But she came worshipping him, saying, 'Lord, help me'. (15.25)
Rejection:		Then they lifted up their voices and wept again; and Orpah kissed her mother-in-law, but Ruth	And he said to her, 'Let the children first be fed, for it is not pleasing to God to	But he answered, saying, 'It is not pleasing to God to take the children's bread

97. The last sentence is a formula statement for certain miracle stories and therefore, not the focal point of the story. See 'And the (Centurion's) servant was healed at that very moment ($\dot{\epsilon}\nu$ $\tau\hat{\eta}$ $\mathring{\omega}\rho\alpha$ $\dot{\epsilon}\kappa\epsilon\acute{\iota}\nu\eta$)' (Mt. 8.13b); 'And instantly ($\dot{\alpha}\pi\grave{o}$ $\tau\hat{\eta}\varsigma$ $\mathring{\omega}\rho\alpha\varsigma$ $\dot{\epsilon}\kappa\epsilon\acute{\iota}\nu\eta\varsigma$) the (hemorrhaging) woman was made well' (9.22); 'and the boy was cured instantly ($\dot{\alpha}\pi\grave{o}$ $\tau\hat{\eta}\varsigma$ $\mathring{\omega}\rho\alpha\varsigma$ $\dot{\epsilon}\kappa\epsilon\acute{\iota}\nu\eta\varsigma$)' (17.18b).

clung to her. (1.14)	take the children's bread and throw it to the dogs'. (7.27)	and throw it to the dogs'. (15.26)
4. Request: And she said, 'See, your sister-in-law has gone back to her people and to her gods; return after your sister-in-law'. (1.15)	But she answered him, 'Yes, Lord; yet even the dogs under the table eat the children's crumbs'. (7.28)	But she said, 'Yes, Lord, yet even the dogs eat the crumbs that fall from the table of their masters'. (15.27)
Response: But Ruth said, 'Entreat me not to leave you or to return from following you; for where you go I will go, and where you lodge I will lodge; your people shall be my people, and your God my God…' (1.16)	And he said to her, 'For this saying you may go your way; the demon has left your daughter'.	Then Jesus answered, saying to her, 'O woman, great is your faith! Be it done for you as you will'.
Resolution: And when Naomi saw that she was determined to go with her, she said no more. (1.18)	And she went home, and found the child lying in bed, and the demon gone. (7.29-30)	And her daughter was healed at that hour. (15.28)

The synopsis shows that the woman from Tyre and Sidon in Matthew's story first asks for Jesus' help by telling him that her daughter is demonized, but Jesus ignores her. She persists by crying along behind the group of disciples with Jesus, and this time he answers her with the Exclusivity Logion that the evangelist has already used in 10.6, indicating that Jesus is only ministering to those of the Jewish faith and since she is a Canaanite from Tyre and Sidon, she is not one of them. She does not go away, however; she comes back even more humbled, only to be stung more deeply by Jesus' words about dogs. To his retort, she responds with a fourth and final request: 'Yes, Lord, yet even the dogs eat the crumbs that fall from the table of their masters' (Mt. 15.27). The woman from Tyre and Sidon is commended for her faith and her daughter is healed.

As the first three steps of the conversion ritual proceed, Matthew portrays the woman in a progressively more humbled stance. Conversely, Matthew describes Jesus in a manner that gets progressively more terse:

	Woman from Tyre and Sidon	*Jesus*
1.	asks for mercy	does not answer
2.	Cries	defines exclusion
3.	Worships	compares her to dogs

The woman's fourth request is still spoken with words of respect ('Yes, Lord, yet...'), but with obvious resolution as well ('even the dogs eat the crumbs that fall from the table of their masters'). According to *Pseudo-Clementine*, the woman's attitude at this point is an indication that she has ceased to be a Gentile by abstaining from forbidden foods.[98]

> But she, hearing this, and begging to partake like a dog of the crumbs that fall from this table, having changed what she was, by living like the sons of the kingdom, she obtained healing for her daughter, as she asked. (*Ps.-Clem.* 2.19)

The woman passes the test for admission that Jesus administers.[99] Matthew purposely poses Jesus, not as being rude, but as ritually testing the Canaanite woman's desire to become a member of the community of faith by turning her away three times and accepting her after she pursues him a fourth.[100]

5. *The Matthean Evangelist*

Since Matthew applies a rabbinic formula to the story of the woman from Tyre and Sidon, a legitimate question arises about the Matthean evangelist: Was Matthew working directly with the book of Ruth, simply familiar with the rabbinic form derived from Ruth, or was Matthew a rabbinic exegete?[101] There are three related issues which were also discussed in the Introduction: Matthew's religious identity, the 'Jewishness of Jesus' and the religious identity of Matthew's community. While the religious background of Jesus is often of more concern than the other two aspects of the

98. *ANF*, VIII, p. 232.

99. There is very little known about the requirements for converts to Judaism during the first century. It is certain, however, according to Scot McKnight (*A Light Among the Gentiles: Jewish Missionary Activity in the Second Temple Period* [Minneapolis: Fortress Press, 1991], p. 88), that 'converts were expected to join Judaism, worship the one God, repent from sin and idolatry, and obey the law'.

100. According to N. Taylor ('Social Nature of Conversion', p. 129), there are three independent but overlapping aspects of 'conversion' which would appear to me to be happening in Matthew's story: (1) conviction/acknowledgement of divinity, essentially cerebral but potentially involving worship; (2) conformity/observance, involving practice, either negative or positive, of the Law; and (3) socialization, involving affiliation and integration into the community.

101. Alan F. Segal ('Matthew's Jewish Voice', in Balch [ed.], *Social History*, pp. 3-37 [5]) writes that Matthew's Gospel demonstrates 'an intimate acquaintance with rabbinic exegesis' and points to the use of antithesis (5.22-48) and *qal vahomer* (12.9-14).

issue,[102] the quest for the 'historical Matthew' is fulfilled in part by this examination of the story of the Canaanite Woman.[103]

The influence of Old Testament texts on Matthew's choice of geographical and ethnic designations for the story of the Canaanite Woman has been demonstrated in Chapters 1 and 2; the influence of rabbinic form has been advanced in this chapter. In addition to this building of a foundation for the Gospel in Hebrew Scriptures, Matthew posits Jesus as the fulfillment of Jewish Law and as an advocate for abiding the Law:

'Think not that I have come to abolish the law and the prophets; I have come not to abolish them but to fulfil them'. (5.17)

And Jesus said to him, 'See that you say nothing to any one; but go, show yourself to the priest, and offer the gift that Moses commanded, for a proof to the people'. (8.4)

When they came to Capernaum, the collectors of the half-shekel tax went up to Peter and said, 'Does not your teacher pay the tax?' He said, 'Yes'...Jesus said to [Peter],...'go to the sea and cast a hook, and take the

102. See, for example, a review by Daniel J. Harrington ('The Jewishness of Jesus: Facing Some Problems', *CBQ* 49 [1987], pp. 1-13) who cites three major scholars on the subject: *idem, Jesus the Jew*; Vermes, *The Gospel of Jesus the Jew* (Newcastle upon Tyne: University of Newcastle upon Tyne, 1981); *idem, Jesus and the World of Judaism* (Philadelphia: Fortress Press, 1984); E.P. Sanders, *Jesus and Judaism* (Philadelphia: Fortress Press, 1985); E.P. Sanders, *The Historical Figure of Jesus* (New York: Penguin Books, 1993); H. Falk, *Jesus the Pharisee: A New Look at the Jewishness of Jesus* (New York: Paulist Press, 1985). See Albert Schweitzer, *The Quest of the Historical Jesus: A Critical Study of Its Progress from Reimarus to Wrede* (trans. W. Montgomery; New York: Macmillan, 1961 [*Von Reimarus zu Wrede* (Tübingen: J.C.B. Mohr, 1906)]). More recent studies on the historical Jesus include the work of Funk, Hoover and The Jesus Seminar, *The Five Gospels* and Funk and the Jesus Seminar *The Acts of Jesus*; John Dominic Crossan, *The Historical Jesus: The Life of a Mediterranean Jewish Peasant* (San Francisco: HarperCollins, 1991) and *idem, A Revolutionary Biography* (San Francisco: HarperSanFrancisco, 1994); Meier *Marginal Jew*; Marcus Borg, *Jesus in Contemporary Scholarship* (Valley Forge, PA: Trinity Press International, 1994).

103. In addition to commentaries on Matthew which include the issue of authorship, others addressing Matthew's identity include France, *Matthew*, especially pp. 50-80; Harrington, *Matthew*; Philip L. Shuler, *A Genre for the Gospels: The Biographical Character of Matthew* (Philadelphia: Fortress Press, 1982). Le Déaut ('Targumic Literature', pp. 243-89) emphasizes the necessity of looking at Hebrew sources in trying to understand New Testament interpretation. For an anti-Jewish view of Matthew, see Fred W. Burnett, 'Exposing the Anti-Jewish Ideology of Matthew's Implied Author: The Characterization of God As Father', *Semeia* 59 (1992), pp. 155-91.

first fish that comes up, and when you open its mouth you will find a shekel; take that and give it to them for me and for yourself'. (17.24-25a, 27)

Gunther Bornkamm reflects scholars who agree that Matthew connects Jesus and his teaching with Jewish tradition:

> Matthew understands the law in a way which does not differ in principle from that of Judaism—or better—which in principle 'does not' differ, i.e., he deliberately inserts his understanding of the law into the Jewish scribal tradition.[104]

A comparison of a final phrase from the story of the Canaanite Woman with the two instances that its cognate appears in Matthew illustrates one further aspect of Matthew's loyalty to Jewish tradition:

> Thy kingdom come, thy will be done (γενηθήτω τὸ θέλημα σου). (6.10)

> O woman, great is your faith! Be it done for you as you will (γενηθήτω σοι ὡς θέλεις). (Mt. 15.28; cf. 8.13 [the Centurion's servant]; 9.29 [the two blind men])

> My Father, if this cannot pass unless I drink it, thy will be done (γενηθήτω τὸ θέλημά σου). (26.42)

The Rabbis say, 'Annul your will in the face of his will' (*m. Ab.* 2.4).[105] Davies and Allison confirm the rabbinic antecedent for Matthew: 'the kingdom comes whenever a human being takes upon him/[her]self the yoke of the kingdom of God to do it'.[106] Nock supports the position that a pious Jew would have no difficulty in uttering the petitions, 'Thy kingdom come, Thy will be done', because the 'hope of Israel' involves the fulfillment of the Law; in the Kingdom, the Law would be perfectly observed.[107] The Canaanite Woman in Matthew's story has observed the Law fully by petitioning Jesus three times and coming back a final and successful fourth time.

The religious identity of Matthew's community is the third part of the issue. Tertullian believed that it was to 'Jewish persons' that Jesus spoke and so Matthew used the story of the Canaanite Woman as an example of that belief.[108] According to Overman:

---

104. Gunther Bornkamm, 'End-Expectation and Church in Matthew', in Bornkamm, Barth and Held (ed.), *Tradition*, p. 31.

105. Cf. *t. Ber.* 3.7; *b. Ber.* 29b; *b. Meg.* 27b; *b. Yoma* 53b.

106. Davies and Allison, *Matthew*, I, p. 605.

107. Arthur Darby Nock, *St. Paul* (London: Butterworth, 1938), p. 36.

108. *ANF*, III, p. 247. Gregory Thaumaturgus ('The Second Homily: On the

the people of Matthew's community did not understand themselves as 'Christians'. On the contrary they were Jews. Like many of their contemporaries and competitors, however, they understood themselves as the 'true Israel' and set themselves over against those they believed to be the false covenant people and false leaders who would lead the people astray. The Gospel of Matthew is full of such exclusive claims and the tension and conflict these claims inevitably provoke.[109]

The story of the Canaanite Woman reinforces Overman's view: Gentile converts had to become Jews, not Christians.[110] The writer of Matthew's Gospel was indeed faithful to Judaism,[111] as is confirmed by the story of the Canaanite Woman.[112]

Annunciation of the Holy Virgin Mary', [*ANF*, VI, p. 65]) 'Christianized' the crumbs for which the woman of Canaan pleaded and consequently lost the Jewish intent of the story.

109. Overman, *Gospel*, p. 5. So already Harnack, *Mission*, I, p. 45; Patricia G. Kirkpatrick, *The Old Testament and Folklore Study* (JSOTSup, 62; Sheffield: JSOT Press, 1988), pp. 118-20; Trilling, *Das Wahre Israel: Studien zur Theologie des Matthäus-Evangeliums* (Munich: Kösel, 1964).

110. For recent studies of early Jewish Christianity, see, for example, Craig C. Hill, *Hellenists and Hebrews: Reappraising Division within the Earliest Church* (Minneapolis: Fortress Press, 1992); Malina, 'Jewish Christianity or Christian Judaism: Toward a Hypothetical Definition', *JSJ* 7 (1990), pp. 46-57. Anthony Saldarini ('The Gospel of Matthew and Jewish-Christian Conflict', in Balch [ed.], *Social History*, pp. 38-61 [60]) tackles both sides of the issue: 'Though many contemporary Christians cannot conceive of Matthew retaining a Jewish identity, Matthew in fact accepts the identity of the Jewish community because it is the overwhelming, real presence in his life world... Matthew insists on his allegiance to Jesus by carving out a deviant Jewish identity for his sectarian Jewish community... Matthew lost the battle for Judaism. Within Christianity his way of following Jesus died out for the most part during the following generation.' See also Stanton and Stroumsa (eds.), *Tolerance and Intolerance*; Anthony Saldarini, 'Jews and Christians in the First Two Centuries: The Changing Paradigm', *Shofar* 10.2 (1992), pp. 16-34. Saldarini lists the Matthean texts that illustrate 'reinterpretations of Jewish customs, laws, and traditions to fit the viewpoint of Jewish believers-in-Jesus', but overlooks the story of the Canaanite Woman (p. 28).

111. For an opposing view, see, for example, Clark, *Gentile Bias*, pp. 1-8.

112. Against scholars such as Bernard J. Lee (*The Galilean Jewishness of Jesus: Retrieving the Jewish Origins of Christianity* [Studies in Judaism and Christianity; New York: Paulist Press, 1988], p. 70), who argues for Jesus' upholding of Jewish tradition, but erroneously concedes the Canaanite woman as exemplary of 'Jesus find[ing] genuine faith outside of Israel', that is, implying that she is still 'outside of Israel'. Theissen (*Social Reality*, p. 219) argues that the 'Jews were an *ethnos*... Christians, in contrast, were interethnic. They were proud of embracing different

6. *Summary*

While the Markan evangelist may have used the story of the Syro-phoenician Woman to demonstrate inclusivity as an ideal and/or how it came about in the community, the author of Matthew expanded it into a paradigm for gaining acceptance into the Jewish in-group. The story of the Canaanite Woman, therefore, is not merely a description of the rewards of faith, as it has been viewed in tradition history, but is a reinforcement of Jewish law for the purpose of attaining membership in the Matthean community.

In the story of the Canaanite Woman, the person in need is a female, a non-Jew, and living outside the immediate area where Jesus and his disciples normally reside. She is as far removed from the inner circle of male Jews as she can be and even if the plot of the story is to be taken literally—that is, she wants to get her daughter healed—the woman must first get Jesus' attention. She, therefore, becomes 'like them' and demonstrates her familiarity with Jewish Law and customs.

The evangelist consciously draws on Hebrew tradition in the telling of this story by imposing the language of the 'Psalmist in lament' on the Canaanite Woman's lips. The lament is then placed in a rabbinic form that demonstrates how one becomes a member of the Jewish community to which Jesus and his disciples belong. One of Bail's conclusions of the female psalmist (Ps. 54, LXX) is that the articulation of the lament may have been the woman's self empowerment to a new identity;[113] as a result of the story of the Canaanite Woman, enemy women can also now have new identities, that of becoming full members of Matthew's Jewish community.

nations and peoples.' A concept of interethnicity may be true for some early Christians, but I would argue that Matthew's Gospel does not reflect it. The story of the Canaanite Woman is a case where the traditional assumption is that Matthew used bits and pieces from an 'old' story world of exclusivity to create a 'new' story of inclusivity. The new story of inclusion, however, is not 'Christianity', but a Judaism that will be reunited with the old 'enemies'. Ironically, the Great Commission then becomes a statement of Jewish proselytism for Matthew's community.

113. Bail, 'O God', p. 261.

CONCLUSION: THE HEALING: A PARADIGM FOR PROSELYTISM

Matthew 15.28

τότε ἀποκριθεὶς ὁ᾽Ἰησοῦς εἶπεν αὐτῇ	Then Jesus answered her, saying,
ὦ γύναι, μεγάλη σου ἡ πίστις	O woman, great is your faith!
γενηθήτω σοι ὡς θέλεις.	Be it done for you as you will'.
καὶ ἰάθη ἡ θυγάτηρ αὐτῆς ἀπὸ	And her daughter was healed instantly.
τῆς ὥρας ἐκείνης.	

Jesus acquiesces and heals the woman's daughter. For many scholars, the real miracle of the story is the woman's great faith and Jesus' recognition of his own universalism. It is at this point, however, that the emphasis on the story inaugurating Jesus' mission to the Gentiles has too often been distorted. The flawed presumption has been that it is the mission to the Gentiles that constitutes Matthean Christianity, rather than a continuation of the Jewish tradition that allows Gentiles into the faith.

Once again, the story of the Canaanite Woman imitates Ruth:

> But Ruth said, 'Entreat me not to leave you, or to return from following you; for wherever you go, I will go, and wherever you lodge, I will lodge; your people shall be my people, and your God my God... The Lord do so to me and more also if I leave you, for death only will divide between you and me'. (Ruth 1.16, 17b)[1]

According to the Rabbis, Ruth's words follow Naomi's admonishment that if Ruth is so eager to share Israel's sufferings, she must be tireless in the fulfillment of commandments and the doing of good deeds in this world. Ruth's response is a commitment to a covenant; if she is allowed to follow Naomi, she will be faithful to Naomi's God. The same is true in reverse for the Canaanite woman: if she is faithful to Jewish Law, she will be allowed to gain entry into the community.

It is clear in Matthew's Gospel that the author is familiar with a variety

---

1.   See 1 Sam. 3.17, where similar words are spoken by Eli to Samuel and a three-time misunderstanding occurs.

of Old Testament texts and rabbinic forms. The story of the Canaanite Woman exemplifies the use that Matthew makes of those sources, for example, a reinforcement of the Jewish tradition of inclusiveness to the Gentiles. For the Matthean evangelist, the trajectory for the original covenant begins with Abraham (1.1), continues through Ruth (1.5), culminates in the story of the Canaanite Woman (15.21-28), and is further dramatized in the remainder of the Gospel. It is, therefore, in the story of the Canaanite Woman that the Gospel writer strengthens the concept of universal covenant-making within Judaism, now continuing through Jesus.

The form of Jesus' responses to the Canaanite woman reinforces the Jewish conversion formula regarding proselytes, thereby corroborating Matthew's portrait of Jesus as a good Jew; the anti-Jewish polemic that has been a part of the history of interpretation of this text is non-existent. Furthermore, the evangelist's redaction of this story places proselytism into Judaism at the very center of Matthew's concerns. The story of Jesus' encounter with the Canaanite Woman was not included in Matthew's Gospel for the purpose of recording the evangelizing of Gentiles, but for the purpose of supporting the Jewish tradition of gaining entrance into the community as a proselyte.

Mark's story of Jesus' encounter with a Syrophoenician is expedient for Matthew to appropriate for several reasons: the evangelist is able to capitalize on its female specificity and transform the woman from Tyre (and Sidon) into one of the noted enemies of Israel, a Canaanite, who according to rabbinic interpretations of Old Testament texts can convert to Judaism only if female; many of Mark's words and phrases that already hint of proselytism are multiplied and magnified; and Mark has provided the beginnings of a request/rejection formula which Matthew places in a rabbinic form for conversion. Any study that ignores the dimension of proselytism in the story of the Canaanite Woman is truncated.

The story also strengthens Matthew's interest and support for the role of women in the community. This study has reinforced the position that conventional thought on women's status and role in the first century CE does not necessarily reflect the actual situation. A fresh analysis of the form for Mt. 15.21-28 exposes one more activity in which women of the first century were actively involved. As it happens, the interpretation I have suggested is found already in the second or third century, when the author of the Pseudo-Clementine Homilies not only names this woman—gives her an identity (Justa)—but actually describes her, defines her, as a 'Proselyte'. In fact, so the homily goes, 'she being a Gentile, and remaining in the same course of life, He [the Lord] would not have healed had she remained a Gentile, on account of its not being lawful to heal her as a Gentile'.[2] The author of that homily was exactly right after all.

2.   ANF, VIII, p. 232.

APPENDIX 1:
GEOGRAPHICAL SETTINGS IN THE GOSPEL OF MATTHEW

A list of the geographical settings in the Gospel of Matthew (in the order of appearance, with subsequent listings)

Babylon—1.11, 12, 17
Bethlehem of Judea—2.1, 3, 5 [see 'Bethlehem' below]
Jerusalem—2.1; 3.5; 4.25; 5.35; 15.1; 16.21; 20.17, 18; 21.1, 10; 23.37
Bethlehem—2.6, 8, 16 [see 'Bethlehem of Judea' above]
   own country—2.12
Egypt—2.13, 14, 15, 19
land of Israel—2.20, 21
Judea—2.22; 3.5; 4.25; 19.1; 24.16 [see 'wilderness of Judea' below]
district of Galilee—2.22; 4.12, 15 [see 'Galilee' below and 'Sea of Galilee' below]
Nazareth—2.23; 4.13; 21.11
wilderness of Judea—3.1 [see 'wilderness' below and 'Judea' above]
(river) Jordan—3.5, 6, 13; 4.15; 4.25; 19.1
Galilee—3.13; 4.12, 15, 23, 25; 17.22; 19.1; 21.11; 26.32; 27.55; 28.7, 10, 16 [see 'district of Galilee' above and 'Sea of Galilee' below]
wilderness—4.1; 11.7; 24.26 [see 'wilderness of Judea' above]
holy city—4.5
Capernaum—4.13; 8.5; 11.23; 17.24
territory of Zebulan and Naphtali—4.13, 15
Sea of Galilee—4.18; 15.29 [see 'district of Galilee' and 'Galilee' above]
Syria—4.24
Decapolis—4.25
mountain—4.8; 5.1; 8.1; 14.23; 15.29; 17.1; 24.16; 28.16
city—5.14; 8.34; 21.10 [see 'their cities' and 'the cities' below]
on the sea—8.24; 14.26 [see 'into the sea' below]
Country of the Gadarenes—8.28
own city—9.1
that district—9.26, 31
all the cities and villages—9.35 [see 'their cities' and 'the cities' below]
town of the Samaritans—10.5
house of Israel—10.6; 15.24 [see 'towns of Israel' below]

Sodom and Gomorrah—10.15; 11.23, 24

towns of Israel—10.23 [see 'house of Israel' above]

their cities—11.1 [see 'city', 'own city', 'all the cities and villages' above and see 'the cities' below]

the cities—11.20 [see 'all the cities and villages' and 'their cities' above]

Chorazin and Bethsaida—11.21

Tyre and Sidon—11.21, 22; 15.21

Nineveh—12.41

beside the sea—13.1

home town—13.54

lonely place apart—14.13, 15

Gennesaret—14.34

Magadan—15.39

Caesarea Philippi—16.13

Jericho—20.29

Bethphage—21.1 [see 'Mount of Olives' below]

Bethany—21.17; 26.6

into the sea—21.21 [see 'on the sea' above]

Mount of Olives—24.3; 26.30 [see 'Bethphage' above]

Gethsemane—26.36

field of blood—27.8

Cyrene—27.32

Golgotha—27.33

Arimathea—27.57

APPENDIX 2:
GENTILES IN THE GOSPEL OF MATTHEW

1. Gentiles as examples of negative ethical behavior:

And if you salute your brethren, what more are you doing than others? Do not even the Gentiles do the same? (5.47//Lk. 6.34)[1]

And in praying do not heap up empty phrases as the Gentiles do; for they think that they will be heard for their many words. (6.7)

Therefore do not be anxious, saying, 'What shall we eat?' or 'What shall we drink?' or 'What shall we wear?' For the Gentiles seek all these things; and your heavenly Father knows that you need them all. (6.31-32//Lk. 12.29-30)[2]

And if he refuses to listen even to the church, let him be to you as a Gentile and a tax collector. (18.17b)

Behold, we are going up to Jerusalem; and the Son of man will be delivered to the chief priests and scribes, and they will condemn him to death, and deliver him to the Gentiles to be mocked and scourged and crucified, and he will be raised on the third day. (20.18-19//Mk 10.33-34//Lk. 18.31b-33)

You know that the rulers of the Gentiles lord it over them, and their great men exercise authority over them. (20.25//Mk 10.42//Lk. 22.25)

2. Gentiles as outsiders to the faith:

Now when he heard that John had been arrested, he withdrew into Galilee; and leaving Nazareth he went and dwelt in Capernaum by the sea, in the territory of Zebulun and Naphtali, so that what was spoken by the prophet Isaiah might be fulfilled: 'The land of Zebulun and the land of Naphtali, toward the sea, across the Jordan, Galilee of the Gentiles—the people who sat in darkness have seen a great light, and for those who sat in the region and shadow of death light has dawned'. (4.12-16)

---

1. There is no parallel in Mark; Luke uses the word 'sinner' instead of Gentile.
2. Luke's ἔθνη is translated 'nations' in the NRSV (12.30).

These twelve Jesus sent out, charging them, 'Go nowhere among the Gentiles, and enter no town of the Samaritans, but go rather to the lost sheep of the house of Israel'. (10.5-6)

Behold, I send you out as sheep in the midst of wolves...and you will be dragged before governors and kings for my sake, to bear testimony before them and the Gentiles. (10.16a, 18b)

For nation shall rise against nation, and kingdom against kingdom, and there will be famines and earthquakes in various places: all this is but the beginning of the birth-pangs. (24.7-8//Mk 13.8//Lk. 21.10-11)

Then they will deliver you up to tribulation, and put you to death; and you will be hated by all nations for my name's sake...and this gospel of the kingdom will be preached throughout the whole world, as a testimony to all nations; and then the end will come. (24.9, 14//Mk 13.10//Lk. 21.13)[3]

3. Gentiles as exemplars of the faith that Israel should have:

The Centurion (8.5-13//Lk. 7.1-10).

The Canaanite Woman (15.21-28//Mk 7.24-30).

4. Gentiles as participants in the salvation of the Jews:

Then he began to upbraid the cities where most of his mighty works had been done, because they did not repent. 'Woe to you, Chorazin! woe to you, Bethsaida! For if the mighty works done in you had been done in Tyre and Sidon, they would have repented long ago in sackcloth and ashes. But I tell you, it shall be more tolerable on the day of judgment for Tyre and Sidon than for you'. (11.21-22//Lk. 10.13-14)

This was to fulfil what was spoken by the prophet Isaiah: 'Behold, my servant whom I have chosen, my beloved with whom my soul is well pleased. I will put my Spirit upon him, and he shall proclaim justice to the Gentiles. He will not wrangle or cry aloud, nor will any one hear his voice in the streets; he will not break a bruised reed or quench a smoldering wick, till he brings justice to victory; and in his name will the Gentiles hope'. (12.17-21)

Jesus said to them, 'Have you never read in the scriptures: "The very stone which the builders rejected has become the head of the corner; this was the Lord's doing, and it is marvelous in our eyes?" Therefore I tell you, the kingdom of God will be taken away from you and given to a nation producing the fruits of it'. (21.42-44)[4]

3.   Mark's ἔθνη is translated 'nations' in the NRSV; the parallel in Luke does not use the term.
4.   Mark (12.1-12) and Luke (20.9-19) both carry the parable of the Wicked Husbandmen, but do not include the statement about the kingdom of God.

Before him will be gathered all the nations, and he will separate them one from another as a shepherd separates the sheep from the goats, and he will place the sheep at his right hand, but the goats at the left. (25.32-33)

Go therefore and make disciples of all nations, baptizing them in the name of the Father and of the Son and of the Holy Spirit, teaching them to observe all that I have commanded you; and lo, I am with you always, to the close of the age. (28.19-20//cf. Lk. 24.47)

Additional References to ἔθνος in Mark and Luke:

1. In the pericope of the cleansing of the temple, Matthew (21.13) drops 'for all the nations' from the Isa. 56.7 quote which Mark (11.17) keeps; Luke also drops it.
2. The story of Jesus' circumcision and presentation in the temple Luke (2.21-28) adds the Isaian passage, 'a light for revelation to the Gentiles, and for glory to thy people Israel' (v. 32).
3. In the tradition of the desolating sacrilege (Mt. 24.15-22//Mk 1.14-20//Lk. 21.20-24), Luke adds, 'and Jerusalem will be trodden down by the Gentiles, until the times of the Gentiles are fulfilled' (v. 24).
4. In the trial before Pilate (Mt. 27.11-14//Mk 15.2-5//Lk. 23.2-5//Jn 18.29-38), Luke begins with 'And they began to accuse him, saying, "We found this man perverting our nation, and forbidding us to give tribute to Caesar, and saying that he himself is Christ a king"' (v. 2).

APPENDIX 3:
WOMEN WITH DIRECT SPEECH IN THE GOSPELS AND ACTS

Matthew
1. The woman with a hemorrhage 'speaks to herself' (9.21).
2. The daughter of Herodias (14.8).
3. The Canaanite woman (15.22, 25, 27).
4. The mother of the sons of Zebedee (20.21).
5. The wise and foolish maidens (25.8, 9, 11).
6. A maid (26.69, 71).
7. The wife of Pilate (27.19).

Mark
1. The woman with a hemorrhage (5.28).
2. Herodias and her daughter (6.24-25).
3. The Syrophoenician woman (7.28).
4. A maid (14.67, 69).
5. Mary Magdalene, Mary the mother of James and Salome (16.3).

Luke-Acts
1. Mary, the mother of Jesus (1.34, 38, 46-55).
2. Elizabeth (1.25, 42-45, 60).
3. Mary (2.48).
4. Martha (10.40).
5. A maid (22.56).
6. Sapphira (Acts 5.8).
7. Lydia (Acts 16.15).
8. A slave girl (Acts 16.17).

John
1. Mary, the mother of Jesus (2.3, 5).
2. The Samaritan woman (4.9, 11-12, 15, 17, 19-20, 25, 29).
3. The adulterous woman (8.11).
4. Mary and Martha (11.3).
5. Martha (11.21, 24, 27, 28, 39).
6. Mary (11.32).
7. Mary Magdalene (20.2, 13, 15, 16, 18).

APPENDIX 4:

THE GEOGRAPHICAL SETTINGS OF THE
MARK//MATTHEW MIRACLE STORIES

	Story	Mark	Matthew
1.	Mk 1.29-31//Mt. 8.14-15 Peter's Mother-in-Law	Capernaum	Capernaum
2.	Mk 1.40-45//Mt. 8.1-4 Cleansing of the Leper	Galilee	Down from the mountain
3.	Mk 2.1-12//Mt. 9.1-8 Healing of the Paralytic	Capernaum (home)	[Capernaum]
4.	Mk 3.1-6//Mt. 12.9-14 Man with Withered Hand	Synagogue	Synagogue
5.	Mk 5.1-20//Mt. 8.28-34 Gerasene Demoniac	Country of Gerasenes Gergesenes, or Gadarenes	Country of Gadarenes Gergesenes, or Gerasenes
6.	Mk 5.21-24, 35-43// Mt. 9.18-19, 23-26 Jairus's Daughter	Jairus's house	Ruler's house
7.	Mk 5.25-34//Mt. 9.20-22 Hemorrhaging Woman	Walking to Jairus's house	Walking to ruler's house
8.	Mk 7.24-30//Mt. 15.21-28 Canaanite Woman's Daughter	Tyre	Tyre and Sidon
9.	Mk 7.31-37//Mt. 15.29-31 Deaf Mute and Others	Sea of Galilee	Up on the mountain
10.	Mk 9.14-29//Mt. 17.14-21 Epileptic Boy	Down from the mountain	Down from the mountain
11.	Mk 10.46-52// Mt. 20.29-34 Healing of the Blind Men	Jericho	Jericho

APPENDIX 5:
PLACE-NAMES IN THE GOSPELS
(PERSONS WITH GEOGRAPHICAL TITLES IN THE GOSPELS)

Place Names in Matthew (and Parallels)

Mt. 2.23
And he went and dwelt in a city called Nazareth, that what was spoken by the prophets might be fulfilled, 'He shall be called a *Nazarene*'.

Mt. 8.28
And when he came to the other side, to the country of the *Gadarenes*, two demoniacs met him, coming out of the tombs, so fierce that no one could pass that way.

[Gerasenes = Mk 5.1//Lk. 8.26; Gergesenes = variant readings]

Mt. 10.1, 4a//Mk 3.18
And he called to him his twelve disciples and gave them authority over unclean spirits, to cast them out, and to heal every disease and every infirmity...Simon the *Cananaean*...

[Simon the Zealot = Lk. 6.15//Acts 1.13]

Mt. 10.4b; 26.14//Mk 3.19; 14.10//Lk. 6.16; 22.3//Jn 13.2
...and Judas *Iscariot*, who betrayed him.

Mt. 10.5
These twelve Jesus sent out, charging them, 'Go nowhere among the Gentiles, and enter no town of the *Samaritans*, but go rather to the lost sheep of the house of Israel'.

Mt. 15.22
And behold, a *Canaanite* woman from that region came out and said, 'Have mercy on me, O Lord, Son of David'.

[a Greek, a Syrophoenician = Mk 7.26a]

Mt. 26.69//Mk 14.66-72//Lk. 22.54-71; 23.6//Jn 18.25-27
Now Peter was sitting outside in the courtyard. And a maid came up to him, and said, 'You also were with Jesus the *Galilean*'.

[Nazarene = Mk 14.67; Peter is called the Galilean in v. 70]

Mt. 27.55-56, 61; 28.1//Mk 15.40, 47; 16.1, 9//Lk. 8.2; 24.10//Jn 19.25; 20.1, 18
There were also many women there, looking on from afar, who had followed Jesus from Galilee, ministering to him; among whom were Mary Magdalene, and Mary the

mother of James and Joseph, and the mother of the sons of Zebedee… Mary Magdalene and the other Mary were there, sitting opposite the sepulchre… Now after the sabbath, toward the dawn of the first day of the week, Mary Magdalene and the other Mary went to see the sepulchre.

Additional Place-Names in Luke

(There are no additional placenames in Mark.)

Lk. 9.52
And he sent messengers ahead of him, who went and entered a village of the *Samaritans*, to make ready for him; but the people would not receive him, because his face was set toward Jerusalem.

Lk. 10.33
But a *Samaritan*, as he journeyed, came to where he was; and when he saw him, he had compassion…

Lk. 13.1-2
There were some present at that very time who told him of the *Galileans* whose blood Pilate had mingled with their sacrifices. And he answered them, 'Do you think that these *Galileans* were worse sinners than all the other *Galileans*, because they suffered thus?'

Lk. 17.16
And he fell on his face at Jesus' feet, giving him thanks. Now he was a *Samaritan*.

Lk. 23.6
When Pilate heard this, he asked whether the man [Jesus] was a *Galilean*.

Additional PlaceNames in John

Jn 1.47
Jesus saw Nathanael coming to him, and said of him, 'Behold, an *Israelite* indeed, in whom is no guile'!

Jn 4.9
The *Samaritan* woman said to him, 'How is it that you, a Jew, ask a drink of me, a woman of Samaria?'

Jn 4.39-40
Many *Samaritans* from that city believed in him because of the woman's testimony, 'He told me all that I ever did'. So when the *Samaritans* came to him, they asked him to stay with them; and he stayed there two days.

Jn 4.45
So when he came to Galilee, the *Galileans* welcomed him, having seen all that he had done in Jerusalem at the feast, for they too had gone to the feast.

Jn 7.35
The Jews said to one another, 'Where does this man intend to go that we shall not find him? Does he intend to go to the Dispersion among the *Greeks* and teach the *Greeks*?'

Jn 8.48
The Jews answered him, 'Are we not right in saying that you are a *Samaritan* and have a demon?'

Jn 12.20
Now among those who went up to worship at the feast were some *Greeks*.

APPENDIX 6:
'CANAAN' AND ITS DERIVATIVES (LXX)

Reference Genesis	Male/Land/People/Female (M/L/P/F)	Evaluation
9.18	M	neutral
9.22	M	neutral
9.25	M	negative
9.26	M	negative
9.27	M	negative
10.6	M	neutral
10.15	M	neutral
10.18	P	neutral
10.19	P	neutral
11.31	L	neutral
12.5 (twice)	L	neutral
12.6	P	neutral
13.7	P	neutral
13.11	L	neutral
15.20	P	neutral
16.3	L	neutral
17.8	L	positive
23.2	L	neutral
23.19	L	neutral
24.3	F	negative
24.37	F	negative
28.1	F	negative
28.6	F	negative
28.8	F	negative
31.18	L	neutral
33.18	L	positive
34.30	P	negative
35.6	L	positive
35.27	L	neutral
36.2	F	negative
36.5	L	neutral
36.6	L	neutral

36.7	L	neutral
37.1	L	neutral
38.2	F	neutral
42.5	L	negative
42.7	L	neutral
42.13	L	neutral
42.29	L	neutral
42.32	L	neutral
44.8	L	neutral
45.17	L	neutral
45.25	L	neutral
46.6	L	neutral
46.10	F	neutral
46.12	L	neutral
46.31	L	neutral
47.1	L	neutral
47.4	L	neutral
47.13	L	neutral
47.14	L	neutral
47.15	L	neutral
48.3	L	positive
48.7	L	neutral
49.30	L	neutral
50.5	L	neutral
50.11	P	positive
50.13	L	neutral
Exodus		
3.8	L/P	positive
3.17	L/P	positive
6.4	L	positive
12.40	L	neutral
13.5	L/P	positive
13.11	L/P	positive
15.15	L/P	negative
23.23	P	negative
23.28	P	negative
33.2	P	negative
34.11	P	negative
Leviticus		
14.34	L	neutral
18.3	L/P	negative
25.38	L	positive
Numbers		
13.2	L/P	negative
13.17	L/P	negative

13.29	P	neutral
14.25	P	neutral
14.43	P	negative
14.45	P	negative
21.1	M	negative
21.3	P	negative
26.19	L	neutral
27.12	L	neutral
32.30	L	neutral
32.32	L	neutral
33.40	M	negative
33.40	L	neutral
33.51	L/P	negative
34.2 (twice)	L	neutral
34.29	L	neutral
35.10	L	neutral
35.14	L	positive
Deuteronomy		
1.7	L/P	neutral
7.1	P	negative
11.30	L/P	negative
20.17	P	negative
32.49	L	neutral
Joshua		
3.10	P	negative
7.8	P	negative
9.1	P	negative
11.2	P	negative
12.8	P	negative
13.3	P	negative
13.4	P	negative
13.13	P	negative
14.1	L	positive
16.10 (twice)	P	negative
17.12	P	negative
17.13	P	negative
17.16	P	negative
17.18	P	negative
21.2	L	neutral
22.9	L	neutral
22.10	L	neutral
22.11	L/P	negative
22.32	L	neutral
24.3	L	positive
24.11	P	negative

Judges		
1.1	P	negative
1.3	P	negative
1.4	P	negative
1.5	P	negative
1.9	P	negative
1.10	P	negative
1.17	P	negative
1.27	P	negative
1.28	P	negative
1.29 (twice)	P	negative
1.30	P	negative
1.32	P	negative
1.33	P	negative
3.1	L	negative
3.3	P	negative
3.5	P	negative
4.2	M	negative
4.23	M	negative
4.24 (twice)	M	negative
5.19	M	negative
21.12	L	negative
2 Samuel		
23.8	M	neutral
24.7	P	positive
1 Chronicles		
1.8	M	neutral
1.13	M	neutral
2.3	F	neutral
16.18	L	positive
Nehemiah		
9.8 (19.8 LXX)	L	positive
9.24 (19.24 LXX)	L	negative
Psalms		
105.11 (104 LXX)	L	neutral
106.38 (105 LXX)	L	negative
135.11 (134 LXX)	L	negative
Isaiah		
19.18	L	neutral
23.11	P/L	negative
Ezekiel		
16.3	P	negative
17.4	L	negative
Hosea		
4.18	P	negative

12.8	M	negative
Obadiah		
20	P	negative
Zephaniah		
1.11	P	negative
2.5	L	negative
1 Esdras		
8.69	P	negative
2 Esdras		
9.1	P	negative
Judith		
5.3	P	neutral
5.9	L	neutral
5.10	L	neutral
5.16	P	negative
Baruch		
3.22	L	negative
Susanna		
56	P/L	negative
1 Maccabees		
9.37	M/F	negative
Matthew		
15.21	F	negative

BIBLIOGRAPHY

Reference Works

Arndt, William F., and Wilbur F. Gingrich, *A Greek–English Lexicon of the New Testament and Other Early Christian Literature* ([a translation and adaptation of the fifth revised and augmented edition of Walter Bauer's *Griechisch-Deutsches Wörterbuch zu den Schriften desNeuen Testaments und der übrigen urchristlichen Literature*] Chicago: University of Chicago Press, 1979).

Hatch, Edwin, and Henry A. Redpath, *A Concordance to the Septuagint and Other Greek Versions of the Old Testament* (Grand Rapids, MI: Baker Books, 2nd edn, 1998).

Horsley, G.H.R., and S.R. Llewelyn (eds.), *New Documents Illustrating Early Christianity* (8 vols.; The Ancient History Documentary Research Centre; New South Wales, Australia: Macquarie University, 1981–98).

Jastrow, Marcus, *A Dictionary of the Targumim, the Talmud Babli and Yerushalmi, and the Midrashic Literature* (2 vols.; Brooklyn, NY: P. Shalom, 1967).

Laymon, Charles M. (ed.), *The Interpreter's Bible* (12 vols.; New York: Abingdon Press, 1952–57).

—*The Interpreter's One-Volume Commentary on the Bible* (Nashville: Abingdon Press, 1971).

Lightfoot, John, *A Commentary on the New Testament from the Talmud and Hebraica* (4 vols.; Grand Rapids: Baker Book House, 1979).

Metzger, Bruce M., *A Textual Commentary on the Greek New Testament* (New York: United Bible Societies, 2nd edn, 1994).

Montefiore, C.G., and H. Loewe, *A Rabbinic Anthology: Selected and Arranged with Comments and Introductions* (New York: Schocken Books, 1974).

Newsom, Carol A., and Sharon H. Ringe (eds.), *The Women's Bible Commentary* (Louisville, KY: Westminster/John Knox Press, 1992).

Roberts, Alexander, and James Donaldson (eds.), *The Ante-Nicene Fathers: Translations of The Writings of the Fathers down to A.D. 325* (10 vols.; Grand Rapids: Eerdmans, 1985–96).

Rousseau, John J., and Rami Arav, *Jesus and His World: An Archaeological and Cultural Dictionary* (Minneapolis: Fortress Press, 1995).

Schiffman, Lawrence H., and James C. VanderKam (eds.), *Encyclopedia of the Dead Sea Scrolls* (2 vols.; Oxford: Oxford University Press, 2000).

Singer, Isidore (ed.), *The Jewish Encyclopedia* (12 vols.; New York: Ktav, 1964).

Stanton, Elizabeth Cady, *The Woman's Bible* (Seattle: Coalition Task Force on Woman and Religion, repr. 1974 [New York: European Publishing, 1898]).

Strack, Hermann L., and Paul Billerbeck, *Kommentar zum New Testament aus Talmud und Midrash* (6 vols.; Munich: Beck, 7th edn, 1965).

Swanson, Reuben (ed.), *New Testament Greek Manuscripts: Variant Readings Arranged in*

Horizontal Lines Against Codex Vaticanus (4 vols.; Sheffield: Sheffield Academic Press, 1995).

Wigoder, Geoffrey (ed.), *The New Standard Jewish Encyclopedia* (New York: Facts on File, 1992).

Primary Sources

Aland, Kurt (ed.), *Synopsis of the Four Gospels* (London: United Biblical Societies, 6th edn, 1985).

Braude, William G. (trans.), *The Midrash on Psalms* (2 vols.; New Haven: Yale University Press, 1959).

Diogenes, Laertius, *Lives of Eminent Philosophers* (LCL; 2 vols.; Cambridge, MA: Harvard University Press, London: Heinemann, 1925).

Murphy, Roland E., and Bruce M. Metzger (eds.), *The New Oxford Annotated Bible with the Apocryphal/Deuterocanonical Books* (New York: Oxford University Press, 1994).

Nestle, Eberhard, *et al.* (eds.), *Novum Testamentum Graece* (Stuttgart: Deutsche Bibelgesellschaft, 27th edn, 1983).

Neusner, Jacob, *The Mishnah: A New Translation* (New Haven: Yale University Press, 1988).

Rahlfs, Alfred, *Septuaginta* (Stuttgart: Deutsche Bibelgesellschaft, 1979).

Robinson, James M. (ed.), *The Nag Hammadi Library in English* (New York: E.J. Brill, 4th edn, 1996).

Secondary Sources

Achtemeier, Paul, '*Omne verbum sonat*: The New Testament and the Oral Environment of Late Western Antiquity', *JBL* 109 (1990), pp. 3-27.

—*Romans* (Interpretation; Atlanta: John Knox Press, 1985).

Ahlström, G.W., *Who Were the Israelites?* (Winona Lake, IN: Eisenbrauns, 1986).

Albright, William F., and C.S. Mann, *Matthew* (AB, 26; Garden City, NY: Doubleday, 1971).

Alexander, Philip S., ' "The Parting of the Ways" from the Perspective of Rabbinic Judaism', in Dunn (ed.), *Jews and Christians*, pp. 1-25.

Allison, Dale C., Jr, *The New Moses: A Matthean Typology* (Minneapolis: Fortress Press, 1993).

Alvarez, Ofelia, 'Bible Study III—Matthew 15.21-28', *Ministerial Formation* (Geneva: World Council of Churches, 1998), pp. 12-15.

Amaru, Betsy Halpern, 'Portraits of Biblical Women in Josephus' Antiquities', *JJS* 39 (1988), pp. 143-70.

Amico, Eleanor B., 'The Status of Women at Ugarit' (unpublished Doctoral dissertation, University of Wisconsin, 1989).

Anderson, A.A., *Psalms* (NCB; 2 vols.; Grand Rapids: Eerdmans, 1985).

Anderson, G.W., P.A.H. DeBoer, Henry Cazelles, J.A. Emerton, W.L. Holladay, R.E. Murphy, E. Nielsen, R. Smend and J.A. Soggin (eds.), VTSup 28 (Congress Volume; Leiden: E.J. Brill, 1975).

Anderson, Janice Capel, 'Mary's Difference: Gender and Patriarchy in the Birth Narratives', *JR* 67 (1987), pp. 183-202.

—'Matthew: Gender and Reading', *Semeia* 28 (1983), pp. 3-28.

Aptowitzer, V., *Parteipolitik der Hasmonaerzeit im Rabbinischen und Pseudoepigraphischen Schrifttum* (Vienna: Verlag der Kohut-Foundation, 1927).

Astour, Michael C., 'The Origin of the Terms "Canaan", "Phoenician", and "Purple" ', *JNES* 24 (1965), pp. 346-50.

Auffret, Pierre, 'Note complementaire sur la structure litteraire du Psaume 6', *BN* 42 (1988), pp. 7-13.

Bacon, Benjamin W., *Studies in Matthew* (2 vols.; New York: Holt, Rinehart & Winston, 1930).

Bail, Ulrike, ' "O God, hear my prayer": Psalm 55 and Violence against Women', in Brenner and Fontaine (eds.), *Wisdom and Psalms*, pp. 242-63.

Balch, David L. (ed.), *The Social History of the Matthean Community: Cross-Disciplinary Approaches* (Minneapolis: Fortress Press, 1991).

Balentine, Samuel E., *The Hidden God: The Hiding of the Face of God in the Old Testament* (Oxford Theological Monographs; Oxford: Oxford University Press, 1983).

—'Prayers for Justice in the Old Testament: Theodicy and Theology', *CBQ* 51 (1989), pp. 597-616.

—'Prayers in the Wilderness Traditions: In Pursuit of Divine Justice', *HAR* 9 (1985), pp. 53-74.

Bamberger, Bernard, *Proselytism in the Talmudic Period* (New York: Ktav, 1968).

Banks, R.J., 'Setting "The Quest for the Historical Jesus" in a Broader Framework', in France, Wenham and Blomberg (eds.), *Gospel Perspectives*, II, pp. 61-82.

Baron, Salo W., *A Social and Religious History of the Jews* (2 vols.; New York: Columbia University Press; Philadelphia: Jewish Publication Society, 2nd edn, 1952).

Bassler, Jouette M., 'The Galileans: A Neglected Factor in Johannine Community Research', *CBQ* 43 (1981), pp. 243-57.

Bauckham, Richard, 'Tamar's Ancestry and Rahab's Marriage: Two Problems in the Matthean Genealogy', *NovT* 37 (1995), pp. 313-29.

Bauer, David R., 'The Kingship of Jesus in the Matthean Infancy Narrative: A Literary Analysis', *CBQ* 57 (1995), pp. 306-23.

—'The Literary and Theological Function of the Genealogy in Matthew's Gospel', in Bauer and Powell (eds.), *Treasures*, pp. 129-59.

—*The Structure of Matthew's Gospel: A Study in Literary Design* (Bible and Literature Series, 15; Sheffield: Almond Press, 1988).

Bauer, David R., and Mark Allan Powell (eds.), *Treasures New and Old: Recent Contributions to Matthean Studies* (SSSBL; Atlanta: Scholars Press, 1996).

Baumgarten, Albert I., 'Myth and Midrash: Genesis 9.20-29', in Neusner (ed.), *Christianity, Judaism and Other Greco-Roman Cults*, III, pp. 55-71.

Beare, Francis Wright, *The Gospel According to Matthew* (San Francisco: Harper & Row, 1981).

Beattie, D.R.G., *Jewish Exegesis of the Book of Ruth* (JSOTSup, 2; Sheffield: JSOT, 1977).

Beckwith, Roger, *The Old Testament Canon of the New Testament Church and its Background in Early Judaism* (Grand Rapids: Eerdmans, 1985).

Berger, Klaus, 'Die königlichen Messianstraditionen des Neuen Testaments', *NTS* 20 (1973), pp. 1-44.

—'Zur Problem der Messianität Jesu', *ZTK* 71 (1974), pp. 1-30.

Berlin, Adele, 'Ruth and the Continuity of Israel', in Kates and Reimer (eds.), *Reading Ruth*, pp. 255-60.

Bickerman, Elias J., *The Jews in the Greek Age* (Cambridge, MA: Harvard University Press, 1988).

Bird, Phyllis A., 'The Harlot as Heroine: Narrative Art and Social Presupposition in Three Old Testament Texts', *Semeia* 46 (1989), pp. 119-39.

Black, Matthew, *The Gospel of Matthew* (NCB; London: Marshall, Morgan & Scott, 1972).

Blanchard, Diane, 'The Gentile Woman: Engagement with Suffering', *Consensus* 20.2 (1994), pp. 11-23.

Blomberg, Craig L., 'The Liberation of Illegitimacy: Women and Rulers in Matthew 1–2', *BTB* 21 (1991), pp. 145-50.

Boccaccini, Gabriele, *Middle Judaism: Jewish Thought 300 B.C.E. to 200 C.E.* (Minneapolis: Fortress Press, 1991).

Boers, Hendrikus, *Who Was Jesus? The Historical Jesus and the Synoptic Gospels* (San Francisco: Harper & Row, 1989).

Bolin, Thomas M., ' "A stranger and an alien among you" (Genesis 23.4): The Old Testament in Early Jewish and Christian Self-Identity', in Hills (ed.), *Common Life*, pp. 57-76.

Boling, Robert G., and Ernest G. Wright, *Joshua* (AB, 6; Garden City, NY: Doubleday, 1982).

Booij, T., 'Some Observations on Psalm LXXXVII', *VT* 37 (1987), pp. 16-24.

Borg, Marcus J., *Jesus in Contemporary Scholarship* (Valley Forge, PA: Trinity Press International, 1994).

Bornkamm, Gunther, 'End-Expectation and Church in Matthew', in Bornkamm, Barth and Held , *Tradition*, pp. 15-51.

—*Jesus of Nazareth* (New York: Harper & Row, 1960).

Bornkamm, Gunther, Gerhard Barth and Heinz Joachim Held, *Tradition and Interpretation in Matthew* (Philadelphia: Westminster Press, 1963).

Bossman, David M., 'Authority and Tradition in First Century Judaism and Christianity', *BTB* 17 (1987), pp. 3-9.

Brandt, Pierre-Yves, 'De l'usage de la frontière dans la recontre entre Jésus et al Syrophénicienne (Mc 7/24-30)', *ETR* 74 (1999), pp. 173-88.

Brenner, Athalaya, *A Feminist Companion to Ruth* (The Feminist Companion to the Bible, 3; Sheffield, England: Sheffield Academic Press, 1993).

—*The Israelite Woman: Social Role and Literary Type in Biblical Narrative* (JSOTSup 21; Sheffield: JSOT Press, 1989).

Brenner, Athalaya and Carole Fontaine (eds.), *Wisdom and Psalms: A Feminist Companion to the Bible* ([second series]; Sheffield: Sheffield Academic Press, 1998).

Broadhead, Edwin K., 'Jesus the Nazarene: Narrative Strategy and Christological Imagery in the Gospel of Mark', *JSNT* 52 (1993), pp. 3-18.

Brown, Colin, 'Synoptic Miracle Stories: A Jewish Religious and Social Setting', *Forum* 2.4 (1986), pp. 55-76.

Brown, Raymond E., *The Birth of the Messiah: A Commentary on the Infancy Narratives in Matthew and Luke* (ABRL; New York: Doubleday, 1977).

—'Gospel Infancy Narrative Research from 1976 to 1986: Part I (Matthew)', *CBQ* 48 (1986), pp. 468-83.

—'*Rachab* in Mt 1,5 Probably is Rahab of Jericho', *Bib.* 63 (1982), pp. 79-80.

Brown, Schuyler, 'The Matthean Community and the Gentile Mission', *NovT* 22 (1980), pp. 193-221.

Broyles, Craig C., *The Conflict of Faith and Experience in the Psalms: A Form-Critical and Theological Study* (JSOTSup, 52; Sheffield: JSOT Press, 1989).

Buckley, Jorunn Jacobsen, ' "The Holy Spirit is a Double Name": Holy Spirit, Mary, and Sophia in the *Gospel of Philip*', in King (ed.), *Images of the Feminine*, pp. 211-27.

Bultmann, Rudolf, *The Gospel of John: A Commentary* (Philadelphia: Westminster Press, 1971).

—*History of the Synoptic Tradition* (New York: Harper & Row, rev. edn, 1963).

Bundy, Walter E., *Jesus and the First Three Gospels: An Introduction to the Synoptic Tradition* (Cambridge, MA: Harvard University Press, 1955).

Burkill, T.A., 'The Historical Development of the Story of the Syrophoenician Woman (Mark vii.24-30)', *NovT* 9 (1967), pp. 161-77.

—*New Light on the Earliest Gospel* (Ithaca, NY: Cornell University Press, 1972).

—'The Syrophoenician Woman: The Congruence of Mark 7.24-31', *ZNW* 57 (1966), pp. 23-37.

Burnett, Fred W., 'Exposing the Anti-Jewish Ideology of Matthew's Implied Author: The Characterization of God As Father', *Semeia* 59 (1992), pp. 155-91.

Callan, Terrance, 'The Background of the Apostolic Decree (Acts 15.20, 29; 21.25)', *CBQ* 55 (1993), pp. 284-97.

Carter, Warren, 'Kernels and Narrative Blocks: The Structure of Matthew's Gospel', *CBQ* 54 (1992), pp. 463-81.

Casey, P.M., *From Jewish Prophet to Gentile God* (Louisville, KY: Westminster/John Knox Press, 1991).

Chilton, Bruce D., 'Jesus ben David: Reflections on the *Davidssohnfrage*', *JSNT* 14 (1982), pp. 88-112.

Chilton, Bruce, and Jacob Neusner, *Judaism in the New Testament: Practices and Beliefs* (London: Routledge, 1995).

Clark, Kenneth Willis, 'The Gentile Bias in Matthew'. *JBL* 66 (1947), pp. 165-72.

—*The Gentile Bias and Other Essays* (NovTSup, 54; Leiden: E.J. Brill, 1980).

Clifford, Richard J., *The Cosmic Mountain in Canaan and the Old Testament* (Cambridge, MA: Harvard University Press, 1972).

Coats, George W., 'The King's Loyal Opposition: Obedience and Authority in Exodus 32–34', in Coats and Long (eds.), *Canon and Authority*, pp. 91-109.

Coats, George W., and Burke O. Long (eds.), *Canon and Authority* (Philadelphia: Fortress Press, 1977).

Cohen, Shaye J.D., *The Beginnings of Jewishness: Boundaries, Varieties, Uncertainties* (Berkeley: University of California Press, 1999).

—'Crossing the Boundary and Becoming a Jew', *HTR* 82 (1989), pp. 13-34 (reprinted in Cohen, *Beginnings of Jewishness*, pp. 140-74).

—'From the Bible to the Talmud: The Prohibition of Intermarriage', *HAR* 7 (1983), pp. 23-39.

—'The Rabbinic Conversion Ceremony', *JJS* 41 (1990), pp. 177-203 (reprinted in Cohen, *Beginnings of Jewishness*, pp. 198-238).

Cole, Robert L., *The Shape and Message of Book III (Psalms 73–89)* (JSOTSup, 307; Sheffield: Sheffield Academic Press, 2000).

Connolly, A.L., 'κυνάριον'; in Horsley and Llewelyn (eds.), *Documents*, IV, pp. 158-59.

Conzelmann, Hans, *Acts of the Apostles* (Hermeneia; Philadelphia: Fortress Press, 1987).

—*Gentiles, Jews, Christians: Polemics and Apologetics in the Greco-Roman Era* (Minneapolis: Fortress Press, 1992).

Coogan, Michael D., 'Canaanites: Who Were They and Where Did They Live?', *BR* 9 (1993), pp. 44-45.

Cope, O. Lamar, *Matthew: A Scribe Trained for the Kingdom of Heaven* (CBQMS, 5; Washington: Catholic Biblical Association, 1976).

Corrington, Gail Paterson, *Her Image of Salvation* (Louisville, KY: Westminster/John Knox Press, 1992).

Cranfield, C.E.B., *The Gospel According to Saint Mark* (CGTC; Cambridge: Cambridge University Press, rev. edn, 1957).

Creach, Jerome F.D., *Yahweh as Refuge and the Editing of the Hebrew Psalter* (JSOTSup, 217; Sheffield: Sheffield Academic Press, 1996).

Crockett, L.C., 'Luke 4.25-27 and Jewish–Gentile Relations in Luke–Acts', *JBL* 88 (1969), pp. 177-83.

Cross, Frank Moore, *Canaanite Myth and Hebrew Epic* (Cambridge, MA: Harvard University Press, 1973).

Crossan, John Dominic, *The Historical Jesus: The Life of a Mediterranean Jewish Peasant* (San Francisco: HarperSanFrancisco, 1991).

—*Jesus: A Revolutionary Biography* (San Francisco: HarperSanFrancisco, 1994).

Cryer, Frederick H., and Thomas L. Thompson, *Qumran Between the Old and New Testaments* (JSOTSup, 290; Copenhagen International Seminar, 6; Sheffield: Sheffield Academic Press, 1998).

Culpepper, R. Alan, *Anatomy of the Fourth Gospel: A Study in Literary Design* (New Testament Foundations and Facets; 2 vols.; Philadelphia: Fortress Press, 1983).

Dahlen, Robert W., 'The Savior and the Dog: An Exercise in Hearing', *WW* 17 (1997), pp. 269-77.

D'Angelo, Mary Rose, '(Re)Presentations of Women in the Gospels: John and Mark' in Kraemer and D'Angelo (eds.), Women and Christian Origins, pp. 129-49.

Daube, David, *Ancient Jewish Law: Three Inaugural Lectures* (Leiden: E.J. Brill, 1981).

—*Appeasement or Resistance and Other Essays on New Testament Judaism* (Berkeley: University of California Press, 1987).

—*The New Testament and Rabbinic Judaism* (Jordan Lectures, 1952; London: Athlone Press, 1956).

Davies, Philip R., *In Search of 'Ancient Israel'* (JSOTSup, 148; Sheffield Academic Press, 1992).

—'Introduction: Minimum or Maximum?', in Fritz and Davies (eds.), *Origins*, pp. 11-21.

—'Method and Madness: Some Remarks on Doing History with the Bible', *JBL* 114 (1995), pp. 699-705.

—'Whose History? Whose Israel? Whose Bible? Biblical Histories, Ancient and Modern', in Grabbe (ed.), *Can a 'History of Israel' Be Written?*, pp. 104-22.

Davies, Philip R., and David J.A. Clines (eds.), *The World of Genesis: Persons, Places, Perspectives* (JSOTSup, 257; Sheffield: Sheffield Academic Press, 1998).

Davies, W.D., *Christian Engagements with Judaism* (Harrisburg, PA: Trinity Press International, 1999).

—*Invitation to the New Testament: A Guide to Its Main Witnesses* (Garden City, NY: Doubleday, 1966).

Davies, W.D., and Dale C. Allison, Jr, *A Critical and Exegetical Commentary on the Gospel According to Saint Matthew* (ICC; 3 vols.; Edinburgh: T. & T. Clark, 1991–97).

de Boer, Martinus C., 'The Nazoreans: Living at the Boundary of Judaism and Christianity', in G. Stanton and G. Stroumsa (eds.), *Tolerance and Intolerance in Early Judaism and Christianity* (Cambridge: Cambridge University Press, 1998), pp. 239-62.

de Chazal, Nancy, 'The Women in Jesus' Family Tree', *Theology* 97 (1994), pp. 413-19.

Dearman, J.A., 'The Tophet in Jerusalem: Archaeology and Cultural Profile', *JNSL* 22.1 (1996), pp. 59-71.

Deissmann, G. Adolf, *Light From the Ancient East: The New Testament Illustrated by Recently Discovered Texts of the Graeco-Roman World* (London: Hodder & Stoughton, 1908).
—*New Light on the New Testament: From Records of the Graeco-Roman Period* (Edinburgh: T. & T. Clark, 1908).
Dennis, T., *Sarah Laughed: Women's Voices in the Old Testament* (London: SPCK, 1994).
Dermience, Alice, 'La péricope de la Cananéenne (Mt 15, 21-28): Rédaction et théologie', *ETL* 58 (1982), pp. 25-49.
Derrett, J. Duncan M., 'Law in the New Testament: The Syro-Phoenician Woman and the Centurion of Capernaum', *NovT* 15 (1973), pp. 161-86.
Deutsch, Celia M., 'Christians and Jews in the First Century: The Gospel of Matthew', *Thought* 67 (1992), pp. 399-408.
—*Lady Wisdom, Jesus, and the Sages* (Valley Forge, PA: Trinity Press International, 1996).
Dibelius, Martin, *From Tradition to Gospel* (New York: Charles Scribner's Sons, 1935).
Dobschütz, Ernst von, 'Matthew as Rabbi and Catechist', *ZNW* 27 (1928), pp. 338-48 (reprinted in Stanton [ed.], *Interpretation*, pp. 19-29).
Dollinger, John J.I., *The Gentile and the Jew in the Courts of the Temple of Christ: An Introduction in the History of Christianity* (2 vols.; London: Longman, Green, Longman, Roberts, & Green, 1962).
Donahoe, John R., *Are You the Christ? The Trial Narrative in the Gospel of Mark* (SBLDS, 10; Atlanta: Scholars Press, 1973).
Donaldson, Terence L., *Jesus on the Mountain: A Study in Matthean Theology* (JSNTSup, 8; Sheffield: JSOT, 1985).
—'The Law That Hangs (Matthew 22.40): Rabbinic Formulation and Matthean Social World', *CBQ* 57 (1995), pp. 689-709.
—'Proselytes or "Righteous Gentiles"? The Status of Gentiles in Eschatological Pilgrimage Patterns of Thought', *JSP* 7 (1990), pp. 3-27.
—' "Riches for the Gentiles" (Rom 11.12): Israel's Rejection and Paul's Gentile Mission', *JBL* 112 (1993), pp. 81-98.
Dossin, G., 'Une mention de Cananéens dans une lettre de Mari', *Syria* 50 (1973), pp. 277-83.
Douglas, Mary, *Natural Symbols: Explorations in Cosmology* (New York: Pantheon, 1970).
—*Purity and Danger: An Analysis of Concepts of Pollution and Taboo* (New York: Pantheon, 1970).
Dube, Musa W., 'Consuming a Colonial Cultural Bomb: Translating *Badimo* into "Demons" in the Setswana Bible (Matthew 8.28-34; 15.22; 10.8)', *JSNT* 73 (1999), pp. 33-59.
—'Readings of Semoya: Batswana Women's Interpretations of Mt. 15.21-28', *Semeia* 73 (1996), pp. 111-29.
Duling, Dennis, 'Solomon, Exorcism, and the Son of David', *HTR* 68 (1975), pp. 235-52.
—'The Therapeutic Son of David: An Element in Matthew's Christological Apologetic', *NTS* 24 (1978), pp. 392-410.
Dunn, James D.G., *The Partings of the Ways between Christianity and Judaism and their Significance for the Character of Christianity* (London: SCM Press, 1991).
Dunn, James D.G. (ed.), *Jews and Christians: The Parting of the Ways A.D. 70 to 135* (Tübingen: J.C.B. Mohr [Paul Siebeck], 1992).
Edelman, Diana (ed.), *The Fabric of History* (JSOTSup, 127; Sheffield: JSOT Press, 1991).
Edwards, Richard A., 'Uncertain Faith: Matthew's Portrait of the Disciples', in Segovia (ed.), *Discipleship*, pp. 47-61.

Eichhorn, David Max (ed.), *Conversion to Judaism: A History and Analysis* (New York: Ktav, 1965).

Eltester, W. (ed.), *Jesus in Nazareth* (BZNW, 40; Berlin: W. de Gruyter, 1972).

Engelken, Karen, 'Kanaan als nicht-territorialer Terminus', *BN* 52 (1990), pp. 47-63.

Eskanazi, Tamara C., 'Out From the Shadows: Biblical Women in the Postexilic Era', *JSOT* 54 (1992), pp. 25-43.

Esler, Philip F. (ed.), *Modelling Early Christianity: Social-Scientific Studies of the New Testament in its Context* (London: Routledge, 1995).

Evans, Craig A., and W. Richard Stegner (eds.), *The Gospels and the Scriptures of Israel* (JSNTSup 104; Sheffield: JSOT Press, 1994).

Evans, G.R., 'Crumbs, Gleanings and Fragments: An Exegetical Topos', *Recherches de Théologie ancienne et médiévale* 50 (1983), pp. 242-45.

Exum, J. Cheryl, *Fragmented Women* (Valley Forge, PA: Trinity Press International, 1993).

Falk, H., *Jesus the Pharisee: A New Look at the Jewishness of Jesus* (New York: Paulist Press, 1985).

Farmer, William R. (ed.), *Anti-Judaism and the Gospels* (Harrisburg, PA: Trinity Press International, 1999).

Feeley-Harnik, Gillian, 'Naomi and Ruth: Building Up the House of David', in Niditch (ed.), *Text and Tradition*, pp. 163-84.

Feldman, Louis H., *Jew and Gentile in the Ancient World: Attitudes and Interactions from Alexander to Justinian* (Princeton, NJ: Princeton University Press, 1993).

Fensham, F.C., 'A Few Observations on the Polarisation Between Yahweh and Baal in I Kings 17–19', *ZAW* 92 (1980), pp. 227-36.

Fenton, J.C., *Saint Matthew* (Westminster Pelican Commentaries; Philadelphia: Westminster, Press, 1963).

Fewell, Danna Nolan, and David Miller Gunn, *Compromising Redemption: Relating Characters in the Book of Ruth* (Literary Currents in Biblical Interpretation; Louisville: Westminster/John Knox Press, 1990).

Filson, Floyd V., *A Commentary on the Gospel According to St. Matthew* (BNTC; London: A. & C. Black, 1960).

Finkelstein, Israel, *The Archaeology of the Israelite Settlement* (Jerusalem: Israel Exploration Society, 1988).

—'Searching for Israelite Origins', *BARev* 14.5 (1988), pp. 34-45, 58.

Fishbane, Mona DeKoven, 'Ruth: Dilemmas of Loyalty and Connection', in Kates and Reimer (eds.), *Reading Ruth*, pp. 298-308.

Fitzmyer, Joseph A., *The Gospel According to Luke I–IX* (AB, 28; New York: Doubleday, 1981).

Flammer, Barnabas, 'Die Syrophoenizerin: Mk 7, 24-30', *TQ* 148 (1968), pp. 463-78.

Flusser, D., 'Paganism in Palestine', in Safrai and Stern (eds.), *The Jewish People*, II, pp. 1065-100.

Foerster, W., 'δαίμων', *TDNT*, II, pp. 1-19.

Ford, G.E., 'The Children's Bread and the Gods (Mt. xv. 21-28; Mk. vii. 24-30)', *ExpTim* 23 (1911–12), pp. 329-30.

France, R.T., *Matthew: Evangelist and Teacher* (Exeter: Paternoster Press, 1989).

—'Scripture, Tradition and History in the Infancy Narratives of Matthew', in France, Wenham and Blomberg (eds.), *Gospel Perspectives*, II, pp. 239-66.

France, R.T., David Wenham and Craig Blomberg (eds.), *Gospel Perspectives: Studies of History and Tradition in the Four Gospels* (6 vols.; Sheffield: JSOT Press, 1981–86).

Frankemölle, Hubert, *Jahwebund und Kirche Christi: Studien zur Form-und Traditionsgeschichte des 'Evangeliums' nach Matthäus* (Münster: Aschendorff, 1974).

Frankiel, Tamar, 'Ruth and the Messiah', in Kates and Reimer (eds.), *Reading Ruth*, pp. 321-35.

Freed, Edwin D., 'The Women in Matthew's Genealogy', *JSNT* 29 (1987), pp. 3-19.

Freyne, Sean, *Galilee, Jesus and the Gospels: Literary Approaches and Historical Investigations* (Philadelphia: Fortress Press, 1988).

—'Vilifying the Other and Defining the Self: Matthew's and John's Anti-Jewish Polemic in Focus', in Neusner and Frerichs (eds.), *'To See Ourselves'*, pp. 117-44.

Frisch, P., 'Über die lydisch-phrygischen Sühneinschriften and die "Confessiones" des Augustinus', *EA* 2 (1983), pp. 41-45.

Fritz, Volkmar, and Philip R. Davies (eds.), *The Origins of the Ancient Israelite States* (JSOTSup 228; Sheffield: Sheffield Academic Press, 1996).

Funk, Robert W., *Honest to Jesus: Jesus for a New Millennium* (San Francisco: Harper & Row, 1996).

Funk, Robert W., and The Jesus Seminar, *The Acts of Jesus: The Search for the Authentic Deeds of Jesus* (San Francisco: HarperSanFrancisco, 1998).

Funk, Robert W., Roy W. Hoover and The Jesus Seminar, *The Five Gospels: The Search for the Authentic Words of Jesus* (New York: Macmillan, 1993).

Garland, David E., *The Intention of Matthew 23* (SNT, 52; Leiden: E.J. Brill, 1979).

—*Reading Matthew: A Literary and Theological Commentary on the First Gospel* (New York: Crossroad, 1993).

Garsiel, Moshe, 'The Story of David and Bathsheba: A Different Approach', *CBQ* 55 (1993), pp. 244-62.

Georgi, Dieter, *The Opponents of Paul in Second Corinthians* (Philadelphia: Fortress Press, 1986).

Gnilka, Joachim, *Das Evangelium nach Markus* (EKKNT; 2 vols.; Zürich: Benzinger Verlag, 1978).

—*Das Matthäusevangelium* (2 vols.; Freiburg: Herder, 1986).

Goldenberg, Robert, 'The Place of Other Religions in Ancient Jewish Thought, with Particular Reference to Early Rabbinic Judaism', in Marty and Greenspahn (eds.), *Pushing the Faith*, pp. 27-40.

Goldstein, Albert A., 'Conversion to Judaism in Bible Times', in Eichhorn (ed.), *Conversion to Judaism*, pp. 9-32.

Golomb, D.M. (ed.), *Working With No Data: Semitic and Egyptian Studies Presented to Thomas O. Lambdin* (Winona Lake, IN: Eisenbrauns, 1988).

Good, Deirde, 'The Verb ΑΝΑΧΩΡΕΟ in Matthew's Gospel', *NovT* 32 (1990), pp. 1-12.

Goodman, Martin, *Mission and Conversion: Proselytizing in the Religious History of the Roman Empire* (Oxford: Clarendon Press, 1994).

—'Proselytising in Rabbinic Judaism', *JJS* 40 (1989), pp. 175-85.

—'Jewish Proselytizing in the First Century', in Lieu, North and Rajak (eds.), *The Jews*, pp. 53-78.

Gordon, Robert P. (ed.), *'The Place Is Too Small for Us': The Israelite Prophets in Recent Scholarship* (Winona Lake, IN: Eisenbrauns, 1995).

Gottwald, Norman K., 'Domain Assumptions and Societal Models in the Study of Pre-Monarchic Israel', in G.W. Anderson, P.A.H. DeBoer, Henry Cazelles, J.A. Emerton, W.L. Holladay, R.E. Murphy, E. Nielsen, R. Smend and J.A. Soggin (eds.), VTSup 28 (Leiden: E.J. Brill, 1975), pp. 89-100.

—*The Hebrew Bible: A Socio-Literary Introduction* (Philadelphia: Fortress Press, 1985).

Grabbe, Lester L. (ed.), *Can a 'History of Israel' Be Written?* (JSOTSup, 245; ESHM, 1; Sheffield: Sheffield Academic Press, 1997).

Graue, Joyce M., 'A Problem...or a Moonbeam? Sermon Study on Matthew 15.21-28', *Lutheran Theological Journal* 30 (1996), pp. 75-80.

Greimas, A.J. (ed.), *De Jésus et des Femmes* (Montréal: Bellarmin, 1987).

Grundman, Walter, 'κράζω', *TDNT*, III, pp. 898-903.

Guardiola-Saenz, Leticia, 'Borderless Women and Borderless Texts: A Cultural Reading of Matthew 15.21-28', *Semeia* 78 (1997), pp. 69-81.

Gundry, Robert Horton, *Matthew: A Commentary on His Handbook for a Mixed Church Under Persecution* (Grand Rapids: Eerdmans, 2nd edn, 1994).

—*The Use of the Old Testament in St. Matthew's Gospel* (Leiden: E.J. Brill, 1967).

Gundry-Volf, Judith, 'Spirit, Mercy, and the Other', *TT* (1995), pp. 508-23.

Gunkel, Hermann, and Joachim Begrich, *Introduction to Psalms: The Genres of the Religious Lyric of Israel* (trans. James D. Nogalski; Mercer Library of Biblical Studies; Macon, GA: Mercer University Press, 1998).

Haenchen, Ernest, *The Acts of the Apostles: A Commentary* (Philadelphia: Westminster Press, 1971).

—*A Commentary on the Gospel of John* (Hermeneia; 2 vols.; Philadelphia: Fortress Press, 1984, 1987).

Hagner, Donald A., 'The *Sitz im Leben* of the Gospel of Matthew', in Bauer and Powell (eds.), *Treasures*, pp. 27-68.

Hallbäck, Geert, 'Sted og Anti-sted: Om forholdet mellem person og lokalitet i Markusevangeliet', *Religionsvidenskabeligt Tidsskrift* 11 (1987), pp. 55-73.

Halpern, Bruce, 'Dialect Distribution in Canaan and the Deir Alla Inscriptions', in Golomb (ed.), *Working With No Data*, pp. 119-39.

Hare, Douglas R.A., and Daniel J. Harrington, ' "Make Disciples of All the Gentiles" (Mt 28.19)', *CBQ* 37 (1975), pp. 359-69.

Harnack, Adolf, *The Mission and Expansion of Christianity in the First Three Centuries* (2 vols.; New York: Putnam's Sons, 1908).

Harrington, Daniel J., *The Gospel of Matthew* (Sacra Pagina, 1; Collegeville, MN: Liturgical Press, 1991).

—'The Jewishness of Jesus: Facing Some Problems', *CBQ* 49 (1987), pp. 1-13.

Harrisville, Roy A., 'The Woman of Canaan: A Chapter in the History of Exegesis', *Int* 20 (1966), pp. 274-87.

Harvey, Dorothea, 'Book of Ruth', *IDB*, IV, pp. 131-34.

Haskins, Susan, *Mary Magdalen: Myth and Metaphor* (New York: Harcourt, Brace Company, 1993).

Hasler, J. Ireland, 'The Incident of the Syrophoenician Woman (Matt. xv. 21-28; Mark vii. 24-30)', *ExpTim* 45 (1934), pp. 459-61.

Heil, John Paul, 'The Narrative Roles of the Women in Matthew's Genealogy', *Bib* 72 (1991), pp. 538-45.

—'Significant Aspects of the Healing Miracles in Matthew', *CBQ* 41 (1979), pp. 274-87.

Held, Heinz Joachim, 'Matthew as Interpreter of the Miracle Stories', in Bornkamm, Barth and Held (eds.) *Tradition*, pp. 165-299.

Hengel, Martin, *Judaism and Hellenism: Studies in their Encounter in Palestine during the Early Hellenistic Period* (2 vols.; Philadelphia: Fortress Press, 1974).

Heschel, Susannah, 'Anti-Judaism in Christian Feminist Theology', *Tikkun* 5.3 (1990), pp. 25-28, 95-97.

—'Jesus as Theological Transvestite', in Peskowitz and Levitt (eds.), *Judaism Since Gender*, pp. 188-99.

Hill, Craig C., *Hellenists and Hebrews: Reappraising Division within the Earliest Church* (Minneapolis: Fortress Press, 1992).

Hillers, Delbert R., 'Analyzing the Abominable: Our Understanding of Canaanite Religion', *JQR* 75 (1985), pp. 253-69.

Hills, Julian V. (ed.), *Common Life in the Early Church: Essays Honoring Graydon F. Snyder* (Harrisburg, PA: Trinity Press International, 1998).

Hjelm, Ingrid, *The Samaritans and Early Judaism: A Literary Analysis* (JSOTSup, 303; CIS, 7; Sheffield: Sheffield Academic Press, 2000).

Hoenig, Sidney B., 'Conversion During the Talmudic Period', in Eichhorn (ed.), *Conversion*, pp. 33-66.

Holloway, Steven W., and Lowell K. Handy (eds.), *The Pitcher is Broken: Memorial Essays for Gösta W. Ahlström* (JSOTSup, 190; Sheffield: Sheffield Academic Press, 1995).

Holmberg, Bengt, 'Debatten Jesus inte vann', *SEÅ* 63 (1998), pp. 167-76.

Hood, Rodney T., 'The Genealogies of Jesus', in Wikgren (ed.), *Early Christian Origins*, pp. 1-15.

Hooker, Morna D., *The Gospel According to Saint Mark* (BNTC; Peabody, MA: Hendrickson, 1991).

Horbury, William, *Jews and Christians in Contact and Controversy* (Edinburgh: T. & T. Clark, 1998).

Horsley, Richard A., *Jesus and the Spiral of Violence: Popular Jewish Resistance in Roman Palestine* (Minneapolis: Fortress Press, 1993).

Hubbard, Benjamin, *The Matthean Redaction of a Primitive Apostolic Commissioning: An Exegesis of Mt 28.16-20* (SBLDS, 19; Missoula, MT: Scholars Press, 1974).

Hubbard, Robert L., *The Book of Ruth* (Grand Rapids: Eerdmans, 1988).

Isenberg, Wesley W., 'The Gospel of Philip (II.3)', in James M. Robinson (ed.), *The Nag Hammadi Library in English*, pp. 139-60.

Jackson, Glenna S., 'Are the "Nations" Present in Matthew?', *Hervormde Teologiese Studies* 56 (2000), pp. 935-48.

—'Jesus as First-Century Feminist: Christian Anti-Judaism?', *FemTh* 19 (1998), pp. 85-98.

Jacobson, Arland D., *The First Gospel: An Introduction to Q* (Sonoma, CA: Polebridge Press, 1992).

—'Wisdom Christology in Q' (unpublished Doctoral dissertation, Claremont Graduate School, 1978).

Jeansonne, Sharon, *The Women of Genesis: From Sarah to Potiphar's Wife* (Minneapolis: Fortress Press, 1990).

Jeremias, Joachim, *Jesus' Promise to the Nations* (SBT, 1/24; London: SCM Press, 1958).

Jobling, David, *The Sense of Biblical Narrative: Structural Analyses in the Hebrew Bible* (JSOTSup, 39: Sheffield: JSOT Press, 1978).

Johnson, Marshall D., *The Purpose of the Biblical Genealogies* (Cambridge: Cambridge University Press, 1988).

Jones, John Mark, 'Subverting the Textuality of Davidic Messianism: Matthew's Presentation of the Genealogy and the Davidic Title', *CBQ* 56 (1994), pp. 256-72.

Kampen, John, 'Communal Discipline in the Social World of the Matthean Community', in Hills (ed.), *Common Life*, pp. 158-74.

Kates, Judith A., and Gail Twersky Reimer (eds.), *Reading Ruth: Contemporary Women Reclaim a Sacred Story* (New York: Ballantine Books, 1994).

Kee, Howard Clark, *Christian Origins in Sociological Perspective: Methods and Resources* (Philadelphia: Westminster Press, 1980).

—*Community of the New Age* (Philadelphia: Westminster Press, 1977).

—*Jesus in History: An Approach to the Study of the Gospels* (New York: Harcourt Brace Jovanovich, 2nd edn, 1977).

—*Miracle in the Early Christian World* (New Haven: Yale University Press, 1983).

Kelber, Warner H., *The Oral and the Written Gospel: The Hermeneutics of Speaking and Writing in the Synoptic Tradition, Mark, Paul, and Q* (Philadelphia: Fortress Press, 1983).

Kilpatrick, G.D., *The Origins of the Gospel According to St. Matthew* (Oxford: Clarendon Press, 1946).

King, Karen L. (ed.), *Images of the Feminine in Gnosticism* (Studies in Antiquity and Christianity; Philadelphia: Fortress Press, 1988).

Kingsbury, Jack Dean, 'The Developing Conflict Between Jesus and the Jewish Leaders in Matthew's Gospel: A Literary-Critical Study', *CBQ* 49 (1987), pp. 57-73.

—*Matthew* (Proclamation Commentaries; Philadelphia: Fortress Press Press, 1977).

—*Matthew: Structure, Christology, Kingdom* (Minneapolis: Fortress, 1975).

—'Reflections on "The Reader" of Matthew's Gospel', *NTS* 34 (1988), pp. 442-60.

—'The Title "Kyrios" in Matthew's Gospel', *JBL* 94 (1975), pp. 246-55.

—'The Verb *Akolouthein* ("to Follow") as an Index of Matthew's View of his Community', *JBL* 97 (1978), pp. 56-73.

Kirkpatrick, Patricia G., *The Old Testament and Folklore Study* (JSOTSup, 62; Sheffield: JSOT Press, 1988).

Klassen, William, *Judas: Betrayer or Friend of Jesus?* (Minneapolis: Fortress Press, 1996).

Koester, Helmut, *Ancient Christian Gospels: Their History and Development* (London: SCM Press; Philadelphia: Trinity Press International, 1990).

—*Introduction to the New Testament* (2 vols.; Berlin: W. de Gruyter, 1982).

Kohler, Kaufman, 'Amorites—In Rabbinical and Apocryphal Literature', in Singer (ed.), *The Jewish Encyclopedia*, XII, p. 529.

Korpel, Marjo Christina Annette, *A Rift in the Clouds: Ugaritic and Hebrew Descriptions of the Divine* (Münster: Ugarit-Verlag, 1990).

Kraemer, Ross Shepard, and Mary Rose D'Angelo (eds.), *Women and Christian Origins* (New York: Oxford University Press, 1999).

Klijn, A.F.J., *Jewish-Christian Gospel Tradition* (Leiden: E.J. Brill, 1992).

Kwok, Pui-Lan, *Discovering the Bible in the Non-Biblical World* (Maryknoll: Orbis Books, 1995).

Laato, Antti, 'Psalm 132 and the Development of the Jerusalemite/Israelite Royal Ideology', *CBQ* 54 (1992), pp. 49-66.

Lachs, Samuel Tobias, *A Rabbinic Commentary on the New Testament: The Gospels of Matthew, Mark, and Luke* (Hoboken, NJ: Ktav, 1987).

—'Rabbinic Sources for New Testament Studies—Use and Misuse', *JQR* 74 (1983), pp. 159-73.

LaCocque, Andre, *The Feminine Unconventional: Four Subversive Figures in Israel's Tradition* (Overtures to Biblical Theology; Minneapolis: Fortress Press, 1990).

Laffey, Alice L., *An Introduction to the Old Testament: A Feminist Perspective* (Philadelphia: Fortress Press, 1988).

LaGrand, James, *The Earliest Christian Mission to 'All Nations' in the Light of Matthew's Gospel* (Atlanta: Scholars Press, 1995).

Lambe, Anthony J., 'Genesis 38: Structure and Literary Design', in Davies and Clines (eds.), *The World of Genesis*, pp. 102-20.

Landy, Francis, 'Ruth and the Romance of Realism, or Deconstructing History', *JAAR* 62 (1994), pp. 285-317.

Lane, Eugene N., *Paganism and Christianity, 100–425 C. E.: A Sourcebook* (Minneapolis: Fortress Press, 1992).

Langley, Wendell E., 'The Parable of the Two Sons (Matthew 21.28-32) against its Semitic and Rabbinic Backdrop', *CBQ* 58 (1996), pp. 228-43.

Le Déaut, Roger, 'Targumic Literature and New Testament Interpretation', *BTB* 4 (1974), pp. 243-89.

Lee, Bernard J., *The Galilean Jewishness of Jesus: Retrieving the Jewish Origins of Christianity* (Studies in Judaism and Christianity; New York: Paulist Press, 1988).

Legasse, S., 'L'épisode de la Cananéenne d'apres Mt 15, 21-28', *BLE* 73 (1972), pp. 21-40.

Lemche, Niels Peter, *Ancient Israel: A New History of Israelite Society* (The Biblical Seminar, 5; Sheffield: JSOT Press, 1988.

—*The Canaanites and Their Land* (JSOTSup, 110; Sheffield: JSOT Press, 1991).

—*Early Israel: Anthropological and Historical Studies on the Israelite Society Before the Monarchy* (Leiden: E.J. Brill, 1985).

—'Greater Canaan: the Implications of a Correct Reading of EA 151.49-67', *BASOR* 310 (1998), pp. 19-24.

—'Is it Still Possible to Write a History of Ancient Israel?', *SJOT* 8 (1994), pp. 165-90.

—*The Israelites in History and Tradition* (Louisville, KY: Westminster/John Knox Press, 1998).

—'New Perspectives on the History of Israel', in Martinez and Noort (eds.), *Perspectives*, pp. 42-60.

—'The Origin of the Israelite State—A Copenhagen Perspective on the Emergence of Critical Historical Studies of Ancient Israel in Recent Times', *SJOT* 12 (1998), pp. 44-63.

—*Prelude to Israel's Past: Background and Beginnings of Israelite History and Identity* (Peabody, MA: Hendrickson, 1998).

—'The Understanding of Community in the Old Testament and in the Dead Sea Scrolls', in Cryer and Thompson (eds.), *Qumran*, pp. 181-93.

—'Where Should We Look for Canaan? A Reply to Nadav Na'aman', *UF* 28 (1996), pp. 767-72.

Levine, Amy-Jill, 'Anti-Judaism and the Gospel of Matthew', in Farmer (ed.), *Anti-Judaism and the Gospels*, pp. 9-36.

—'Matthew', in Newsom and Ringe (eds.), *Women's Bible Commentary*, pp. 252-62.

—'Ruth', in Newsom and Ringe (eds.), *Women's Bible Commentary*, pp. 78-84.

—*The Social and Ethnic Dimensions of Matthean Social History* (Studies in the Bible and Early Christianity, 14; Lewiston, NY: Edwin Mellen Press, 1988).

—*'Women Like This': New Perspectives on Jewish Women in the Greco-Roman World* (SBL Early Judaism and Its Literature, 1; Atlanta: Scholars Press, 1991).

Levine, Etan, *The Aramaic Version of Ruth* (AnBib, 58; Rome: Biblical Institute Press, 1973).

Lieberman, Saul, *Greek in Jewish Palestine: Studies in the Life and Manners of Jewish Palestine in the II–IV Centuries C. E.* (New York: Jewish Theological Seminary of America, 1942).

Bibliography 173

Lieu, Judith M., 'The "Attraction of Women" in/to Early Judaism and Christianity: Gender and the Politics of Conversion', *JSNT* 72 (1998), pp. 5-22.

Lieu, Judith M., John North and Tessa Rajak (eds.), *The Jews Among Pagans and Christians in the Roman Empire* (New York: Routledge, 1992).

Lindars, Barnabas, *The Gospel of John* (NCB; Grand Rapids: Eerdmans, 1972).

Livingstone, E.A. (ed.), *Studia Biblica 1978*, II. *Papers on the Gospels* (JSNTSup, 2; Sheffield: JSOT, 1980).

Loader, William, 'Challenged at the Boundaries: A Conservative Jesus in Mark's Tradition', *JSNT* 63 (1996), pp. 45-61.

Lohfink, Gerhard, *Jesus and Community* (Philadelphia: Fortress Press, 2nd edn, 1989).

Lohfink, Norbert, and Erich Zenger, *The God of Israel and the Nations: Studies in Isaiah and the Psalms* (trans. Everett R. Kalin; Collegeville, MN: Liturgical Press, 2000).

Lohmeyer, Ernst, *Das Evangelium des Markus* (Meyer's Kommentar zum Neue Testament, 2; Göttingen: Vandenhoeck & Ruprecht, 1963).

Long, Asphodel P., 'Book Review: Schüssler Fiorenza, Elisabeth, *But She Said: Feminist Practices of Biblical Interpretation*', *FemTh* 7 (1994), pp. 135-39.

Long, V. Philips (ed.), *Israel's Past in Present Research: Essays on Ancient Israelite Historiography* (SBTS; Winona Lake, IN: Eisenbrauns, 1999).

Luz, Ulrich, 'The Disciples in the Gospel According to Matthew', in Stanton (ed.), *Interpretation*, pp. 98-128.

—*Matthew 1–7: A Commentary* (Minneapolis: Augsburg, 1989).

—*Matthew in History: Interpretation, Influence, and Effects* (Minneapolis: Fortress Press, 1994).

—*The Theology of the Gospel of Matthew* (Cambridge: Cambridge University Press, 1995).

Maccoby, Hyam, *Early Rabbinic Writings* (Cambridge Commentaries on Writings of the Jewish and Christian World 200 BC to AD 200; Cambridge: Cambridge University Press, 1988).

—*Judas Iscariot and the Myth of Jewish Evil* (Glencoe: Free Press, 1992).

MacDonald, Dennis Ronald, 'From Audita to Legenda: Oral and Written Miracle Stories', *Forum* 2.4 (1986), pp. 15-26.

Mack, Burton, L., *A Myth of Innocence: Mark and Christian Origins* (Philadelphia: Fortress Press, 1988).

Mack, Burton, and Vernon K. Robbins, *Patterns of Persuasion in the Gospels* (Sonoma, CA: Polebridge Press, 1989).

MacLennan, Robert S., *Early Christian Texts on Jews and Judaism* (BJS, 194; Atlanta: Scholars Press, 1990).

MacMullen, Ramsey, *Paganism in the Roman Empire* (New Haven: Yale University Press, 1981).

MacMullen, Ramsey, and Eugene N. Lane, *Paganism and Christianity, 100–425 C.E.: A Sourcebook* (Minneapolis: Fortress Press, 1992).

Malbon, Elizabeth Struthers, 'Echoes and Foreshadowing in Mark 4–8: Reading and Rereading', *JBL* 112 (1993), pp. 211-30.

—'Fallible Followers: Women and Men in the Gospel of Mark', *Semeia* 28 (1983), pp. 29-48.

—'Galilee and Jerusalem: History and Literature in Marcan Interpretation', *CBQ* 44 (1982), pp. 242-55.

—'The Jesus of Mark and the Sea of Galilee', *JBL* 103 (1984), pp. 363-77.

—'Mythic Structure and Meaning in Mark: Elements of a Levi-Straussian Analysis', *Semeia* 16 (1979), pp. 97-132.

—*Narrative Space and Mythic Meaning in Mark* (San Francisco: Harper & Row, 1986).

Malherbe, Abraham J., *Social Aspects of Early Christianity* (Philadelphia: Fortress Press, 2nd edn, 1983).

Malina, Bruce J., 'Jewish Christianity or Christian Judaism: Toward a Hypothetical Definition', *JSJ* 7 (1990), pp. 46-57.

—*The New Testament World: Insights from Cultural Anthropology* (Louisville, KY: John Knox Press, 1981).

Malina, Bruce J., and Jerome H. Neyrey, *Calling Jesus Names: The Social Value of Labels in Matthew* (Sonoma, CA: Polebridge Press, 1988).

Malina, Bruce J., and Richard L. Rohrbaugh, *Social-Science Commentary on the Synoptic Gospels* (Minneapolis: Fortress Press, 1992).

Margoliouth, D.S., 'The Syro-Phoenician Woman', *The Expositor* 22 (1921), pp. 1-10.

Martinez, Florentino Garcia, and Ed Noort, *Perspectives in the Study of the Old Testament and Early Judaism: A Symposium in Honour of Adam S. Van der Woude on the Occasion of His 70th Birthday* (VTSup, 73; Leiden: E.J. Brill, 1998).

Marty, Martin E., and Frederick E. Greenspahn (eds.), *Pushing the Faith: Proselytism and Civility in a Pluralistic World* (New York: Crossroad, 1988).

Marxen, Willi, *Mark the Evangelist: Studies on the Redaction History of the Gospel* (Nashville: Abingdon Press, 1969).

Matera, Frank, *Passion Narratives and Gospel Theologies: Interpreting the Synoptics through their Passion Stories* (Theological Inquiries; New York: Paulist Press, 1986).

—'The Plot of Matthew's Gospel', *CBQ* 49 (1987), pp. 233-53.

McKenzie, John, *The World of the Judges* (Englewood Cliffs, NJ: Prentice–Hall, 1966).

McKnight, Scot, *A Light Among the Gentiles: Jewish Missionary Activity in the Second Temple Period* (Minneapolis: Fortress Press, 1991).

McNeile, Alan Hugh, *The Gospel According to St. Matthew* (London: Macmillan, 1915).

Meeks, Wayne A., 'Breaking Away: Three New Testament Pictures of Christianity's Separation from the Jewish Communities', in Neusner and Frerichs (eds.), *'To See Ourselves'*, pp. 93-116.

Meier, John P., *A Marginal Jew: Rethinking the Historical Jesus* (ABRL; 2 vols.; New York: Doubleday, 1991–94).

—*Matthew* (New Testament Message, 3; Wilmington, DE: Michael Glazier, 1980).

Mendels, Doran, *The Land of Israel as a Political Concept in Hasmonean Literature: Recourse to History Second Century B.C. Claims to the Holy Land* (Texte und Studien zum Antiken Judentum, 15; Tübingen: J.C.B. Mohr, 1987).

Mendenhall, George, 'The Hebrew Conquest of Palestine', *BA* 25 (1962), pp. 66-87.

Meyers, Carol, *Discovering Eve* (New York: Oxford University Press, 1988).

Michel, Otto, 'κύων', in TDNT, III, pp. 1101-14.

Miller, Patrick D., *They Cried to the Lord: The Form and Theology of Biblical Prayer* (Minneapolis: Fortress Press, 1994).

Mitchell, David C., *The Message of the Psalter: An Eschatological Programme in the Book of Psalms* (JSOTSup, 252; Sheffield: Sheffield Academic Press, 1997).

Moeser, A.G., 'The Death of Judas', *BibTod* 30 (1992), pp. 145-51.

Monro, Anita, 'Alterity and the Canaanite Woman: A Postmodern Feminist Theological Reflection on Political Action', *Colloquium: The Australian and New Zealand Theological Review* 26 (1994), pp. 264-78.

Montague, George T., *Companion God: A Cross-Cultural Commentary on the Gospel of Matthew* (New York: Paulist Press, 1989).

Moore, George Foot, *Judaism in the First Centuries of the Christian Era: The Age of the Tannaim* (3 vols.; Peabody, MA: Hendrickson, 1997).

Moore, Michael S., 'Ruth the Moabite and the Blessing of Foreigners', *CBQ* 60 (1998), pp. 203-17.

Moscati, S. (ed.), *The Phoenicians* (New York: Abbeville, 1988).

Mowinkel, Sigmund, *The Psalms in Israel's Worship* (2 vols.; New York: Abingdon Press, 1962).

Murphy-O'Connor, Jerome, 'The Structure of Matthew XIV–XVII', *RB* 3 (1975), pp. 360-84.

Mussies, Gerard, 'Matthew's Pedigree of Jesus', *NovT* 38 (1986), pp. 32-47.

Na'aman, Nadav, 'The Canaanites and Their Land: A Rejoinder', *UF* 26 (1995), pp. 397-418.

Nash, Peter Theodore, 'Ruth: An Exercise in Israelite Political Correctness or a Call to Proper Conversion?', in Holloway and Handy (eds.), *Pitcher is Broken*, pp. 347-54.

Neary, Michael, 'The Importance of Lament in the God/Man Relationship in Ancient Israel', *ITQ* 52 (1986), pp. 180-92.

Neill, Margaret James, 'Racism and the Soul: The Canaanite Woman's Challenge', *The Other Side* 34 (1998), pp. 42-44.

Neiman, David., 'Phoenician Place-Names', *JNES* 24 (1965), pp. 113-15.

Neusner, Jacob, *Eliezer ben Hyrcanus: The Tradition and The Man* (SJLA, 32; 2 vols.; Leiden: E.J. Brill, 1973).

—*From Scripture to 70: The Pre-Rabbinic Beginnings of the Halakhah* (SFSHJ; Atlanta: Scholars Press, 1998).

—*The Judaism Behind the Texts: The Generative Premises of Rabbinic Literature* (SFSHJ, 4; Atlanta: Scholars Press, 1994).

—*The Midrash Compilations of the Sixth and Seventh Centuries: An Introduction to the Rhetorical, Logical, and Topical Program: Ruth Rabbah* (BJS, 189; 4 vols.; Atlanta: Scholars Press, 1989).

—*The Mother of the Messiah in Judaism: The Book of Ruth* (Valley Forge, PA: Trinity Press International, 1993).

—*Rabbinic Literature and the New Testament: What We Cannot Show, We Do Not Know* (Valley Forge, PA: Trinity Press International, 1994).

—*Ruth Rabbah: An Analytic Translation* (Atlanta: Scholars Press, 1989).

—'Was Rabbinic Judaism Really "Ethnic"?', *CBQ* 57 (1995), pp. 281-305.

Neusner, Jacob (ed.), *Christianity, Judaism and Other Greco-Roman Cults* (SJLA, 12; 4 vols.; Leiden: E.J. Brill, 1975).

Neusner, Jacob and E.S. Frerichs (eds.), *'To See Ourselves as Others See Us': Christians, Jews, 'Others' in Late Antiquity* (Chico, CA: Scholars Press, 1985).

Newsom, Carol A., 'A Maker of Metaphors: Ezekiel's Oracles Against Tyre', in Gordon (ed.), *'The Place Is Too Small'*, pp. 191-204.

Neyrey, Jerome H., 'Decision Making in the Early Church: The Case of the Canaanite Woman (Mt 15.21-28)', *Science et Esprit* 33 (1981), pp. 373-78.

Nibbi, Alessandra, *Canaan and Canaanite in Ancient Egypt* (Hawksworth: Bocardo, 1989).

Nickelsburg, George W.E., *Jewish Literature Between the Bible and the Mishnah* (Philadelphia: Fortress Press, 1981).

Niditch, Susan, 'Notes and Observations: The Wronged Woman Righted: An Analysis of Genesis 38', *HTR* 72 (1979), pp. 143-49.

Niditch, Susan (ed.), *Text and Tradition: The Hebrew Bible and Folklore* (SBLSS; Atlanta: Scholars Press, 1990).

Nock, Arthur Darby, *Conversion: The Old and the New in Religion from Alexander the Great to Augustine of Hippo* (London: Oxford University Press, 1933).

—*Early Gentile Christianity and Its Hellenistic Background* (New York: Harper & Row, 1964).

—*St. Paul* (London: Butterworth, 1938).

Nolan, Albert, *Jesus Before Christianity* (Maryknoll, NY: Orbis Books, 1976).

Nolland, John, 'The Four (Five) Women and Other Annotations in Matthew's Genealogy', *NTS* 43 (1997), pp. 527-39.

Novak, David, *The Image of the Non-Jew in Judaism: An Historical and Constructive Study of the Noahide Laws* (Toronto Studies in Theology, 14; New York: Edwin Mellen Press, 1983).

O'Connor, M., 'The Rhetoric of the Kilamuwa Inscription', *BASOR* 226 (1977), pp. 15-29.

O'Day, Gail O., 'Surprised by Faith: Jesus and the Canaanite Woman', *Listening: Journal of Religion and Culture* 24 (1989), pp. 290-301.

Onwu, Neenanya, 'Jesus and the Canaanite Woman (Mt. 15.21-28)', *Bible Bhashyam* 11 (1985), pp. 130-43.

Orrieux, Claude, *'Proselytisme Juif'? Histoire d'une erreur* (Paris: Belles, 1992).

Overman, J. Andrew, *Church and Community in Crisis: The Gospel According to Matthew* (The New Testament in Context; Valley Forge: Trinity Press International, 1996).

—'The God-Fearers: Some Neglected Features', *JSNT* 32 (1988), pp. 17-26.

—*Matthew's Gospel and Formative Judaism: The Social World of the Matthean Community* (Minneapolis: Fortress Press, 1990).

Pagels, Elaine, 'Pursuing the Spiritual Eve: Imagery and Hermeneutics in the *Hypostasis of the Archons* and the *Gospel of Philip*', in King (ed.), *Images of the Feminine*, pp. 187-206.

Paget, James Carleton, 'Jewish Proselytism at the Time of Christian Origins: Chimera or Reality?' *JSNT* 62 (1996), pp. 65-103.

Patte, Daniel, *The Gospel According to Matthew: A Structural Commentary on Matthew's Faith* (Philadelphia: Fortress Press, 1987).

Perelmuter, Hayim Goren, *Siblings: Rabbinic Judaism and Early Christianity at their Beginnings* (New York: Paulist Press, 1989).

Perkinson, Jim, 'A Canaanite Word in the Logos of Christ; or the Difference the Syro-Phoenician Woman Makes to Jesus', *Semeia* 75 (1996), pp. 61-85.

Pervo, Richard I., 'Aseneth and Her Sisters: Women in Jewish Narrative and in the Greek Novels', in A.-J. Levine (ed.), *'Women Like This'*, pp. 145-60.

Pesch, Rudolf, ' "He will be called a Nazorean": Messianic Exegesis in Matthew 1–2', in Evans and Stegner (eds.), *Gospels and the Scriptures of Israel*, pp. 129-78.

Peskowitz, Miriam, and Laura Levitt (eds.), *Judaism Since Gender* (New York: Routledge & Kegan Paul, 1997).

Plaskow, Judith, 'Anti-Judaism in Feminist Christian Interpretation', in Schüssler Fiorenza (ed.), *Searching the Scriptures*, I, pp. 117-29.

—'Blaming Jews for Inventing Patriarchy', *Lilith* 7 (1980), pp. 11-12.

—'Feminist Anti-Judaism and the Christian God', *JFSR* 7.2 (1991), pp. 99-108.

Plummer, Alfred, *An Exegetical Commentary on the Gospel According to Saint Matthew* (London: Scott, 1915).

Porton, Gary G., *Gentiles and Israelites in Mishnah-Tosefta* (BJS, 155; Atlanta: Scholars Press, 1988).

Powell, J. Enoch, *The Evolution of the Gospel: A New Translation of the First Gospel with Commentary and Introductory Essay* (New Haven: Yale University Press, 1994).

Powell, Mark Allan, 'A Typology of Worship in the Gospel of Matthew', *JSNT* 57 (1995), pp. 3-17.

Pregeant, Russell, 'The Wisdom Passages in Matthew's Story', in Bauer and Powell (eds.), *Treasures*, pp. 197-232.

Pritz, R., 'He Shall Be Called a "Nazarene" ', *Jerusalem Perspective* 4 (1991), pp. 3-4.

Provan, Iain W., 'Ideologies, Literary and Critical: Reflections on Recent Writing on the History of Israel', *JBL* 114 (1995), pp. 585-606.

Quinn, Jerome D., 'Is "PAXAB" in Mt 1,5 Rahab of Jericho'? *Bib.* 62 (1981), pp. 225-28.

Rabinowitz, L., *Midrash Rabbah: Ruth* (New York: Soncino, 1983).

Rainey, Anson F., 'Who is a Canaanite? A Review of the Textual Evidence', *BASOR* 304 (1996), pp. 1-15.

Rhoads, David, 'Jesus and the Syrophoenician Woman in Mark: A Narrative-Critical Study', *JAAR* 62 (1994), pp. 343-75.

Ricci, Carla, *Mary Magdalene and Many Others: Women Who Followed Jesus* (Minneapolis: Fortress Press, 1994).

Ringe, Sharon, 'A Gentile Woman's Story', in Letty M. Russell (ed.), *Feminist Interpretation*, pp. 65-72.

Robbins, Vernon K., 'Pronouncement Stories from a Rhetorical Perspective', *Forum* 4.2 (1988), pp. 3-32.

Ruether, Rosemary Radford, *Sexism and God-Talk: Toward a Feminist Theology* (Boston: Beacon Press, 1983).

Russell, E.A., 'The Canaanite Woman and the Gospels (Mt 15.21-28)', in Livingstone (ed.), *Studia Biblica*, pp. 263-300.

Russell, Letty M. (ed.), *Feminist Interpretation of the Bible* (Philadelphia: Westminster Press, 1985).

Safrai, S., and M. Stern (eds.), *The Jewish People in the First Century* (2 vols.; Philadelphia: Fortress Press, 1974, 1984).

Sakenfield, Katharine Doob, 'Feminist Perspective on Bible and Theology: An Introduction to Selected Issues and Literature', *Int* 42 (1988), pp. 5-18.

Saldarini, Anthony J., 'Delegitimation of Leaders in Matthew 23', *CBQ* 54 (1992), pp. 659-80.

—'The Gospel of Matthew and Jewish–Christian Conflict', in Balch (ed.), *Social History*, pp. 38-61.

—'The Gospel of Matthew and Jewish–Christian Conflict in the Galilee', in L. Levine (ed.), *Galilee*, pp. 23-38.

—'Jews and Christians in the First Two Centuries: The Changing Paradigm', *Shofar* 10.2 (1992), pp. 16-34.

—*Matthew's Christian–Jewish Community* (Chicago: University of Chicago Press, 1994).

Sanders, E.P., *The Historical Figure of Jesus* (New York: Penguin Books, 1993).

—*Jesus and Judaism* (Philadelphia: Fortress Press, 1985).

—*Judaism: Practice and Belief 63 BCE–66 CE* (Philadelphia: Trinity Press International, 1992).

Sanders, Jack T., *Schismatics, Sectarians, Dissidents, Deviants: The First One Hundred Years of Jewish–Christian Relations* (Valley Forge, PA: Trinity Press International, 1993).

Sanders, James A., 'Ναζωραῖος in Matthew 2.23', in Evans and Stegner (eds.), *Gospels and the Scriptures of Israel*, pp. 116-28.

Sandmel, Samuel, *The First Century in Judaism and Christianity: Certainties and Uncertainties* (New York: Oxford University Press, 1969).

—*Judaism and Christian Beginnings* (New York: Oxford University Press, 1978).

Sasson, Jack M., 'A Genealogical "Convention" in Biblical Chronography?', *ZAW* 90 (1978), pp. 171-85.

—*Ruth: A New Translation with a Philological Commentary and a Formalist-Folklorist Interpretation* (The Biblical Seminar, 10; Sheffield: JSOT Press, 1989).

Sawicki, Marianne, *Seeing the Lord: Resurrection and Early Christian Practices* (Minneapolis: Fortress Press, 1994).

Schaberg, Jane, *The Father, the Son and the Holy Spirit: The Triadic Phrase in Matthew 28.19b* (SBLDS, 61; Chico: CA: Scholars Press, 1982).

—'Feminist Interpretations of the Infancy Narrative of Matthew', *JFSR* 13 (1997), pp. 35-62.

—*The Illegitimacy of Jesus* (San Francisco: Harper & Row, 1987).

Schechter, S., *Studies in Judaism* (New York: Meridian, 1958).

Schneider, Johannes, 'κλαίω', in *TDNT*, III, pp. 722-25.

Schrage, Wolfgang, *The Ethics of the New Testament* (Philadelphia: Fortress Press, 1988).

Schroer, Silvia, ' "Under the shadow of your wings": The Metaphor of God's Wings in the Psalms, Exodus 19.4, Deuteronomy 32.11 and Malachi 3.20, as Seen Through the Perspectives of Feminism and the History of Religion', in Brenner and Fontaine (eds.), *Wisdom and Psalms*, pp. 264-82.

Schüssler Fiorenza, Elisabeth, *Bread Not Stone: The Challenge of Feminist Biblical Interpretation* (Boston: Beacon Press, 1984).

—*But She Said: Feminist Practices of Biblical Interpretation* (Boston: Beacon Press, 1992).

—*In Memory of Her: A Feminist Theological Reconstruction of Christian Origins* (New York: Crossroad, 1983).

—*Jesus: Miriam's Child, Sophia's Prophet: Critical Issues in Feminist Christology* (New York: Continuum, 1994).

Schüssler Fiorenza, Elisabeth (ed.), *Aspects of Religious Propaganda in Judaism and Early Christianity* (University of Notre Dame Center for the Study of Judaism and Christianity in Antiquity, 2; Notre Dame: University of Notre Dame Press, 1976).

—*Searching the Scriptures: A Feminist Introduction* (2 vol.; New York: Crossroad, 1995).

—'The Power of Naming: Jesus, Women, and Christian Anti-Judaism', in Fiorenza (ed.), *Sharing Her Word*, pp. 67-96.

—*Sharing Her Word: Feminist Biblical Interpretation in Context* (Boston: Beacon Press, 1998).

Schwarz, G., 'ΣΥΡΟΦΟΙΝΙΚΙΣΣΑ—ΧΑΝΑΝΑΙΑ (MARKUS 7.26/MATTHÄUS 15.22', *NTS* 30 (1984), pp. 626-28.

Schweitzer, Albert, *The Quest of the Historical Jesus: A Critical Study of Its Progress from Reimarus to Wrede* (trans. W. Montgomery; New York: Macmillan, 1961 [*Von Reimarus zu Wrede* (Tübingen: J.C.B. Mohr, 1906)]).

Schweizer, Eduard, *The Good News According to Matthew* (Atlanta: John Knox Press, 1975).

—'Matthew's Church', in Stanton (ed.), *Interpretation*, pp. 129-55.

Scott, Bernard Brandon, 'The Birth of the Reader', *Semeia* 52 (1990), pp. 83-102.

Scott, J. Martin C., 'Matthew 15.21-28: A Test-Case for Jesus' Manners', *JSNT* 63 (1996), pp. 21-44.

Segal, Alan F., 'Matthew's Jewish Voice', in Balch (ed.), *Social History*, pp. 3-37.

Segovia, Frank (ed.), *Discipleship in the New Testament* (Philadelphia: Fortress Press, 1985).

Seltzer, Robert M., 'Joining the Jewish People from Biblical to Modern Times', in Marty and Greenspahn (eds.), *Pushing the Faith*, pp. 41-63.

Selvidge, Marla J., *Daughters of Jerusalem* (Kitchener, Ontario: Herald Press, 1987).

—'Violence, Woman, and the Future of the Matthean Community: A Redactional Critical Essay', *USQR* 39 (1984), pp. 213-23.

—*Woman, Cult, and Miracle Recital: A Redactional Critical Investigation on Mark 5.24-34* (London, NJ: Associated University Presses; Lewisburg: Bucknell University Press, 1990).

Senior, Donald, 'Between Two Worlds: Gentiles and Jewish Christians in Matthew's Gospel', *CBQ* 61 (1999), pp. 1-23.

Sheffield, Julian, 'The Canaanite Woman, Mat. 15.21-28: A Slave Proselyte?' (unpublished paper delivered at the SBL Annual Meeting, Boston, 1999).

Shuler, Philip L., *A Genre for the Gospels: The Biographical Character of Matthew* (Philadelphia: Fortress Press, 1982).

Siker, Jeffrey S., ' "First to the Gentiles": A Literary Analysis of Luke 4.16-30', *JBL* 111 (1992), pp. 73-90.

Sim, David C., *The Gospel of Matthew and Christian Judaism: The History and Social Setting of the Matthean Community* (Studies of the New Testament and Its World; Edinburgh: T. & T. Clark, 1998).

—'The Gospel of Matthew and the Gentiles', *JSNT* 57 (1995), pp. 19-48.

—'The Magi: Gentiles or Jews?', *Hervormde Teologiese Studies* 55 (1999), pp. 980-1000.

Smart, James D., 'Jesus, the Syro-Phoenician Woman—and the Disciples', *ExpTim* 50 (1938–39), pp. 469-72.

Smulders, P., *Hilary of Poitiers' Preface to His Opus Historicum: Translation and Commentary* (Leiden: E.J. Brill, 1995).

Soggin, J. Alberto, *Joshua* (OTL; Philadelphia: Westminster Press, 1972).

Spieckermann, Hermann, ' "Die ganze Erde ist seiner Herrlichkeit voll" Pantheismus im Alten Testament?', *ZTK* 87 (1990), pp. 415-36.

Stager, Lawrence E., 'Why Were Hundreds of Dogs Buried at Ashkelon?', *BARev* 17 (1991), pp. 26-42, 34-53, 72.

Stanton, Graham, *A Gospel for a New People: Studies in Matthew* (Edinburgh: T. & T. Clark, 1992).

—'The Origin and Purpose of Matthew's Gospel: Matthean Scholarship from 1945-1980', in H. Temporini and W. Haase (eds.), *Aufstieg und Niedergang der Römischen Welt* II.25.3 (5 vols.; Berlin: W. de Gruyter, 1983), pp. 1889-951.

Stanton, Graham (ed.), *The Interpretation of Matthew* (Studies in New Testament Interpretation; Edinburgh: T. & T. Clark, 2nd rev. edn,1995).

Stanton, Graham N., and Guy G. Stroumsa (eds.), *Tolerance and Intolerance in Early Judaism and Christianity* (Cambridge: Cambridge University Press, 1998).

Stegner, William Richard, 'Leadership and Governance in the Matthean Community', in Hills (ed.), *Common Life*, pp. 147-57.

Steinmetz, Franz-Josef, 'Jesus bei den Heiden: Aktuelle Überlegungen zur Heilung der Syrophönizierin', *GuL* 55 (1982), pp. 177-84.

Stendahl, Krister, 'Quis et Unde? An Analysis of Mt 1–2', in Stanton (ed.), *Interpretation*, pp. 56-66.

—*The School of St. Matthew and Its Use of the Old Testament* (Philadelphia: Fortress Press, 1968).

Stramare, T., 'Sara chiamato Nazareno: Era stato detto dai Profeti', *BibOr* 36 (1994), pp. 231-49.

Strecker, Georg, 'The Concept of History in Matthew', in Stanton (ed.), *Interpretation*, pp. 67-84.

—*Der Weg der Gerechtigkeit: Untersuchung zur Theologie des Matthäus* (FRLANT, Testaments 82; Göttingen: Vandenhoeck & Ruprecht, 1966).

Streeter, B.H., *The Four Gospels* (New York: Macmillan, 1956).

Strong, John T., 'Tyre's Isolationist Policies in the Early Sixth Century BCE: Evidence from the Prophets', *VT* 47 (1997), pp. 207-19.

Stroup, George W., 'Between Echo and Narcissus: The Role of the Bible in Feminist Theology', *Int* 42 (1988), pp. 19-32.

Tagawa, Kenza, *Miracles et Evangile: La Pensée Personnelle de L'Evangéliste Marc* (Paris: Presses Universitaires de France, 1966).

Tannehill, Robert C., 'The Mission of Jesus According to Luke ix 16-30 in Eltester (ed.), *Jesus in Nazareth*, pp. 51-75.

—'Varieties of Synoptic Pronouncement Stories', *Semeia* 20 (1981), pp. 101-19.

Tanner, Beth LaNeel, 'Hearing the Cries Unspoken: An Intertextual-Feminist Reading of Psalm 109', in Brenner and Fontaine (eds.), *Wisdom and Psalms*, pp. 283-301.

Taylor, Miriam S., *Anti-Judaism and Early Christian Identity: A Critique of the Scholarly Consensus* (Leiden: E.J. Brill, 1995).

Taylor, Nicholas H., 'The Social Nature of Conversion in the Early Christian World', in Esler (ed.), *Modelling Early Christianity*, pp. 128-36.

Taylor, Vincent, *The Gospel According to St. Mark* (London: Macmillan, 2nd edn, 1966).

Telford, William (ed.), *The Interpretation of Mark* (Issues in Religion and Theology, 7; Philadelphia: Fortress Press, 1985).

Theissen, Gerd, *The Gospels in Context: Social and Political History in the Synoptic Tradition* (Minneapolis: Fortress Press, 1991).

—'Lokal-und Sozialkolorit in der Geschichte von der syrophönikischen Frau (Mk 7.2-30)', *ZNW* 75 (1984), pp. 202-25.

—*The Miracle Stories of the Early Christian Tradition* (Philadelphia: Fortress Press, 1983).

—*Social Reality and the Early Christians: Theology, Ethics and the World of the New Testament* (Minneapolis: Fortress Press, 1992).

—*Sociology of Early Palestinian Christianity* (Philadelphia: Fortress Press, 1988).

—'Die Tempelweissagung Jesu: Prophetie in Spannungsfeld von Stadt und Land', *TZ* 32 (1976), pp. 144-58.

Thériault, Jean-Yves, 'Le Maitre Maitrisé! Mathieu 15, 21-28', in Greimas (ed.), *De Jesus et des Femmes*, pp. 19-34.

Thomas, D. Winton, 'KELEBH "Dog": Its Origin and Some Usages of It in the Old Testament', *VT* 10 (1960), pp. 410-27.

Thompson, T.L., *Early History of the Israelite People: From the Written and Archaeological Sources* (SHANE, 4; Leiden: E.J. Brill, 1992).

—*The Historicity of the Patriarchal Narratives: The Quest for the Historical Abraham* (BZAW, 133; Berlin: W. de Gruyter, 1974).

—'Historiography in the Pentateuch: Twenty-Five Years After Historicity', *SJOT* 13 (1999), pp. 258-83.

—*The Mythic Past: Biblical Archaeology and the Myth of Israel* (New York: Basic Books, 1999).

—'A Neo-Albrightean School in History and Biblical Scholarship?', *JBL* 114 (1995), pp. 683-98.

—*The Origin Tradition of Ancient Israel*. I. *The Literary Formation of Genesis and Exodus 1–23* (JSOTSup, 55; Sheffield: JSOT Press, 1987).

—'Text, Context, and Referent in Israelite Historiography', in Edelman (ed.), *The Fabric of History*, pp. 65-92.

Thompson, William G., 'An Historical Perspective in the Gospel of Matthew', *JBL* 93 (1974), pp. 243-62.

Tiede, David Lenz, *The Charismatic Figure as Miracle Worker* (SBLDS, 1; Missoula, MT: Society of Biblical Literature, 1972).

Tisera, Guido, *Universalism According to the Gospel of Matthew* (Frankfurt am Main: Peter Lang, 1993).

Torn, Susan Reimer, 'Ruth Reconsidered', in Kates and Reimer (eds.), *Reading Ruth*, pp. 336-46.

Treat, James, 'The Canaanite Problem', *Daughters of Sarah* 20 (1994), pp. 20-24.

Trible, Phyllis, 'Ruth: A Text in Therapy', *USQR* 51 (1997), pp. 33-42.

Trilling, Wolfgang, *The Gospel According to Matthew* (New Testament for Spiritual Reading, 2; London: Burns & Oates, 1981).

—*Das Wahre Israel: Studien zur Theologie des Matthäus-Evangeliums* (Munich: Kösel, 1964).

Ulanov, Ann Belford, *The Female Ancestors of Christ* (Boston: Shambhala, 1993).

Ulfgard, Håkan, 'The Branch in the Last Days: Observations on the New Covenant Before and After the Messiah' (unpublished paper presented at 'The Dead Sea Scrolls in their Historical Context', conference 5-6 May 1998, Edinburgh).

Vale, Ruth, 'Literary Sources in Archaeological Description: The Case of Galilee, Galilees and Galileans', *JSJ* 18 (1987), pp. 209-26.

van Aarde, Andries G., 'The *Evangelium Infantium*, the Abandonment of Children, and the Infancy Narrative in Matthew 1 and 2 from a Social Scientific Perspective', in Eugene H. Lovering (ed.), *Society of Biblical Literature Seminar Papers* 31 (Atlanta: Scholars Press, 1992), pp. 435-49.

van de Sandt, Huub, 'An Explanation of Acts 15.6-21 in the Light of Deuteronomy 4.29-35 (LXX)', *JSNT* 6 (1992), pp. 73-97.

van Houten, Christiana, *The Alien in Israelite Law* (JSOTSup, 107; Sheffield: JSOT Press, 1991).

van Wolde, E., *Ruth en Noomi, twee vreemdgangers* (Baarn: Ten Have, 1993).

Van Seters, John, *Abraham in History and Tradition* (New Haven: Yale University Press, 1975).

—*Prologue to History: The Yahwist as Historian in Genesis* (Louisville, KY: Westminster/ John Knox Press, 1992).

Vermes, Geza, *The Gospel of Jesus the Jew* (Newcastle upon Tyne: University of Newcastle upon Tyne Press, 1981).

—*Jesus and the World of Judaism* (Philadelphia: Fortress Press, 1985).

—*Jesus the Jew: A Historian's Reading of the Gospels* (Philadelphia: Fortress Press, rev. edn, 1981).

—*Scripture and Tradition in Judaism: Haggadic Studies* (SPB, 40; Leiden: E.J. Brill, 1961).

Verseput, Donald J., 'The Faith of the Reader and the Narrative of Matthew 13.53–16.20', *JSNT* 46 (1992), pp. 3-24.

Viviano, Benedict T., 'The Genres of Matthew 1-2: Light from 1 Timothy 1.4', *RB* (1990), pp. 31-53.

Waetjen, Herman C., 'The Genealogy as the Key to the Gospel According to Matthew', *JBL* 95 (1976), pp. 205-30.

Wainwright, Elaine Mary, 'The Gospel of Matthew', in Schüssler Fiorenza (ed.), *Searching the Scriptures*, II, pp. 642-43.

—*Towards a Feminist Critical Reading of the Gospel According to Matthew* (BZNW, 60; New York: W. de Gruyter, 1991).

Ward, B. Horace, 'Our Lord's Hard Saying to the Syro-Phoenician Woman: Matt. xv. 26; Mark vii. 27', *ExpTim* 13 (1901–1902), p. 48.

Weber, David, 'Jesus' Use of Echoic Utterance', *Notes on Translation* 12.2 (1998), pp. 1-10.

Wegner, Judith Romney, *Chattel or Person? The Status of Women in the Mishnah* (Oxford: Oxford University Press, 1988).

Weippert, Manfred, *The Settlement of the Israelite Tribes in Palestine* (SBT, 21; Naperville, IL: Allenson, 1967).

Weiser, Artur, *The Psalms* (Philadelphia: Westminster Press, 1959).

Wellhausen, Julius, *Prolegomena to the History of Ancient Israel* (New York: Meridian, 1957).

Weren, Wim J.C., 'The Five Women in Matthew's Genealogy', *CBQ* 59 (1997), pp. 288-305.

Westermann, Claus, *Genesis* (BKAT, I/1; 2 vols.; Neukirchen–Vluyn: Neukirchener Verlag, 1974).

—*Praise and Lament in the Psalms* (Atlanta: John Knox Press, 1981).

White, L. Michael, 'Crisis Management and Boundary Maintenance', in Balch (ed.), *Social History*, pp. 211-47.

Whitelam, Keith W., *The Invention of Ancient Israel: The Silencing of Palestinian History* (London: Routledge, 1996).

—'Recreating the History of "Israel" ', *JSOT* 35 (1986), pp. 45-70.

Whybray, Norman, *Reading the Psalms as a Book* (JSOTSup, 222; Sheffield: Sheffield Academic Press, 1996).

Wikgren, Allen (ed.), *Early Christian Origins* (Chicago: Quadrangle, 1961).

Wilkins, Michael J., *The Concept of Disciples in Matthew's Gospel* (NovTSup, 59; Leiden: E.J. Brill, 1988).

Wilson, Stephen G., *Related Strangers: Jews and Christians, 70–170 C.E.* (Minneapolis: Fortress Press, 1995).

Wire, Antoinette Clark, 'The Structure of the Gospel Miracle Stories and Their Tellers', *Semeia* 11 (1978), pp. 83-113.

—'The Social Functions of Women's Asceticism in the Roman East', in King (ed.), *Images of the Feminine*, pp. 308-23.

Woschitz, Karl Matthäus, 'Erzählter Glaube: Die Geschichte vom starken Glauben als Ge-schichte Göttes mit Juden und Heiden (Mt 5, 21-28 par)', *ZKT* 107 (1985), pp. 319-32.

Zakowitch, Yair, 'Rahab als Mutter des Boas in der Jesus-Genealogie (Matth. I 5)', *NovT* 17 (1975), pp. 1-5.

Zeitlin, Solomon, *Studies in the Early History of Judaism* (4 vols.; New York: Ktav, 1974).

—'Who Were the Galileans?', *JQR* 64 (1974), pp. 189-203.

Ziderman, I. Irving, 'Seashells and Ancient Purple Dyeing', *BA* 53 (1990), pp. 98-101.

INDEXES

INDEX OF REFERENCES

OLD TESTAMENT

JOURNAL FOR THE STUDY OF THE NEW TESTAMENT
SUPPLEMENT SERIES